THE DECALOGUE

THE DECALOGUE

BEING

THE WARBURTON LECTURES

DELIVERED IN

LINCOLN'S INN AND WESTMINSTER ABBEY

1919–1923

BY

R. H. CHARLES, D.D., D.Litt., LL.D.

ARCHDEACON OF WESTMINSTER
FELLOW OF THE BRITISH ACADEMY

Eugene, Oregon

Wipf and Stock Publishers
199 W 8th Ave, Suite 3
Eugene, OR 97401

The Decalogue
Being the Warburton Lectures Delivered in Lincoln's Inn
and Westminster Abbey 1919-1923
By Charles, R.H.
ISBN: 1-59244-840-2
Publication date 8/26/2004
Previously published by T and T Clark, 1923

PREFACE

THE subject of these Warburton Lectures I have treated from three standpoints — the critical, the historical and the practical.

The Critical. — In the *Introduction* (pp. vii–lxiv) I have studied the Decalogue critically and have shown that it existed in various forms—at least five—its earliest dating from the close of the fourteenth century B.C., and its latest from the close of the third. The latest is preserved in the Nash Hebrew Papyrus (pp. vii–xxxiii). In its earliest and tersest form, in which each Commandment consisted of one brief crisp command (pp. xliv–xlviii), it comes from the great lawgiver, Moses. In the centuries that followed it received various accretions which were on the whole in keeping with the spirit of the original Commandments, save in the case of the Fourth as it is transmitted in Exodus xx. 11.

In order to represent the results of my research briefly and clearly, I have given on p. lv a genealogical tree, which shows the descent and relations of the successive forms of the Mosaic Decalogue, and on p. lxiii another which exhibits the relations subsisting between the original Mosaic Decalogue and the two later documents —the Book of the Covenant and the Ritual Decalogue in Exodus xxxiv.

The Historical.—In the Lectures I have sought to ascertain the meaning and measure of obedience which were assigned to the Ten Commandments at various stages in the history of Israel and Judah, and particularly to the Second and Fourth. In my study of the Fourth it gradually became clear that a new and Judaistic conception of the Sabbath conflicting with the original one was introduced into Exodus xx. 11 about 500 B.C. or later, and that this later conception henceforward held the field in Judaism.

With the advent of Christianity the Decalogue was reinterpreted for the most part and given a new and spiritual significance. During the first three centuries no difficulties arose within the Church in connection with the Decalogue save that the Sabbath was observed by Jewish Christians as well as the Lord's Day. But in the subsequent centuries difficulties did arise and particularly in the case of the Second and Fourth Commandments. Gradually, though unwittingly, the entire Church abandoned the true conception of the Lord's Day, and substituted in its stead the later conception of the Jewish Sabbath, and clung to this wrong and Judaistic conception to the period of the

PREFACE

Reformation. In the case of the Second Commandment it was otherwise. This Commandment the Church misinterpreted for the most part wittingly, because it condemned absolutely the growing practice of image worship within the Church. From the thirteenth century, if not earlier, it jettisoned the Second Commandment bodily from the Decalogue, and published as authoritative a mutilated Decalogue till the time of the Reformers.

The Practical.—But deeply as I have been interested in the critical and historical study of the Decalogue, it has been my main aim to reinterpret the Decalogue on the spiritual and ethical lines already laid down in the N.T., and to apply its lessons to the crying needs of our own day.

For the very full Indexes I am indebted to the efficient services of the Rev. A. Ll. Davies, Vicar of Llanrhos, Llandudno.

R. H. C.

4 LITTLE CLOISTERS,
WESTMINSTER ABBEY,
September 1923.

CONTENTS

INTRODUCTION

PAGES

ABBREVIATIONS AND BRACKETS USED IN THIS
EDITION vi

I. SUMMARY OF CONCLUSIONS ARRIVED AT . vii–xii

II. THE NASH PAPYRUS OF THE DECALOGUE . xiii–xvi

III. HEBREW TEXT OF THE NASH PAPYRUS (i.e. N)
AND CRITICAL NOTES . . . . xvi–xxii

IV. TRANSLATION OF THIS TEXT AND CRITICAL
NOTES . . . . . . xxii–xxvii

V. RELATIONS OF N TO DECALOGUE IN EX 20 AND
D 5. N—Egyptian in character—§ 1. Agrees
generally with D 5 against Ex 20—§ 2. Agrees
occasionally with Ex 20 against D 5—§ 3.
Agrees with LXX more than with any other
authority—§ 6 . . . . xxvii–xxxiii

VI. DATE OF ORIGINAL TEXT OF N—§ 1. Divergences between Ex 20 and D 5 in II. IV. V. IX.
X.—§ 2. D 5 secondary to Ex 20 in V. IX. X.—
§ 3. Original form of II.—§ 4. Various forms
of IV.—§ 5. Comparison of Decalogue (II.
III.–V. IX.–X.) in E (8th Cent. B.C.) with Decalogue in D 5 (7th Cent.)—§ 6. Decalogue as it
existed about 750 B.C. or earlier—§ 7 . xxxiii–xliv

VII. ORIGINAL FORM OF III. IV. X.—§ 1. Decalogue
purged of accretions goes back to Moses—§ 2.
Objections dealt with—§ 3. Mosaic Decalogue and its subsequent revisions and accre-

CONTENTS

tions down to 200 B.C.—genealogical tree—
§ 4. Book of Covenant presupposes Mosaic
Decalogue—§ 5. Decalogue in Ex 34 presupposes Mosaic Decalogue—§ 6. Influence
of Ex 34 on later forms of Decalogue in D 5
and Ex 20—§§ 7–8 . . . . . xlv–lxiv

LECTURES

FIRST COMMANDMENT	1–13
SECOND COMMANDMENT—	
First Lecture	14–35
Second Lecture	36–58
Third Lecture	59–88
THIRD COMMANDMENT	89–109
FOURTH COMMANDMENT—	
First Lecture	110–131
Second Lecture	132–151
Third Lecture	152–172
FIFTH COMMANDMENT	173–184
SIXTH COMMANDMENT—	
First Lecture	185–198
Second Lecture	199–211
SEVENTH COMMANDMENT	212–228
EIGHTH COMMANDMENT	229–245
NINTH COMMANDMENT	246–257
TENTH COMMANDMENT	258–272

INDEX

I. Subjects	273–286
II. Passages from the Biblical and other writers dealt with in the text	287–294

ABBREVIATIONS AND BRACKETS USED IN THE INTRODUCTION

D	=	Deuteronomy.
E	=	Elohistic source used in the Hexateuch.
Ex.	=	Exodus.
J	=	Jahwistic source used in the Hexateuch.
Jub.	=	Book of Jubilees.
LXX	=	Septuagint.
M	=	Massoretic Text.
N	=	Nash Hebrew Papyrus.
Onk.	=	Targum of Onkelos in Walton's Polyglott.
Ps.-Jon.	=	Targum of Jonathan ben Uzziel.
Sam.	=	Samaritan text of the Pentateuch.
Syr.	=	Syriac version of the O.T.
T Sam.	=	Samaritan Targum in Walton's Polyglott.
Vulg.	=	Vulgate.
< >	=	Words so enclosed are restored by the Editor
( )	=	Words so enclosed are supplied by the Editor.
[ ]	=	Words so enclosed are interpolated.

INTRODUCTION

I

SUMMARY OF THE CRITICAL INVESTIGATIONS MADE AND CONCLUSIONS ARRIVED AT IN THIS INTRODUCTION IN REGARD TO THE MOSAIC DECALOGUE, THE DECALOGUE IN EX. 34 AND THE BOOK OF THE COVENANT

(a) *Hebrew Text of Decalogue about 200 B.C. in Egypt.*—The Nash Papyrus was discovered just over twenty years ago. It was written towards the close of the first century A.D., and was used probably as a Service Book or Catechism. It represents the Hebrew text of the Decalogue that was current in Egypt about 200 B.C., which was based mainly on D.[1] I have given the Hebrew text of the papyrus restored by the help of Ex 20 and D 5,[2] and an English translation,[3] in both cases with critical notes pointing out the affinities of N.

From the above study it follows that N has a definite Egyptian character, that it is mainly descended from D, though in a few passages it is a

[1] See II. §§ 1-3, pp. xiii–xvi; v. § 6, p. xxxii.
[2] See III. pp. xvi–xxii.   [3] IV. pp. xxii–xxvii.

conflate text, and especially so in the fourth Commandment where it follows Ex 20^{11}.[1] In two cases where M and Sam. (*i.e.* the older Semitic authorities) fail, N appears to preserve an older text.[2] It is more closely related to the LXX than any other authority.[3]

(*b*) *Hebrew Text of Decalogue in Egypt (and other localities) about 300 B.C.*—From the text of N we move backwards to the closely related Hebrew text which is presupposed by the LXX of Ex 20 and D 5. The text of these two passages is corrupt in several passages. The LXX of D 5 has reacted on that of Ex 20^{12} in v. (*i.e.* 5th Commandment) so that it adds " that it may be well with thee " before " that thy days," etc., exactly as in D 5^{16}: in x. the LXX of Ex 20^{17} adds " his field " before " nor his manservant," as in D 5^{21}. There are other reactions of the LXX of D 5 on that of Ex 20. On the other hand, there is a reaction of the LXX of Ex 20^{11} on that of D 5^{14} which has led to the insertion in the latter of an entire sentence. Possibly the wrong order of the LXX in VII.–VI.–VIII. in D 5^{17-19} may have led to the anomalous order in Ex 20^{13-15}.

When a critical text of the LXX of these two chapters is published it will be easy to recover the Hebrew it presupposes.

(*c*) *Hebrew Text of Decalogue in Ex 20 in the fifth century B.C. and in D 5 about or before 621 B.C.*—We can now put N aside, which is the latest,[4] and con-

---

[1] See v. §§ 1–3, pp. xxvii–xxxi. [2] See v. § 4, p. xxxi.
[3] See v. § 6, p. xxxii. [4] See VI. § 1, p. xxxiii sq.

INTRODUCTION ix

fine our attention to the two forms of the Decalogue in Ex. and D. These two agree in I. III. VI.–VIII., but diverge from each other in II. IV.–V. IX.–X. Of these five the text of V. IX. X. is secondary in D to that in Ex. and owes its divergencies to the hand of the Deuteronomist.[1]

The real difficulties centre in II. and IV. First, as regards II. In this Commandment both Ex. and D agree. But the Hebrew is impossible. It is ungrammatical, if we attempt to give it an intelligible meaning by translating it thus: " Thou shalt not make unto thee a graven image nor any likeness[2] of that which is in heaven," etc. On the other hand, it is unmeaning, if we translate it as it stands : " nor any likeness that is in heaven." No man makes " a likeness that is in heaven." D 5^{8b-10} (Ex 20^{4b-6}) can therefore be best explained as originally a marginal gloss in D which was afterwards incorporated in the text in the fifth century B.C. and thence passed into Ex 20. But the phrase " nor any likeness " is differently situated. It is a distinctly Deuteronomic phrase and, like many other Deuteronomic phrases in D 5, is to be attributed to the author of D. Hence II. stood most probably as follows in D in 621 B.C.: " Thou shalt not make thee a graven image nor any likeness."[3] All that follows in the present

---

[1] See VI. §§ 2–3, p. xxxiv sq.

[2] There is nothing to justify the rendering of the R.V. "nor *the likeness of* any form that." The R.V., it is true, acknowledges by the italics that it inserts an explanatory phrase.

[3] See VI. § 4, pp. xxxv–xxxix.

INTRODUCTION

Hebrew text of II. is to be regarded as due to the incorporation of a marginal gloss of the fifth century B.C.

In IV. the divergence between Ex 20^{8-11} and D 5^{12-15} is fundamental. All other variations between the two Decalogues may be regarded as explanatory additions or glosses, which are never contrary to the spirit of the original commandment, but it is otherwise in the case of IV. The interpolation of Ex 20^{11} alters essentially the entire character of the original commandment. By virtue of its actual words it was instituted to meet the needs of the Godhead and had no reference originally to man. This interpolation has made the acceptance of the fourth Commandment an impossibility outside a narrow Jewish circle.[1] To this interpolation is most probably due the extrusion of the very ancient clause preserved in D 5^{14}, *i.e.*, "that thy manservant and thy maidservant may rest as well as thou." This clause gives the right note. The Sabbath was made for man.

Thus the Decalogue as it stands at present in Ex 20 does not go back farther than the fifth century B.C., whereas that in D 5 goes back to 621 B.C. or earlier, if we remove the gloss in II., *i.e.* 5^{8b-10}.

(*d*) *Hebrew text of the Decalogue in Ex 20 as it stood in the eighth century B.C. or earlier, especially of II. IV. and V. as compared with the Decalogue in D 5 of 621 B.C.*—The text of II. in D, as we have already

[1] See VI. § 5, pp. xxxix–xl.

INTRODUCTION

seen in the preceding paragraph, ran as follows:
" Thou shalt not make thee a graven image nor any
likeness." But the last phrase "nor any likeness"
is a Deuteronomic phrase and comes most probably
from the Deuteronomist as do many other phrases in
the Decalogue in D. Hence in the eighth century
B.C., II. reads as follows: " Thou shalt not make thee a
graven image."[1]

The eighth century form of IV. can also be re-
covered. It read in all probability as follows:
" Remember the Sabbath day to keep it holy. Six
days shalt thou labour, and do all thy work: but
<on> the seventh day is a Sabbath unto the Lord
thy God: <on it> thou shalt not do any work, thou,
nor thy son, nor thy daughter, thy manservant, nor
thy maidservant, <nor thine ox nor thine ass>, nor
thy cattle,<that thy manservant and thy maidservant
may rest as well as thou>."

V. read simply thus: "Honour thy father and thy
mother." The remaining clauses are from the hand
of the Deuteronomist.[2]

For the rest of the commandments as they stood in
the eighth century, see VI. § 7.

(e) *The fact that there was a steady, though sporadic,
growth of explanatory additions from the eighth century
to the second B.C. leads to the hypothesis that such explanatory clauses as still survive in III. IV. X. of the
eighth century Decalogue are themselves accretions, and
were unknown to the original Decalogue.*—Since I have

[1] See pp. xxxv–xxxix.   [2] See VI. §§ 6–7.

dealt with this question in VII. § 1, in a fashion intelligible to the ordinary reader, it is not necessary to repeat any of the arguments there advanced. I have there concluded that the original form of III. IV. and X. was as follows:

III. " Thou shalt not take the name of the Lord thy God in vain."

IV. " Remember the Sabbath day to keep it holy."

X. " Thou shalt not covet."

Later, in VII. § 5–6, I have sought to prove that the Decalogue, even with certain additions in IV., is older than the Book of the Covenant in E and the Decalogue in Ex 34 (J).

(*f*) *If the above conclusions are valid, it follows, first, that the Decalogue is presupposed by documents of the tenth century or older*; for E and J are merely historians making use of documents such as the Book of the Covenant and the Decalogue in Ex 34: *and*, in the next place, *that, if these things are so, there is no outstanding personality to whom the original Decalogue can be ascribed other than Moses.*[1]

With various objections to this conclusion I have dealt in VII. § 3, and in VII. § 4 (p. lv) I have given a genealogical tree in which I have traced the development of the Decalogue from the time of Moses, ·1320–1300 B.C., down to that of the Nash text of 200 B.C.

[1] See VII. § 2.

II

THE NASH PAPYRUS OF THE DECALOGUE

§ 1. *Its date and character.*—This papyrus was discovered in Egypt in 1902 by W. L. Nash, the Secretary of the Society of Biblical Archæology, and presented by him to the University Library of Cambridge. It is generally assigned to the close of the first century A.D. (Burkitt) or the beginning of the second (Cook and Lévi), and is thus about 600 to 750 years older than the oldest Hebrew MS of the O.T.[1] Hebrew papyri are very rare. Hence independently of its contents the papyrus before us has an interest of its own.

This papyrus, which I shall forthwith designate with some earlier writers as N, consists of four mutilated fragments, which, when duly put together, measures 5 in. by $2\frac{7}{8}$ in. It contains twenty-five lines, but of the last line only the tops of a few of the letters are decipherable. The papyrus contains neither vowel points, accents, nor diacritical marks. There are no verse divisions. Spaces intervene between the words, but the spacing is very irregular. In line 15 עלי־כן is written as one word עלכן. Final letters are employed. For an account of the letters I must refer the reader to Cook's article in the

[1] The oldest MS is in the British Museum (*i.e.* Or. 4445). It is undated, but was written, according to Ginsburg, about A.D. 820-850. The oldest dated Hebrew MS (*i.e.* A.D. 916) is in the Imperial Library of St. Petersburg.

xiv INTRODUCTION

Proceedings of the Society of Biblical Archæology (Jan. 1903, pp. 34–56). This is accompanied by three plates, one of which is a facsimile of the MS, the second of its reproduction fully restored by the editor, and the third of a table of Hebrew alphabets at various periods. To this work I shall frequently refer. In the *Jewish Quarterly Review*, xv. (1903) 392–408, Burkitt deals with this papyrus under the title, "The Hebrew Papyrus of the Ten Commandments," and returns to it in xvi. (1904) 559–561, "The Nash Papyrus, a New Photograph." A German study of the papyrus was published by Peters, *Die älteste Abschrift der zehn Gebote der Papyrus Nash* (Freiburg), in 1905.[1] This work is valuable for its collection of materials, but its conclusions are frequently arbitrary.

The average number of letters in a line of N is 32–33 according to Cook, and 31½ according to Peters. According to my restoration of the text there are 750 (or 749) letters in the first twenty-four lines. Thus the average line contains 31¼ letters. The two longest lines are lines 5 and 10, which consist of 36 letters each. The two shortest are 21 and 23, which consist respectively of 25 and 27 letters. Thus the lines are very irregular in length. At the beginning of each line 2 to 8 letters are lost, except in lines 15–18. The letters are of the square character.

[1] Two other scholars should be mentioned: Israel Lévi, "Un Papyrus Biblique," in the *Revue des Études Juives*, xlvi. (1903) 212–217; von Gall, "Ein neuer hebräischer Text der zehn Gebote und des Schma'," *ZATW* xxiii. 347–351.

INTRODUCTION xv

§ 2. *N was possibly a Service Book or a Catechism.*—
At an early date the Decalogue and the Shema‛
(*i.e.* "Hear, O Israel," etc.) were recited daily in the
Temple Service (Tamid, iv. *ad fin.* v. 1).[1] But, because
the Minim (the Early Jewish Christians) claimed
divine revelation exclusively for the Decalogue and
discarded the other Mosaic laws as temporary enact-
ments, the recital of the Decalogue in the daily
morning liturgy was abolished (J. T. Ber. 3c, 11a;
B. T. Ber. 12a). In the last passage we are told
that Rabba b. bar-Ḥana wished to restore at Sura
the recital of the Decalogue, and that R. Ashi made
the same attempt at Nehardea, but that their efforts
failed.

Now it is most probable that N was simply a
tiny prayer book consisting of the Decalogue and the
Shema‛, and belonged therefore to the period before
the recitation of the Decalogue was forbidden.[2]

§ 3. *N represents a form of the Hebrew text that
circulated in Egypt as early as 200 B.C.*—The evidence

---

[1] לקרות את שמע . . . ברכו וקראו עשרת הדברים = "to recite the Shema‛ . . .
they gave the blessing and recited the ten words." In his commentary on this passage (see Surenhusius, Pars quinta, p. 301)
Maimonides' exposition is given. "Decem vero quotidie verba
legebant . . . Cæterum jam dictum est quod in Terminis (extra
terram Israelis) eas legere volebant, sed quod hoc prohibitum
fuerit propter hæreticos; sed Gemara non declarat quænam sit ista
hæreticorum controversia, sed in principio tractatus Berachoth in
Talmude Jerusalymitano dicitur, fas erat ut decem verba legerentur
quotidie, quare autem non leguntur ? Ob hæreticos, ne dicant, hæc
duntaxat a Mose data sunt in Sinai."

[2] Cook (p. 55) suggests that in N we have a collection of passages
of the Mosaic Law.

xvi INTRODUCTION

for this statement is given on pp. xxxii–xxxiii. The Jews in Egypt copied their sacred writings without the accuracy that was due to them. Thus Aristeas[1] (130–70 B.C.) writes: "The books of the law ... were written in Hebrew characters and language, but they were copied[2] carelessly and not in consonance with the original" (ἀμελέστερον δὲ καὶ οὐχ ὑπάρχει σεσήμανται). One of these copies may have been the ancestor of N. N was based mainly on D; see pp. xxix–xxx.

III

Hebrew Text of the Papyrus restored by help of Ex 20 and Deut 5

(For the Abbreviations and Brackets, see p. vi.)

Ex. xx.		Lines in Papyrus.
1	>אנכי י<הוה אלהיך אשר >הוצא<תיך מארץ מ>צרים<	2
2	>לוא יהיה ל<ך אלהים אחרים >על־פנ<י >לוא תעשה >לך פסל<	3, 4
3	>וכל תמונה< אשר בשמים ממעל ואשר בארץ >מתחת<	
4	>ואשר במי<ם מתחת לארץ לוא תשתחוה להם >ולוא<	5
5	>תעבדם כי< אנכי יהוה אלהיך אל קנוא פק>ד עון אבות<	
6	>על בני<ם על שלשים ועל רבעים לשנאי >ועשה חסד<	6
7	>לאלפים< לאהבי ולשמרי מצותי לוא ת>שא את שם<	7
8	>יהוה א<להיך לשוא כי לוא ינקה יהוה >את אשר<	
9	>ישא את ש<מה לשוא זכור את יום השבת ל>קדשו<	8
10	>ששת ימים< תעבוד ועשית כל מלאכתך וביום >השביעי<	9, 10
11	>שבת ליהוה< אלהיך לוא תעשה בו כל מלאכה >אתה<	
12	>ובנך ובתך< עבדך ואמתך שורך וחמרך וכל בה>מתך<	
13	>וגרך אשר< בשעריך כי ששת ימים עשה י>הוה<	11
14	>את השמי<ם ואת הארץ את הים ואת כל אש>ר בם<	
15	וינח >ביום< השביעי עלכן ברך יהוה את >יום<	

[1] See Charles, *Apoc. and Pseudep.* ii. 98.
[2] Andrews (*op. cit.* ii. 98) renders σεσήμανται by "interpreted."

	Lines in
Ex. xx.	Papyrus.

12	16 השביעי ויקדשיו כבד את אביך ואת אמ<ך למען>
	17 ייטב לך ולמען יאריכן ימיך על האדמה <אשר>
14, 13, 15	18 יהוה אלהיך נתן לך לוא תנאף לוא תרצח לוא
16, 17	19 <תג>נב לוא תענה ברעך עד שוא לוא תחמור <את>
	20 <אשת רעך ל>וא תתאווה את ב<י><ת רעך שד<הו ועבדו>
	21 <ואמתו וש>ורו וחמרו וכל אשר לרעך
Deut. iv. 45	
(vi. 2)	22 <ואלה החק<ים והמשפטים אשר צוא משה את <בני>
„ vi. 4	23 <ישראל> במדבר בצאתם מארץ מצרים שמע
„ vi. 5	24 <ישרא><ל יהוה אלהינו יהוה אחד הוא ואהבת
	25 <את יהוה א><ל><הי><ך <בכ><ל ל<בבך> . . . <

Line 1. N >מבית עבדים, though it is found both in Ex. and D.

l. 3. With כל טמונה (an addition of D; see p. xxxvii sq.) contrast כל תמונת in D 4^{16. 23. 25}. On the ungrammatical structure of the words תמונה אשר, see p. xxxvi sqq. I have restored ו before כל as it is found in M. Sam. T Sam. LXX. Syr. Onk. Ps.-Jon. of Ex 20⁴ and all these authorities in D 5⁸ save M. Onk.

l. 9. For זכור D reads שמור. After לקדשו D adds כאשר צוא יהוה אלהיך.

l. 12. M. Syr. Onk. Ps.-Jon. of D 5¹⁴ read ו before עבדך, but against Sam. LXX. Vulg. In Ex 20¹⁰ many Hebrew MSS with Syr. Ps.-Jon. also insert the ו against all the remaining authorities cited by me. שורך וחמרך. So also D 5¹⁴ (M. Sam. T Sam. LXX. Syr. Onk. Ps.-Jon. Vulg., save that M. Syr. Onk. Ps.-Jon. Vulg. prefix ו). >Ex 20¹⁰ (M. Sam. Syr. Onk. Ps.-Jon. Vulg., but T Sam. LXX. read as in N). וכל. So D 5¹⁴ (M. Sam. T Sam. LXX. Syr. Onk.

xviii   INTRODUCTION

Ps.-Jon. Vulg.). Ex 20¹⁰ (M. Syr. Onk.) כל<
and Sam. Vulg. >וכל. But T Sam. LXX. Jub 50⁷
read וכל.

ll. 13–16. ויקדשיו . . . כי is derived from Ex 20¹¹
(M. Sam. T Sam. LXX. Syr. Onk. Ps.-Jon. Vulg.).
This dogmatic reason has displaced the older ethical
reason which is preserved in D: למען ינוח עבדך ואמתך כמוך.
That the Deuteronomic clause is 200 or 300 years
older than the clauses which have displaced it in
Ex 20¹¹ I have shown elsewhere. D adds a further
reason—and this an historical one—for the observance of the sabbath in 5¹⁵, just as Ex. adds a dogmatic
one in 20¹¹. With the latter compare Ex 31¹⁷.

l. 16. After אמך D makes the same addition that
it has already made after לקדשו in l. 12.

l. 17. On the addition ייטב לך ולמען, see note 6,
p. xxiv.

l. 18. לוא תנאף לוא תרצח. On this Egyptian order
of these commandments, see note 1, p. xxv.

ll. 18–20. For לוא, which occurs here five times
in N, D 5¹⁸⁻²¹ (M. Onk.) reads ולא. But Sam. T Sam.
LXX. Syr. of D 5¹⁸⁻²¹>ו.

ll. 18–20. N in omitting ו before לוא (five times)
is supported by D 5¹⁸⁻²¹ (Sam. T Sam. LXX. Syr.),
Ex 20¹⁴⁻¹⁷ (M. LXX. Syr. Onk.). But T Sam. Vulg.
of Ex 20¹⁴⁻¹⁷ >ו only the first four times and Sam. the
first three. D 5¹⁸⁻²¹ (M. Onk.), which inserts ו in all
five cases, is secondary.

l. 19. שוא. So D 5²⁰ (M. Sam. T Sam.). Ex 20¹⁶
(M. Sam. T Sam.) שקר. The latter is an early ex-

planation or rendering of שוא, as Wellhausen observes, and makes a difficult and indefinite phrase clear. Hence D contains the original reading and Ex. is secondary but gives the right sense. T Sam. gives the same Samaritan equivalent for שוא in D 5¹⁹ as it does for this word in Ex 23¹. The word שוא was a source of difficulty to Jewish scholars. In Ex 23¹, where it occurs twice, Onk. renders it by two different words. The evidence of the Greek and other versions is not helpful here.

את. <Ex. and D.

l. 20. אשת ... בית. So N, following D 5²¹ (M. LXX. Syr. Onk. Ps.-Jon. Vulg.) and Ex 20¹⁷ LXX. But Ex 20¹⁷ (M. Sam. T Sam. Syr. Onk. Vulg.) and D 5²¹ (Sam. T Sam.) preserve the original order בית ... אשת. As Steuernagel (Holzinger, *Deut.* p. 22) observes: "The Deuteronomist seeks also elsewhere to raise the position of the wife; cf. 21¹⁰ˢᵠᵠ· 22¹³ˢᵠᵠ· 24¹ˢᵠᵠ·." The wife is no longer subsumed under the conception "house." תתאוה. Here N follows D 5²¹ (M. Onk. Ps.-Jon.). Sam. T Sam. Syr. read תחמוד; but here the reading of the Samaritan text in Ex 20¹⁷ has reacted on the Samaritan text in D 5²¹, just as the LXX of D has reacted on the LXX of Ex. It is to be observed that אוה occurs three times in D but not in Ex. שדהו. N follows D 5²¹ (M. Sam. T Sam. LXX. Syr. Onk. Ps.-Jon. Vulg.). >Ex 20¹⁷ (M. Syr. Onk. Vulg.), but Sam. T Sam. LXX of Ex 20¹⁷ support D. Here Sam. of D has reacted on Sam. of Ex., and the LXX of Ex. has been affected

xx INTRODUCTION

similarly by the LXX of D. In D 5²¹ שדהו appears to be an addition of the Deuteronomist. By his transposition of בית ... אשת he transformed the meaning of בית, which originally was a comprehensive term for the entire household, and reduced it to the simple meaning of "house" in a material sense. This once done, the addition becomes natural. Ex 20¹⁷ could go back to the nomadic period: D 5²¹ could not unless we take it as predictive in character. Hence Ex 20¹⁷ is superior to D 5²¹ on every ground.

ll. 22–23. But for the LXX text of D 6⁴ we should naturally have concluded (as Swete, *Introd. to O.T. in Greek*, p. 332) that these lines were borrowed from D 4⁴⁵, "These are the testimonies and the statutes and the judgments which Moses spake (so LXX. BAL, but F reads ἐνετείλατο) unto the children of Israel when they came forth out of Egypt" (החקים והמשפטים אשר דבר משה על בני ישראל בצאתם ממצרים), influenced by D 6², "All his statutes and his Commandments which I command thee (אשר אנכי מצוך), thou and thy son, and thy son's son." But the Hebrew in our text, ll. 22–23, agrees almost *verbatim* with the LXX of 6⁴ where it diverges from M (Sam. T Sam. Syr. Onk. Ps.-Jon. Vulg.). The LXX reads: καὶ ταῦτα τὰ δικαιώματα καὶ τὰ κρίματα ὅσα ἐνετείλατο κύριος τοῖς υἱοῖς Ἰσραήλ, ἐξελθόντων αὐτῶν ἐκ γῆς Αἰγύπτου· Ἄκουε, Ἰσραήλ· κύριος ὁ θεὸς ἡμῶν κύριος εἷς ἐστιν. The Lyons O. Latin codex also preserves these words, but in agreement with LXX. B*F reads Moyses for κύριος, and D̄S̄ tuus D̄N̄S̄ unus est for ὁ θεὸς ἡμῶν. Cook

INTRODUCTION

(*Pre-Massoretic Biblical Papyrus*, p. 44 sq.) regards these words as genuine and as having originally formed part of the Hebrew text of D 6^4. It is clear that, as Cook observes (*op. cit.* p. 44), κύριος and ἡμῶν are inconsistent. Cook is of opinion that the subject of the verb commanded was originally unexpressed, and that this introduction to the Shemaʽ (*i.e.* " Hear, O Israel," etc.) is genuine. He thinks that this introduction was omitted " partly because an introduction was already contained in 4^{44} or, better, in 6^1," and " partly to avoid a break in the continuity." Now this last argument makes against the genuineness; for the introduction in the LXX 6^4 constitutes an awkward break in the context. His next argument is that the Palestinian Targums on this passage ascribe the origin of the Shemaʽ to the sons of Jacob which they uttered when urged by the dying Jacob to shun idolatry. Hence this introduction, which ascribes it to Moses, " was dropped either before or at the formation of the Massoretic text." But the passage in the Targums is brought in artificially. Besides, it is found in the Babylonian Talmud, *Pesach*, 56a, where it is attributed to Simeon ben Lakish of the third century A.D. Furthermore, the evidence of Sam. T Sam. and Syr. is wholly adverse to the genuineness of this passage in the Palestinian form of the Hebrew text. There is also the later evidence of Onk. Ps.-Jon. and the Vulg. Hence, since this introduction appears only in N and the LXX (with the versions derived from it), it seems most

xxii INTRODUCTION

reasonable to conclude that it represents a third or fourth (?) century B.C. intrusion in what afterwards became the Egyptian type of the Hebrew text.

l. 23. במדבר. >LXX in D 6⁴.

l. 24. הוא. Elsewhere only in LXX of D 6⁴ ($\dot{\epsilon}\sigma\tau\iota\nu$) and Mk 12²⁹.

IV

TRANSLATION OF THE HEBREW TEXT OF THE PAPYRUS

	Lines in Papyrus.
Ex. xx.	
2 <I am the L>ord thy God which <brought> thee out of the land of E<gypt>.[1]	1
3, 4 Thou <shalt have none> other gods <before> me. Thou shalt not make <unto thee a graven image>,	2
<nor any likeness> that is in heaven above, or that is in the earth <beneath>,	3
5 <or that is in the water>s under the earth: thou shalt not bow down to them <nor>	4
<serve them: for> I the Lord thy God am a jealous God, vis<iting the iniquity of the fathers>	5

[1] Ex. and D add "out of the house of bondage." Its omission by N is probably due (as E. J. Pilcher suggests) to prudential reasons, as the MS was designed for circulation in Egypt.

Ex. xx. Lines in Papyrus.

<upon the child>ren upon [1] the third 6
and upon the fourth generation of them
6 that hate me; <and showing mercy>
<unto thousands of> them that love me 7
7 and keep my commandments. Thou
shalt not t<ake the name of
the Lord thy G>od in vain; for the Lord 8
will not hold him guiltless <that>
8 <taketh his na>me in vain. Remember [2] 9
the sabbath day to <keep it holy>.[3]
9 <Six days> shalt thou labour, and do 10
10 all thy work: but *on* [4] the <seventh>
day is
<the sabbath unto the Lord> thy God: 11
in it [5] thou shalt not do any work,
<thou>
<nor thy son nor thy daughter>, thy [6] 12
manservant nor thy maidservant, *thine*

---

[1] So also D 5⁹ (LXX. Syr. Onk. Ps.-Jon.) and Ex 20⁵ (M. LXX. Syr. Onk.). But D 5⁹ (M. Sam. T Sam.) and Ex 20⁵ (Sam. T Sam.) read "and upon."

[2] D reads "observe."

[3] + "as the Lord thy God commanded thee," D.

[4] >Ex. and D (M. Sam. T Sam. Syr. Onk. Ps.-Jon. in both Decalogues). But LXX and Vulg. (in Ex.) support N: also Ex 23¹² 34²¹). Hence the "on" here appears to be original, though lost early in M and Sam.

[5] >Ex. and D. But N is right, since Sam. T Sam. LXX. Jub. 50⁷, Syr. Onk. Vulg. so read. Cf. Jer 17²⁴ *ad fin.*

[6] So Ex 20¹⁰ (M. Sam. T Sam. LXX. Onk. Vulg., but Syr. Ps.-Jon. Vulg. read "nor thy") and D 5¹⁴ (Sam. T Sam. LXX, but M. Syr. Onk. Ps.-Jon. Vulg. read "nor thy").

xxiv INTRODUCTION

	Lines in Papyrus.
Ex. xx.	

    ox nor thine ass,[1] nor *any*[2] of <thy> ca<ttle>,

    <nor thy stranger that is> within thy 13

11   gates:[3] for in six days the L<ord> made

    <the heav>en and the earth, the sea and 14 all th<at in them is>,

    and rested the seventh day: wherefore 15 the Lord blessed <the day>

12 the *seventh,*[4] and hallowed it. Honour thy 16 father and <thy> mother[5] <*that*>

    it may be well with thee[6] and that thy 17 days may be long upon the land <which>

---

[1] >Ex 20¹⁰ (M. Sam. Syr. Onk. Ps.-Jon., but T Sam. LXX support N). D 5¹⁴ (M. Sam. T Sam. LXX. Syr. Onk. Ps.-Jon. Vulg.) supports N save that for "thine ox" M. Sam. Syr. Onk. Ps.-Jon. read "nor thine ox."

[2] N follows D 5¹⁴ (M. Sam. T Sam. LXX. Syr. Onk. Ps.-Jon.). Ex 20¹⁰ (M. Sam. Syr. Onk. Ps.-Jon.) >"any of." But T Sam. LXX of Ex 20¹⁰ herein follow D.

[3] The words "for in six days . . . which the Lord thy God giveth thee" are an interpolation in Ex 20¹⁵ of the sixth or fifth century B.C. See pp. 110–116. N has adopted this late text.

[4] So only LXX. Syr. Hence this correction, due to Gn 2³, may have originated in Egypt in the third century B.C. But השביעי may be merely a corruption of הבעה.

[5] +as the Lord thy God commanded thee, D.

[6] Ex 20¹² (M. Sam. T Sam. LXX. (A) Onk. Ps.-Jon. Vulg.) >underlined words. LXX (B) supports them in their present position. D 5¹⁶ (M. Sam. T Sam. Syr. Onk. Vulg.) also adds this clause, but transposes it after the clause "that thy days may be long," etc. Hence since LXX of D 5¹⁶ N insert them before "that thy days may be long," etc., and M. Sam. T Sam. Syr. Onk. Vulg. insert them

INTRODUCTION xxv

Ex. xx.

Lines in
Papyrus.

14, 13 the Lord thy God giveth thee. *Thou* 18
*shalt not commit adultery. Thou shalt
do no murder.*[1]

15 Thou shalt not

after this clause; they appear to have been originally a marginal gloss which was afterwards incorporated in the text—by one scribe in one place, by another scribe in another. It is a favourite expression in D. Cf. 4^{40} $5^{29.\ 33}$ $6^{3.\ 18}$ $12^{25.\ 28}$ 19^{13} 22^7. Both clauses, with words coming between, are found in 4^{40} $6^{2.\ 3}$ 22^7, but with a divergence in order. $6^{2.\ 3}$ (with intervening words) supports the order in 5^{16}, while 4^{40} 22^7 reverse this order as in N.

[1] The order of the Commandments, VII.-VI.-VIII., "Thou shalt not commit adultery, Thou shalt do no murder, Thou shalt not steal," is Egyptian. Ex 20^{13-14} (M. Sam. T Sam. LXX (AFL). Syr. Onk. Ps.-Jon. Vulg.) and D 5^{17} (M. Sam. T Sam. LXX (AF). Onk. Ps.-Jon. Vulg.) give the Palestinian and original order, *i.e.* VI. VII. VIII., "Thou shalt do no murder, Thou shalt not commit adultery, Thou shalt not steal." It is found also in Mt 19^{18} ($5^{21.\ 27}$), Mk 10^{19}; Josephus (*Ant.* iii. 5. 5); the Didache, ii. 2, iii. 2 sqq.; Tertullian, Clem. Alex., Origen, etc. The order in N is supported in Ex $20^{13.\ 14}$ by some Greek cursives and B (in part; for its arrangement is VII.-VIII.-VI.); in D by Greek MSS, B and some cursives, Sahidic, Bohairic, Ethiopic; Luke 18^{20}, Ro 13^9, Ja 2^{11}; Philo, Jerome, Augustine, etc. This order seems clearly to have originated in Egypt. If so, the Hebrew text was naturally rearranged as in N for Egyptian Jews. Philo, writing nearly a hundred years before the Hebrew papyrus N was written, says that Moses placed the VII. Commandment before the VI. because he considered the VII. to be the greatest violation of the Law (ἀδικημάτων μέγιστον τοῦτ' εἶναι ὑπολαβών, *De decem Orac.* xxix. *ad fin.*). In the *Jewish Encyc.* iv. 496, an ancient opinion is given that adultery was a breach of seven other Commandments besides the seventh. This is the Jewish view. But Dr. Peters (*Älteste Abschrift d. zehn Gebote*, p. 33), not being acquainted with the attitude of the Jews on this question, thinks that the order VII.-VI.-VIII. is the original one, and that it was changed deliberately into VI.-VII.-VIII. on the theological grounds that murder was a worse sin than adultery. It appears possibly in an ancient Babylonian document. Jeremias[2] (*Das alte Test. in Lichte des alten Orients*, 1906, p. 208) gives the following rendering of it,

xxvi INTRODUCTION

Ex. xx.
Lines in Papyrus.

16, 17 <st>eal. Thou shalt not[1] bear vain[2] 19
witness against thy neighbour. *Thou
shalt not[3] covet*[4]

18 <*thy neighbour's wife. Thou shalt n*>*ot* 20
desire[4] *thy neighbour's house,* <*his*>
fi<*eld*,[5] *or his manservant*>
<*or his maidservant, or his o*>*x or his* 21
ass, or *anything that is thy neighbour's.*

which recalls the v.–viii. Commandments, but the order is peculiar and confused. I prefix the number of the Commandment in the Decalogue:

    (v.) Hat er Vater und Mutter verachtet . . .
   (viii.) Falsche Wage gebraucht,
     Falsches Geld genommen . . .
   (vii.) Hat er seines Nächsten Haus betreten
     Seines Nächsten Weib sich genaht
    vi. Seines Nächsten Blut vergossen
   viii. Seines Nächsten Kleid geraubt?

In Budge's *Books on Egypt and Chaldeans*, vii. 365, quoted by Burney, *JTS*, April 1908, p. 350 sq., there are in the forty-two statements of the Negative Confession parallels to the iii. and vi.–x. Commandments, but in an utterly illogical order.

[1] For "thou shalt not" in Commandments vii.–x. D reads "neither shalt thou"; but see p. xviii, ll. 18–20 for the detailed evidence.

[2] So D (M. Sam. T Sam.). Ex. (M. Sam. T Sam.) reads שוא. See note on l. 19, p. xviii sq.

[3] So Ex. (M. LXX (–A). Syr. Onk. Vulg.): D (Sam. T Sam. LXX. Syr. Vulg.), but Ex. (Sam. T Sam.): D (M. Onk.) read "nor shalt thou."

[4] "Covet . . . desire." Here N follows D 5²⁰. See note on l. 20, p. xix.

[5] "His field." Here N follows D 5²¹ (M. Sam. T Sam.) in this addition. LXX. Syr. Onk. read "nor his field." Sam. of D 5²¹ has reacted on Ex 20¹⁷. Hence Sam. T Sam. of Ex 20¹⁷ insert "his field." See note on l. 20, p. xix sq.

INTRODUCTION xxvii

	Lines in Papyrus.
Deut.	
vi. 4 <And these are the statute>s and the judgments which Moses commanded the <children of>	22
(iv. 45, <Israel> in the wilderness, when they	23
vi. 2) went forth from the land of Egypt.[1]	
4 Hear	
O Is<rael>: the Lord our God is one	24
5 Lord: and thou shalt love	
<the Lord> thy G<od with> a<ll thy hea>rt	25

V

CONCLUSIONS DRAWN FROM THE ABOVE STUDY AS TO N AND ITS RELATIONS TO EX. AND D IN POINT OF TIME AND TRUSTWORTHINESS

§ 1. *N has a definite Egyptian character.*—(a) N was found in Cairo. This fact in itself proves nothing, but when taken in connection with the facts that follow, it possesses some evidential value.

(b) N agrees with the LXX, when the LXX has the Massoretic of D supported by Sam. T Sam. Syr. Onk. Ps.-Jon. Vulg. against it in 6^4. (See notes on ll. 22–23, p. xx above.) In other words, the verse

---

[1] These lines seem to be compounded of D 4^{45} 6^2, and to be an early intrusion in the Hebrew text of the third or fourth (?) cent. which circulated in Egypt. This Egyptian form of the text is supported only by N and the LXX (with the versions made from the latter). See note on lines 22–23, p. xx sq.

xxviii INTRODUCTION

which is interpolated in the LXX of D 6⁴ was unknown in the fourth century B.C. as Sam.[1] (T Sam.) prove, and continued to be unknown in non-Egyptian authorities till the second century A.D. if we assign the Old Latin to that date. This evidence is very strong.

(c) N omits "out of the house of bondage," against Ex. D and their versions. The most reasonable explanation of this omission is that the *Jews in Egypt* refrained from describing Egypt as a house of bondage (see footnote, p. xxii).

(d) N with LXX reads "on the seventh day" (Ex 20¹⁰ D 5¹⁴), where M. Sam. T Sam. Syr. Onk. Ps.-Jon. both in Ex. and D read "the seventh day."

(e) N reads "blessed the seventh day" in the fourth Commandment (Ex 20¹¹), in agreement with LXX and Syr., where M. Sam. T Sam. Onk. Ps.-Jon. Vulg. read "blessed the sabbath day." See footnote 4, p. xxiv.

(f) N reads the Commandments VI.-VII.-VIII. in the order VII.-VI.-VIII. The former order is attested by M. Sam. T Sam. Onk. Ps.-Jon. Vulg. both in Ex 20¹³·¹⁴

---

[1] The Samaritan Pentateuch "has, presumably, escaped the corruptions which have befallen the purely Jewish line of transmission since the fourth century B.C., whence now and then it agrees with the Septuagint in preserving words and letters which have dropped out of the Massoretic text." Burkitt in *Encyc. Bib.* iv. 5015. It is generally accepted that about the year 333 B.C., Manasseh, the grandson of the high priest Eliashib, carried off to Samaria the Hebrew Book of the Law, when Darius Codomannus gave him permission to build a temple on Mount Gerizim (Neh 13²³⁻³¹; Jos. *Ant.* xi. 7. 8).

INTRODUCTION   xxix

and D 5^{17}, Josephus (*Ant.* iii. 5. 5), the Didache, etc. The order VII.–VI.–VIII. clearly originated in Egypt, possibly as early as the third century B.C. But N's only supporters are the Greek MSS B and some cursives. Hence the order of N and the LXX (B) may be later than the third century. Philo supports the order in N. This order is purely Egyptian. See footnote 1, p. xxv.

§ 2. *N agrees with D against Ex. and is dependent essentially on D or a descendant of D.*—(*a*) N adds with D 5^{14} "thine ox and thine ass" against Ex 20^{10}. D has here the support of M. Sam. T Sam. LXX. Syr. Onk. Ps.-Jon., but M. Syr. Onk. Ps.-Jon. insert "and" before "thine ox."

(*b*) N adds "any of" (*i.e.* כל) before "thy cattle," with D 5^{14} against Ex 20^{10}.

(*c*) N and LXX (B) of D 5^{16} add "that it may be well with thee." D 5^{16} (*i.e.* M. Sam. T Sam. Syr. Onk. Ps.-Jon. Vulg.) also makes this addition, but after "that thy days may be long." This addition originated in a marginal gloss in the Hebrew of D. See note 6, p. xxiv.

(*d*) N following D 5^{20} (M. Sam. T Sam.) reads "vain witness" (עד שוא). Here D N preserve the original reading. In Ex 20^{16} (M. Sam. T Sam.) שוא is rendered by שקר (= "false"). See note on l. 19, p. xviii sq.

(*e*) N following D 5^{21} (M. LXX. Syr. Onk. Ps.-Jon. Vulg.) reads "wife . . . house." So also LXX (B) of Ex 20^{17}, but wrongly. Ex 20^{17} (M. Sam. T Sam.

xxx INTRODUCTION

Syr. Onk. Vulg.) and Sam. T Sam. of D 5^{21} preserve the original order "house . . . wife." See note on l. 20, p. xix. Here Sam. of Ex. has reacted on Sam. of D.

(*f*) N following D 5^{21} (M. Onk. Ps.-Jon.) reads "desire" instead of "covet," as in Ex 20^{17}. The change is due to the Deuteronomist. Here Sam. of Ex 20^{17} has reacted on Sam. of D 5^{21} so that Sam. T Sam. agree in both Decalogues. M is right in both Decalogues. See footnote on l. 20, p. xix.

(*g*) N following D 5^{21} (M. Sam. T Sam. LXX. Syr. Onk. Ps.-Jon.) reads "his field." But Ex 20^{17} (M. Syr. Onk. Vulg.) omit this expression and rightly, though Sam. T Sam. LXX support D. Here Sam. of D 5^{21} has reacted on Sam. Ex. 20^{17}. See preceding note for the converse. Here also as in (*f*) M is right. See note on l. 20, p. xix.

§ 3. *N agrees with Ex. against D.*—(*a*) N reads "remember" with Ex 20^8 (M. LXX. Syr. Onk. Ps.-Jon. Vulg.), against D 5^{12} (M. Sam. T Sam. LXX. Onk. Ps.-Jon. Vulg.) which reads "observe." Here Sam. T Sam. of Ex 20^8 read "observe." The text of Sam. in D 5^{12} has here, as in § 2 (*g*) above, reacted on Sam. of Ex 20^8.

(*b*) N follows Ex 20^{11} in adding "for in six days . . . and hallowed it." In Ex. this is an interpolation of the late fifth century: see pp. xviii, xxxix sq. But that such an addition to some texts of D was already made in the third century B.C., is proved by the LXX of D which, after "nor thy stranger that is within thy gates," inserts the following clause from Ex 20^{11} "for

INTRODUCTION xxxi

in six days the Lord made heaven and earth, and the sea, and all that in them is (ἐν γὰρ ἐξ ἡμέραις ἐποίησεν κύριος τόν τε οὐρανὸν καὶ τὴν γῆν καὶ τὴν θάλασσαν καὶ πάντα τὰ ἐν αὐτοῖς). Hence the above agreement between N and Ex. does not necessarily prove any direct dependence of N on Ex.

(c) N agrees with LXX. Syr. Onk. of D 5⁹ in omitting "and" before "upon the third," but M. Sam. T Sam. read it. N agrees with Ex 20⁵ (M. LXX. Syr. Onk.), but again Sam. T Sam. read "and." N therefore agrees with the LXX. Syr. Onk. in both Decalogues; with M in Ex 20⁵, but has M against it in D 5⁹ and Sam. T Sam. in both Decalogues. N has, therefore, Semitic texts of the seventh to fourth centuries B.C. against it, *i.e.* M once and Sam. twice. It is allied to the LXX of the third century. It does not appear to be directly dependent on M in Ex 20⁵.

§ 4. *N right against Ex. and D.*—N rightly reads "in it" before "thou shalt not do any work" (Ex 20¹⁰, D 5¹⁴), since Sam. T Sam. LXX. Syr. Vulg. in both Ex. and D so read: also Jub 50⁷. Also the "on" before "the seventh day," though lost in M. Sam. T Sam., belongs to an ancient form of the text.

§ 5. *N has readings and forms of its own which do not affect the sense.*—N alone inserts את before אשת and בית in Ex 20¹⁷, D 5²¹. N always reads לוא instead of לא. But both forms are found elsewhere in M, the former thirty-five times. Of the compounds הלוא and

xxxii INTRODUCTION

הלא the Books of Samuel always have the former, while Chronicles always have the latter.

§ 6. *N agrees with the LXX more than with any other authority, and apparently represents a form of the Hebrew text current in Egypt at the close of the third century B.C.*—(*a*) N >" and " before " upon the third," with LXX. Syr. Onk. Ps.-Jon., against M. Sam. T Sam. of D 5^9.

(*b*) N represents a later stage of change than the LXX in the fourth Commandment. Thus, whereas the LXX of D 5^{14} borrowed only the clause " for in six days the Lord created the heaven and the earth, and all that in them is," from Ex 20^{11} (itself a late fifth-century interpolation?), N has borrowed this clause and three others from the same source, Ex 20^{11}.

(*c*) N agrees with the LXX against M. Sam. T Sam. Syr. Onk. in giving a different order of the two clauses in the fifth Commandment[1] in D 5^{16}, " that thy days may be long, and that it may go well with thee."

(*d*) N agrees with the LXX of D 5^{17-19} against M. Sam. T Sam. Syr. Onk. Ps.-Jon. (see § 1 (*f*) above) in changing the order of the Commandments VI.–VII.–VIII. into VII.–VI.–VIII. Order of LXX in Ex 20^{13-15} is VII.–VIII.–VI.

---

[1] But as we have seen in note 6, p. xxiv, the clause "that it may be well with thee" originated in a marginal gloss in D 5^{16}, which was subsequently incorporated by one scribe in an MS (which became the ancestor of M. Sam. T Sam. Syr. Onk. Vulg.) after the clause "that thy days may be long," and by another scribe before this clause in an MS which was the archetype of the LXX of D and of N.

(e) N alone with the LXX interpolates in D 6⁴ the following words: "And these are the statutes and the judgments which Moses commanded the children of Israel in the wilderness (>LXX last three words) when they went forth out of the land of Egypt."

VI

§ 1. *The three forms of the Decalogue in Hebrew, i.e., in Exodus 20, Deuteronomy 5 and the Nash Papyrus, and the date of the archetype of the last of these—not earlier than the close of the third century B.C. or the beginning of the second.*—Owing to the discovery of the Nash Papyrus we now possess the Decalogue in Hebrew in three forms. These in the main agree with each other, and yet they differ essentially from each other in important features as regards both contents and dates. With the Nash Papyrus and its relations to the Decalogues in Exodus 20 and Deuteronomy 5 we have already dealt. N is very closely related to the LXX of D. See p. xxxii. Further, it is dependent mainly on D: it reproduces the tenth Commandment in dependence on D where D diverges in three respects from Ex. In the ninth Commandment it again follows D against Ex. Also in the fifth it borrows a clause from D, and in the fourth it borrows twice from D, in all three cases against Ex. See v. § 2 (a) (b) (c) (d) (e–g), pp. xxix–xxx. There can be no question as to its dependence on D, and thus to the date of its archetype as subsequent to 600 B.C.

xxxiv INTRODUCTION

But N has borrowed from Ex. in the fourth Commandment, and from the latter half of that Commandment, which is itself an interpolation of the fifth century B.C. (or later), for the interpolation is either drawn from or based on the Priests' Code. (See p. xxx sq. § 3 (*b*), p. xxx.) Thus the date of N is brought down to the fifth century B.C.

But N is later still; for the conjunctions with the LXX it arranges the Commandments VI.–VII.–VIII. in the order VII.–VI.–VIII.—an order which is unknown in the fourth century, B.C., as the Samaritan text (not to speak of M) of Ex. and D proves. N also is with the LXX in interpolating a sentence composed of three clauses in D 6^4. (See § 6 (*d*) (*e*), p. xxxii.) The date of N thus comes down to the third century B.C.

It is very probable that N belongs to the close of the third or early in the second century B.C. To the latter date rather than to the former; for it agrees very markedly with the LXX against all other authorities, and, furthermore, it represents a still later form of text than the LXX. See v. § 6, pp. xxxii–xxxiii.

§ 2. *The Decalogue in Ex 20 agrees literally with the Decalogue in D 5, in respect of Commandments I. III. VI.–VIII., but differs in respect of II. IV.–V. IX.–X.*—Since the two Decalogues agree verbally in respect of I. III. VI.–VIII. we have only to study the differences in II. IV.–V. IX.–X. Let us deal with the easiest of these problems first: with V. IX. X. first and in this order, and then with II. and IV.

§ 3. A critical examination of V. IX. X. in respect of their differences proves that D 5 is wholly secondary to Ex 20 save in respect of a single word in IX.

(a) In V. the text of D is obviously secondary. First, the Deuteronomist has inserted the familiar "as the Lord thy God commanded thee" after the first clause, just as he has already inserted it after the first clause in IV. Again, we have a marginal gloss on D 5^{16} in the words "that it may be well with thee," for they have been incorporated in one set of authorities after "that thy days may be long," and in another before this clause—a pretty sure sign of interpolation. This is a frequent Deuteronomic clause: cf. 4^{40} $5^{29,\ 33}$ $6^{3,\ 18}$ $12^{25,\ 28}$ 19^{13} 22^{7}. See note 6, p. xxiv.

(b) In IX. the text of D is primary, that of Ex. secondary. D reads "vain witness." This indefinite phrase is made quite definite in Ex., and rendered "false witness." See note 2, p. xxvi; l. 19, p. xviii, for the discussion of this question.

(c) In X. the text of D is secondary in three respects: (1) in transposing the order of "house" and "wife" (see l. 20, p. xix); (2) in reading "desire" for "covet" (see same reference); (3) in adding "his field" (see note 5, p. xxvi; l. 20, p. xix), where the grounds are given for branding D's text in X. as secondary.

§ 4. *The text of II. is most difficult, but yields fruitful results on examination. The evidence tends to prove that in the eighth century B.C. the Commandment consisted of the words "Thou shalt not make unto thee a graven*

xxxvi INTRODUCTION

image," or this with the addition "nor any likeness." But this Deuteronomic phrase is most probably an addition of D. Subsequently the rest of the Commandment, which appeared first as a marginal gloss in D, was incorporated in D during the sixth or early in the fifth century B.C. From D it was copied into Ex. in the fifth century B.C., or not later than the beginning of the fourth.—The evidence for the above statement is as follows: First of all, the evidence of M (save in D) and all the authorities, the Samaritan text, LXX, Syr., etc., alike in Ex 20⁴ and D 5⁸ (see l. 3, p. xvii), prove that the text about 400 B.C. read "thou shalt not make unto thee a graven image, nor[1] any likeness whatever."

So far the problem presents no difficulty, but the moment we pass on to the words that follow we are brought face to face with untranslatable and, in fact, with ungrammatical Hebrew.[2] If we translate the text as it stands it is meaningless, "Thou shalt not make unto thee a graven image, nor any likeness (כל תמונה), which is in heaven above," etc. But the context requires "nor any likeness *of that* which is in heaven above," etc. No craftsman could make

[1] The text of M in D 5⁸, which omits "nor," is simply a late corruption of M without the support of authority; but Onk. Wellhausen and Kuenen assume that M in D 5⁸ is right, and put פסל (="graven image") in the construct state before כל תמונה (="any likeness"). But Dillmann (see Holzinger, *in loc.*) objects that such a construction as is here supposed is not possible. In any case the textual evidence is against this proposal.

[2] For a series of other like ungrammatical constructions in the Hebrew text, where as here genitives follow the absolute state, see Gesenius, *Hebrew Grammar* (Kautzsch), translated by Cowley, p. 414 sq.

a likeness which is in heaven. In order to get over this difficulty, it is proposed by Holzinger, followed by Peters, to read "nor the likeness of anything" (תמונת כל), as in D 4[16. 23. 25]. But the entire textual evidence is against this proposal. Why should all the authorities agree in giving an unmeaning and ungrammatical text in D 5[8] (Ex 20[4]), when in the preceding chapter we find three times these two words sound alike in sense and grammar? It is true that the LXX renders כל תמונה by παντὸς ὁμοίωμα in D 5[8] and Ex 20[4]. Here the LXX preserves the order of the Hebrew words, but gives them an impossible rendering. On the other hand, in D 4[23. 25] the LXX has ὁμοίωμα πάντων (παντός), which is a correct rendering of תמונת כל. Cf. also D 5[16]. Seeing, therefore, that the Sam. LXX, etc., distinguish carefully *the order and ungrammatical form of these words* in D 5[8], Ex 20[4] *from their order and grammatical form* in D 4[16. 23. 25], there is no evading of the conclusion that not only in the third century B.C. as in the LXX and N, but in the fourth century or earlier the text stood as it does at present. This unmeaning and ungrammatical text in D 5[8], Ex 20[4] came therefore into being between the composition of D in the seventh century and the end of the fifth B.C. It could not have come from the hand of the Deuteronomist.

How then is this ungrammatical text to be explained? The evidence suggests that originally in D 5[8] (if not in the copy of the Decalogue current in the eighth century B.C.) this Commandment read as follows: "Thou shalt not make unto thee a graven image nor any likeness," *i.e.* of Yahweh. The word for "likeness" (תמונה) occurs eight times in the Pentateuch, and, of these eight, six times in Deuteronomy. Of the remaining two, one occurs in Ex 20⁴, which is itself, as it appears, borrowed from D 5⁸.[1] It is, therefore, a favourite word of the Deuteronomist. Hence it is natural to conclude that to the original Commandment, "Thou shalt not make unto thee a graven image," the Deuteronomist added, "nor any likeness." Later, by a scribe of the Deuteronomist's school, a gloss was added in the margin = "which is in heaven above . . . in them that keep My commandments" (D 5⁸ᵇ⁻¹⁰). Thus every phrase in 5⁸ᵇ is to be found in D 4³⁹ᶜ and 4¹⁸ᵇ, and not elsewhere in the Pentateuch outside the Decalogue. In 5⁹ the glosser has drawn the clauses, "a jealous God," and "visiting the iniquity of the fathers upon the children and upon the third and fourth generation," from Ex 34¹⁴ᵇ and 34⁷ respectively (which are either J or JE), 5¹⁰ "showing mercy[2] unto thousands of them that love Me and keep My commandments" is almost a verbal reproduction of D 7⁹: "God which keepeth . . . mercy with them that love Him and keep His commandments to a thousand generations."

D 5⁸ᵇ⁻¹⁰, which appeared first as a gloss in the margin, was incorporated in the text by a later scribe

---

[1] Elsewhere in the Pentateuch it is only found in Nu 12⁸ (E).

[2] The Hebrew phrase (עשה חסר) is not found elsewhere in D, though it is a familiar one in J and E in Genesis. Cf. also Jos 2¹². ¹⁴.

without a readjustment of the grammar. From D 5^{8b-10} it was taken over into the Decalogue in Ex 20^{4b-6}, possibly in the fifth century B.C. and not later than the first half of the fourth. This last inference follows from the fact that the Samaritan text (fourth century B.C.) and the LXX reproduce the gloss.

§ 5. *The divergence between IV. in D 5^{12-15} and Ex 20^{8-11} is great. But this divergence is due mainly to the comparatively late (fifth century B.C. ?) interpolation of 20^{11} in Ex. based on Gn 2^{26} and Ex 31^{17} (both verses of the Priests' Code) and to the addition of 5^{15} in D by the Deuteronomist. D 5^{14c} preserves a clause lost in Ex 20^{8-10} and preserves the ancient sense of IV. lost in the present form of Ex 20^{8-11}.*

I have elsewhere dealt with the interpolation in Ex 20^{11}.[1] The author of D would naturally add explanatory clauses but not omit them. Since this interpolation is practically unquestioned, we may turn aside to the additions made in D 5^{15}. Thus the words, " And thou shalt remember that thou wast a servant in the land of Egypt and the Lord thy God brought thee out hence," are found almost verbally in 15^{15} 16^{12} $24^{18,\ 22}$. The next clause of 5^{15} "by a mighty hand and a stretched out arm" have already occurred in 4^{34} (only in the Pentateuch : cf. 6^{21} 7^{8}).

Thus IV. consists of 20^{8-12} in Ex. and 5^{12-14} in D. The last clause in D 5^{14}, "that thy manservant and thy maidservant may rest as well as thou," is without doubt older than D, as it occurs in Ex 23^{12} (E—a

[1] See pp. 112-116.

INTRODUCTION

document over a hundred years older than D), "six days thou shalt do thy work, and on the seventh day thou shalt rest: that thine ox and thine ass may have rest, and the son of thine handmaid, and the stranger may be refreshed." It is probable also that the words "nor thine ox nor thine ass" (which Ex 20^{10} omits) go back to the eighth century B.C., seeing that they occur in Ex 23^{12} as well as in D 5^{14}.

In D 5^{12} the clause "as the Lord thy God commanded thee" is obviously an addition of the Deuteronomist as also in 5^{16}. It is a favourite expression with him: cf. 1^{19} 4^5 5^{32} 6^{25} 20^{17} 24^8, or in the form "which the Lord thy God hath commanded thee": cf. 1^{41} 5^{33} 6^{17} etc. etc.

This Commandment, therefore, on the united evidence of Ex 20^{8-10}, D 5^{12-14} read most probably as follows in the eighth century B.C.:

"Remember [1] the sabbath day, to keep it holy. Six days shalt thou labour and do all thy work; but <on> the seventh day is a sabbath unto the Lord thy God; <in it>[2] thou shalt not do any work, thou nor thy son nor thy daughter nor [3] thy manservant, nor thy maidservant nor [3] thine ox nor thine ass, nor (any of)[3] thy cattle,[4] that thy manservant and thy maidservant may rest as well as thou."

[1] D reads "observe," but wrongly.
[2] The words "in it" though omitted by M in Ex. and D are original; see p. xxiii, note 5.
[3] Found in D, but doubtful.
[4] D adds "nor thy stranger that is within thy gates." See note 2, p. xlii.

INTRODUCTION xli

§ 6. *A comparison of the Decalogue in E as reproduced in Ex 20 (as we conclude from the above investigation it stood in the eighth century or earlier) and the Decalogue in D 5 in respect of Commandments II. III.–V. and IX.–X. (as it stood in the seventh).*

Ex $20^{4-12.\ 17}$
(eighth century B.C.)

D $5^{8-16.\ 21}$ (621 B.C.)

II. *i.e.* (20^4). "Thou shalt not make unto thee a graven image."[1]

(5^{8a}) "Thou shalt not make unto thee a graven image nor any likeness."[2]

IV. (20^{8-10}). "Remember the sabbath day to keep it holy. Six days shalt thou labour, and do all thy work: but <on>[3] the seventh day is a sabbath unto the Lord thy God: <in it>[4] thou shalt not do any work, thou, nor thy son, nor thy daughter, thy manservant, nor thy maidservant, <nor thine

5^{12-14} "Observe the sabbath day to keep it holy, as the Lord thy God commanded thee: six days shalt thou labour, and do all thy work: but the seventh day is a sabbath unto the Lord thy God: <in it>[4] thou shalt not do any work, thou, nor thy son, nor thy daughter, nor thy manservant, nor thy

[1] Here was subsequently added not only the clause from D "nor any likeness," but also the marginal gloss that was incorporated by D between 600 and 500 B.C. See next note and also p. xxxvi sqq.

[2] Here were incorporated ungrammatically the words that formerly stood as a marginal gloss: "that is in heaven above . . . and showing mercy unto thousands of them that love Me and keep My commandments" (D 5^{8b-10}).

[3] The "on" appears to belong to the text of the eighth century. Though lost in the Massoretic it is preserved in N of Ex 20^{10}: also in LXX and Vulg. and in the parallel passages in Ex $23^{12}\ 34^{21}$.

[4] "In it" belongs to the text of the Decalogue in the seventh as well as the eighth century.

xlii INTRODUCTION

ox, nor thine ass>,[1] nor thy cattle,[2] < that thy manservant and thy maidservant may rest as well as thou.">[3]	maidservant, nor thine ox, nor thine ass, nor any of thy cattle, nor thy stranger that is within thy gates; that thy manservant and thy maidservant may rest as well as thou. And thou shalt remember that thou wast a servant in the land of Egypt,[4] and the Lord thy God brought thee out thence by a mighty hand and by a

---

[1] Restored from D 5[14] and Book of Covenant, Ex 23[12] in the same connection. The phrase occurs five times in the Book of the Covenant.

[2] Here D adds "nor thy stranger that is within thy gates." The phrase "within thy ('your' or 'any of thy') gates" occurs nearly thirty times in D and not elsewhere in the Pentateuch save in Ex 20[10] where it has been borrowed from D. The clause "thy stranger that is within thy gates" recurs in D 31[12], and the words "thy stranger" four times in D but not elsewhere in the Pentateuch save in Ex 20[10], where it is a loan from D.

[3] This clause in brackets I have restored. It is found in D 5[14c]: also in the Book of the Covenant in the same connection though in different phraseology, Ex 23[12]. The evidence, therefore, is in favour of the conclusion that it stood originally in Ex 20 after v.[10], but was omitted by the interpolator of Ex 20[11]. Ex 20[11] is based on Gn 2[3].

[4] The words, "that thou wast a servant in the land of Egypt," which follow closely after "the stranger within thy gates," certainly recall the clauses in the Book of the Covenant, Ex 22[21] 23[9], "a stranger shalt thou not wrong (תונה: 'oppress,' תלחץ, Ex 23[9]) . . . for ye were strangers in the land of Egypt." Seeing that the Book of the Covenant to a considerable extent presupposes (see p. liv sqq.) the Mosaic Decalogue, the Deuteronomist, who was acquainted with it, may have been encouraged thereby to add the many explanatory clauses, which as a matter of fact he does.

stretched out arm: therefore the Lord thy God commanded thee to keep the sabbath day."

v. (20¹²). "Honour thy father and thy mother."[1]

(5¹⁶) "Honour thy father and thy mother, as the Lord thy God commanded thee: that thy days may be long[2] upon the land which the Lord thy God giveth thee."

IX. (20¹⁶). "Thou[3] shalt not bear vain[4] witness against thy neighbour."

(5²⁰) "Neither shalt thou bear vain witness against thy neighbour."

X. (20¹⁷). "Thou shalt not covet thy neighbour's house, thou shalt not covet thy neighbour's wife, nor his manservant, nor his

(5²¹) "Neither shalt thou covet thy neighbour's wife; neither shalt thou desire thy neighbour's house, his field, or his

---

[1] The words that follow in Ex 20¹², "that thy days may be long upon the land which the Lord thy God giveth thee," are simply borrowed from D 5¹⁶. The first clause is a Deuteronomic phrase: cf. 4²¹·⁴⁰ 5³³ 6² 11⁹ 17²⁰ 22⁷ 25¹⁵ 30¹⁸ 32⁴⁷. It is not found elsewhere in the Pentateuch save in Ex 20¹², where it is secondary and borrowed. The second clause, "upon the land which the Lord thy God is giving (always the participle נתן) thee," is also a Deuteronomic phrase and not found elsewhere in the Pentateuch save in Ex 20¹², where it is borrowed from D 5¹⁶. With slight variations it is found almost forty times in D.

[2] Here M. Sam. TSam. Syr. Onk. Vulg. add, "and that it may be well with thee," whereas LXX and N insert this clause before "that thy days may be long." This clause originated in a marginal clause about or before 400 B.C. See note 6, p. xxiv.

[3] See p. xviii, ll. 18–20.

[4] I have restored "vain" (i.e. שוא). שקר (= "false") is a rendering which has displaced the original word.

maidservant, nor his ox, nor his ass, nor anything that is thy neighbour's." manservant, or his maidservant, his ox, or his ass, or anything that is thy neighbour's."

§ 7. *The Decalogue as it existed about 750 B.C. or earlier.*

I. "Thou shalt have none other gods before Me."

II. "Thou shalt not make unto thee a graven image."

III. "Thou shalt not take the name of the Lord thy God in vain; for the Lord will not hold him guiltless that taketh His name in vain."

IV. "Remember the sabbath day to keep it holy. Six days shalt thou labour, and do all thy work: but <on> the seventh day is a sabbath unto the Lord thy God: in it thou shalt not do any work, thou, nor thy son, nor thy daughter, thy manservant nor thy maidservant: <nor thine ox nor thine ass>, nor thy cattle, <that thy manservant and thy maidservant may rest as well as thou>."

V. "Honour thy father and thy mother."

VI. "Thou shalt do no murder."

VII. "Thou shalt not commit adultery."

VIII. "Thou shalt not steal."

IX. "Thou shalt not bear false witness against thy neighbour."

X. "Thou shalt not covet thy neighbour's house, thou shalt not covet thy neighbour's wife, nor his manservant, nor his maidservant, nor his ox, nor his ass, nor anything that is thy neighbour's."

VII

§ 1. *The fact that there was, as we have seen, a steady growth of explanatory accretions or changes from the eighth century to the second B.C., leads naturally to the hypothesis that such explanatory clauses as still survive in the eighth century Decalogue in III.-IV. X. are themselves accretions.*—This hypothesis is found first, so far as I am aware, in Ewald (*Hist.* ii. 159), who writes as follows: "If we take from the two copies which have been handed down to us, Ex 20 and Deut 5, the additions and explanations which we find there, they exhibit perfectly that sharp, clear brevity which every law ought to possess." Dillmann is of the same mind. But neither attempted to justify this hypothesis. Let us now study III. IV. and X. in the light of the results we have arrived at on critical grounds in the case of II. V. and partially in the case of IV. First of all as regards III. In this Commandment it seems obvious that the words "for the Lord will not hold him guiltless that taketh His name in vain," are an accretion. The second clause, "that taketh His name in vain," is simply based on the Commandment itself, and the first clause may be drawn verbally from Ex 34^7 if that passage belongs to J.

In IV. the original Commandment was most probably " Remember the sabbath day to keep it holy." *In primitive races ordinary work was sus-*

INTRODUCTION

pended with a view to some religious function—not as in the present day with multitudes, simply and solely with a view to rest. The idea of rest and of recreation was, of course, early associated with that of worship.

Now the question arises: Is the addition in IV. anterior or subsequent to the corresponding commands in the Book of the Covenant, *i.e.* Ex 23^{12} (E) and the Decalogue in Ex 34^{21} (J)? No important result follows, however we decide. But, on the whole, the addition seems to be older than the Book of the Covenant, and also than the Decalogue in Ex 34, and in other words than E and J, as I have to show later in VII. §§ 5–6. Thus Ex 34^{21ab} consists verbally of two clauses occurring in two different parts of the addition in Ex 20^{10}. As for the words of the Book of the Covenant in Ex 23^{12} "Six days shalt thou do thy work, and on the seventh shalt thou rest:[1] that thine ox and thine ass may have rest, and the son of thine handmaid, and the stranger may be refreshed," the first clause agrees in thought with the corresponding phrase in Ex 20^{10}, while the last two clauses agree with the concluding clauses in Ex 20^{10} (as it

---

[1] For "shalt thou rest" the LXX has ἀνάπαυσις, *i.e.* "Sabbath," *i.e.* השבּת instead of תשׁבּת. This seems to be right; but if so, it would be of the nature of a conjecture, since M. Sam. T Sam. Syr. support the former reading. Baentsch (*D. Bundesbuch*, p. 94) states categorically that command "to rest" on the seventh day is more primitive than "to keep it holy." But the analogy of primitive religions proves that the main object is a religious one, and that the command "to rest" is simply with a view to the discharge of the religious obligation.

stood in E) though the diction differs. It is easier to explain 34^{21ab} and 23^{12} as based on Ex 20^{10} than *vice versa*.

In x. the problem is difficult. The analogy of I.–II. V.–IX. and in all probability of III.–IV. suggests that the original form of this Commandment was "Thou shalt not covet," or "Thou shalt not covet thy neighbour's house." If the latter conjecture is accepted, the remaining words are merely a very natural explanation of the Hebrew expression "house." But the more natural assumption is that the original form was simply "Thou shalt not covet," and that the exigencies of the times called for an expansion of this Commandment in the way of explanation. It is further to be observed that there is not the slightest allusion to this Commandment in the Book of the Covenant or in the Decalogue in Ex 34.

It must be acknowledged that this Commandment stands on a higher level than the preceding nine. But this fact in itself does not conflict with the possibility, or rather probability, of its existence in the Decalogue prior to E. For the time being, I assume that x. originally existed in the form, "Thou shalt not covet," without the accretions that accompany it in Ex 20^{17}.

Hence, I conclude that III. IV. and X. originally read as follows:

III. Thou shalt not take the name of the Lord thy God in vain.

INTRODUCTION

IV. Remember the sabbath day, to keep it holy.

X. Thou shalt not covet.[1]

But for this form of the Decalogue we should probably have to go back to the centuries preceding 900 B.C.

§ 2. *If the above conclusions, and the hypothesis in VII. § 1, are valid, it follows that, before E and J were written, the Decalogue existed, each Commandment consisting of one clause, expressed in a few clear and crisp words, in the tenth century or earlier. But if this is so, then there is no outstanding personality to whom this Decalogue can be ascribed other than Moses.*— Before the eighth century B.C. there is only one great outstanding personality to whom Israel attributed its primitive legislation, and this, of course, was Moses. In this attribution the tradition never wavers. No doubt the greater part of this legislation is late, but, whatever else may be of late derivation, the Decalogue, in the form represented in VI. § 7, VII. § 1 above, can hardly be traced to any other person than Moses, the founder of the preprophetic and ethical Yahwism of Israel. For the high ethical Yahwism introduced by Moses has to be distinguished from "the lower and naturalistic conception of the same deity [2] already prevalent in

[1] The Decalogue, including the introductory words, when relieved of the accretions of centuries, would amount to about 159 letters. These could be written on two small tables of stone. But the text as it stands at present in Ex 20 would run to 620 letters, which would require rather formidable stones for their inscription.

[2] That Yahweh was originally an Amorite deity, see Burney, *Judges*, 243 sqq. Sayce was the first to discover the existence of Yahweh as a divine name in Babylon under the first dynasty.

INTRODUCTION

Canaan."[1] Burney maintains that "no sharp line of demarcation can be drawn between the religion of Amos and that of the founder of the national life," and that "the title 'prophetic,' with its implications as applied to the earlier religion of the nation of Israel, is largely a misnomer." This is rather an overstatement. For, though the same ethical character attaches to the religious beliefs of Moses and of the eighth-century prophets, yet the prophetic conception of Yahweh was monotheistic, while that of Moses was henotheistic. In this respect a great intellectual gulf does exist between the religious beliefs of the prophets and of Moses.[2]

§ 3. *Various objections to the conclusion that the Decalogue without the accretions of subsequent ages was Mosaic, stated and answered.* — Baentsch (*Das Bundesbuch*, p. 95) and most O.T. scholars rightly maintain that "the higher the spiritual and moral development of a people rises, the more abstract appear these ethical laws." "The Decalogue in Ex 20 represents throughout the standpoint of that which is *fas*" (or purely ethical). "Confessedly the idea, the abstract is ever younger than the concrete" (p. 96). "The supremacy of abstract thought was reserved in Israel for the prophetic period" (p. 97).

These general observations are deserving of consideration in themselves, but we cannot conclude from

[1] See Burney, *Israel's Settlement in Canaan*, p. 55 sq. *n.*; *JTS*, 1908, 344 sqq.

[2] Burney, of course, recognises this fact elsewhere; see *Judges*, p. 315.

INTRODUCTION

them that the Decalogue is later than the Book of the Covenant and the Decalogue in Ex 34, *unless we maintain at the same time that there was no religious or moral development outside Israel and anterior to Moses.* But no scholar can maintain such a thesis at the present day. According to the universal Hebrew tradition, Moses was acquainted with the learning of the Egyptians, and, accordingly, with the ethical teaching of the Egyptians. Moreover, Egypt was not excluded from intercourse with the great religions of the East —at all events of Babylon. Hence, unless Hebrew thought and religion sprang spontaneously into existence and grew in absolute isolation and continued to grow without any period of reaction, decadence, or obscurantism, the above theory that the Decalogue is not conceivable before the eighth century B.C. cannot be maintained. There are periods of reaction in all religions. That there have been such periods in Christianity is a fact too familiar to require further treatment, though we shall return to it later. In fact, the ethical teaching of Christianity is purest in its beginnings. In Brahmanism the ancient tenfold laws of Manu precede centuries of obscurantism and degradation in that religion. These are: contentment, forgiveness, self-control, abstention from theft, purification, control of the organs, wisdom, knowledge (of the supreme soul), truthfulness, abstention from anger (*SBE* xxv. 215). Buddhism, like Christianity, was at its purest in its beginnings. But even as late as the beginning of the first century A.D. it requires the following ten conditions of the heart: self-control, inward calm, long-suffering, self-restraint, temperance, voluntary subjection to meritorious vows, freedom from wrath and cruelty, truthfulness, purity of heart (*SBE* xxxv. 173 sq.). Zoroastrianism has its ten admonitions in regard to religion, but they are not of a high order (*SBE* xlvii. 167 sqq.).

Apart from these general analogies it should not be forgotten that in the Egyptian Book of the Dead there are several remarkable parallels to the original Mosaic Decalogue. Burney (*JTS*, 1908, 350 sq.) has already drawn attention to these in the Negative Confession, with its forty-two statements (Budge, *Books on Egypt and Chaldæa*, vii. 365 sqq.). I prefix the number of the Mosaic Commandment.

III.	No. 38. I have not cursed the god. No. 42. I have not thought scorn of the god who is in my city.
VI.	No. 5. I have not slain man or woman. (Cf. also No. 12.)
VII.	No. 19. I have not defiled the wife of a man. No. 20. I have not committed any sin against purity. No. 27. I have not committed acts of impurity, neither have I lain with men.

VIII. No. 4. I have not committed theft. Cf. No. 2.
IX. No. 9. I have not uttered falsehood. No. 31. I have not judged hastily.

Here the statements are terse and direct, and certainly remind us of the Mosaic Decalogue. Parallels in the same crisp form are found in an ancient Babylonian document to Commandments V.–VIII. as I have shown elsewhere; see p. xxv sq. n. There is, therefore, no *a priori* objection to the Mosaic Decalogue, while, on the other hand, there are abundant historical analogies that can be cited in support of it.

Again, this objection, that "the abstract is ever younger than the concrete," is in direct conflict with the actual history of the Decalogue from 800 to 200 B.C. The fourth Commandment becomes more concrete with the progress of the centuries: so also does the fifth, and likewise the second and tenth.

Again, a great religious and moral revelation is not the work of a moral syndicate, but is due to the inspiration of some great outstanding personality. Such lofty disclosures may fail in the lifetime of their author to effect their ends, but sooner or later they come into their own. Thus the second Commandment was ignored in Southern Israel till the tenth century (if not later), and in Northern Israel till the Exile. This fact is put forward as irrefragable evidence by many scholars that the second Commandment was non-existent down to the tenth century at all events.

But we can never safely argue from the non-observance of a law at a certain period to the conclusion that no such law existed. Those who study the history of the Christian Church are well aware that from the Seventh General Council, 787 A.D., to the Reformation the second Commandment was either explained away or deliberately omitted from the Decalogue. In fact, this is the treatment meted out to this Commandment by the Roman Church at the present day.[1] Indeed, if we applied the same arguments to the penal laws connected with breaches of the Sabbath day, or of a wife's unfaithfulness in the Priests' Code, we should be obliged to deny their existence there, seeing that these laws were never apparently put into execution by the Jewish authorities except on one or more occasions in the course of all the centuries that have followed since their enactment.

Again, it is maintained that the eighth-century prophets never appeal to the Decalogue, and therefore it did not exist before their time. But surely the reason that they made no such appeal is that they took for granted *Israel's* acquaintance with it. As Burney (*JTS*, 1908, 331) rightly urges: "The eighth-century prophets . . . when they attack the religious and social abuses of their time, appear, in fact, to attack them *as abuses, i.e.*, they seem to regard themselves not as founders of a new type of Yahwe-religion, but as interpreting and insisting upon religious essentials which ought to have been patent to Israel

[1] See pp. 71-74.

liv INTRODUCTION

at large. The whole tenor of their teaching may be said to *presuppose* the Decalogue. It is difficult to understand the severity of their language, if it was aimed, *not against a moral declension, but against a stage of morals which as yet knew of no higher ideal.*"[1]

§ 4. *The Mosaic Decalogue and its subsequent revisions and accretions down to 200 B.C.* See opposite page.

§ 5. *The Book of the Covenant,* i.e. *Ex* 20^{22}–23^{33} *presupposes the Decalogue.*

In order to avoid complications we have hitherto ignored the relation, chronological or other, in which the Decalogue stands to the Book of the Covenant, 20^{22}–23^{33}, and to the Decalogue in Ex 34. This question has been discussed by most of the O.T. scholars. It is too large to be discussed here. And yet it cannot be put aside wholly, though only some of the chief conclusions can be considered. First, as to the relation of the Book of the Covenant[2] to the Decalogue, Rothstein concludes that the former is a commentary on the latter. Klostermann holds that the Book of the Covenant was built on the Decalogue. Both these hypotheses have been rejected by the vast body of scholars.

Notwithstanding, I am constrained to adopt an hypothesis not unrelated to those of the two scholars just mentioned. I have briefly shown in § 3 (p. xlix sqq.) that the main objections to the existence of the

[1] The italics in the last clause are mine.
[2] This designation of this section is found in Ex 24^7.

Mosaic Decalogue, each Commandment consisting of one short clause. *c.* 1320–1300 B.C.

Decalogue with the earliest additions in III. (?),[1] IV.[2] X.[3] *c.* 900 B.C. or earlier.[4]

Decalogue as it stood before its incorporation in E. *c.* 800–750 B.C.

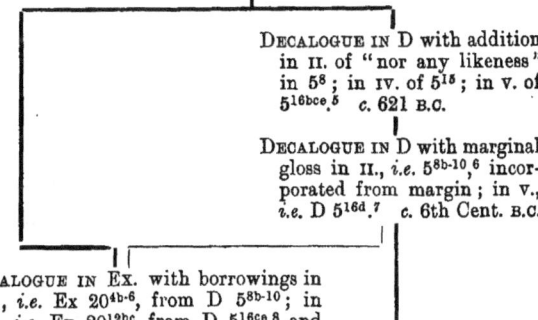

DECALOGUE IN D with addition in II. of "nor any likeness" in 5^8; in IV. of 5^{15}; in V. of 5^{16bce}.[5] *c.* 621 B.C.

DECALOGUE IN D with marginal gloss in II., *i.e.* 5^{8b-10},[6] incorporated from margin; in V., *i.e.* D 5^{16d}.[7] *c.* 6th Cent. B.C.

DECALOGUE IN EX. with borrowings in II., *i.e.* Ex 20^{4b-6}, from D 5^{8b-10}; in V., *i.e.* Ex 20^{12bc}, from D 5^{16ce},[8] and interpolation in IV., *i.e.* Ex 20^{11}, which has displaced the final clause still preserved in D 5^{14}.[9] *c.* 5th Cent. B.C.

Hebrew Archetype used by LXX current in Egypt. *c.* 300 B.C.

NASH HEBREW PAPYRUS. *c.* 200 B.C.

N.B.—Heavy lines denote direct descent, light lines indirect descent.

---

[1] *i.e.* Ex 20^{7b}.   [2] *i.e.* Ex $20^{9,10}$ and last clause in D 5^{14}.

[3] *i.e.* Ex 20^7 "thy neighbour's house, thou shalt not covet . . . anything that is thy neighbour's."

[4] For the ground for this date see § 13 *ad fin.* and the footnotes 2, 3.

[5] 5^{16b} "as the Lord thy God commanded thee" is peculiar to D.

[6] 5^{8b-10} "that is in heaven above . . . keep My commandments."

[7] 5^{16d} "And that it may go well with thee."

[8] Ex 20^{12bc} "that thy days may be long upon the land which the Lord thy God giveth thee."

[9] *i.e.* "that thy manservant and maidservant may rest as well as thou."

lvi INTRODUCTION

Decalogue from the Mosaic period onwards are really without weight.

In the Book of the Covenant there are, as it has been shown, borrowings[1] from the Decalogue in Ex 34, and possibly interpolations.[2] The order is likewise confused.[3] There is an intermingling of ethical, religious (20^{22-26} $22^{17}-23^{19}$) and judicial elements (21^2-22^{17}). But the ethical commands and the judgments (expressed hypothetically) both alike rightly belong to the document. The latter are simply a practical application of the former in specific cases. Their aim is to regulate the life of a people living under primitive conditions and mainly engaged in agriculture.

Now it is to be noted that of the ten Commandments account is taken of seven (or possibly nine). In other words, these seven (or nine) are presupposed. That the tenth is omitted is natural. Such a practical document as the Book of the Covenant can take little or no account of the thoughts of the heart.[4] In the next place, the omission of the second Commandment in a document composed in the Northern Kingdom (for the Book of the Covenant is derived

[1] *i.e.* 23^{14-19} from $34^{18, 22-23, 25-26}$.

[2] 20^{22-23} $22^{23, 21b, 24}$ $23^{10, 11, 13b}$.

[3] Thus 21^{17} should be restored before 21^{16}; 21^{18-25} read in the following order $21^{18-19, 23-25, 22, 20-21}$. The text in 22^{1-4} is also confused.

[4] Some elements which take account of motives appear in $22^{21, 27}$, $23^{4-5, 9}$, but they are probably of later origin. In any case they do not approach the profound and universal ethical character of the tenth Commandment.

INTRODUCTION lvii

from E) would not be astonishing or even remarkable, seeing that it was ignored by Northern Israel as a whole till the Exile. And yet, if 20^{23} is original, then it presupposes both the first and second (?) Commandments.

A priori, therefore, we should not expect a document of this nature to deal with more than eight out of the ten Commandments, and when we examine the Book of the Covenant we find that eight (or seven) are actually dealt with. Clearly the Book of the Covenant is incomplete; else there would be a section on the adulterous wife. The seven (or six) are as follows:

Decalogue before its incorporation in E.	*Book of Covenant, Ex 20^{22}–23^{33}.*
I. "Thou shalt have none other gods before Me."	This Commandment is presupposed in Ex $23^{13.24.32-33}$, 20^{23}. The Israelites are required not even to mention the name of other gods (23^{13}): they are not to make any covenant with them (23^{32}), nor serve them ($23^{24.33}$), nor make images of them in silver or gold (20^{23}). But this last verse is regarded as a secondary addition to the text. If it were original it would implicitly (?) forbid the

I.–II.	making of images of Yahweh (*i.e.* the second Commandment). Ex 20²³ "Ye shall not make other gods¹ with Me; gods of silver or gods of gold, ye shall not make unto you." These words, if original, presuppose the existence of Yahweh and other gods. The prohibition of images of the latter may carry with it the prohibition of images of Yahweh.
III. "Thou shalt not take the name of the Lord thy God in vain."	? Ex 22²⁸ "Thou shalt not revile God." But for "God" we should most probably render "the judges," as in 21⁶ 22⁸. If the latter rendering is right, then only seven of the Commandments are presupposed.
IV. "Remember the sabbath day to keep it holy . . . that thy manservant and thy maidservant may rest as well as thou." (See above, pp. xli sq., xliv.)	Ex 23¹² "Six days thou shalt do thy work, and on the seventh thou shalt rest: that thine ox and thine ass may have rest, and the son of thine handmaid, and the stranger, may be refreshed."

---

¹ The words "other gods" are restored by Dillmann.

INTRODUCTION lix

v. "Honour thy father and thy mother."	Ex 21^{15} "He that smiteth his father, or mother, shall surely be put to death." 21^{17} "And he that curseth his father, or his mother, shall surely be put to death."
vi.	Ex 21$^{12-14\cdot\ 20\cdot\ 23-24\cdot\ 29}$. These are practical applications of vi.
vii.	? Ex 22^{16}. This is not a judgment following logically from vii., *but may be part of a section now lost which dealt with the adulterous wife.* The Book of the Covenant would be incomplete without such a section.
viii.	Ex 22$^{1-5\cdot\ 7-8\cdot\ 12}$.
ix.	Ex 23$^{1-2}$.

That such a document as the Decalogue is presupposed by the Book of the Covenant follows naturally from the above comparison.

§ 6. *The Decalogue in Ex 34 (i.e. J)*[1] *has several*

---

[1] Wellhausen, *Comp. des Hexat.* pp. 331–332, tries to recover the Decalogue in 34. He makes it out as follows: I. Thou shalt worship no other god (34^{14}). II. Thou shalt make thee no molten gods (34^{17}). III. The feast of unleavened bread thou shalt keep (34^{18}). IV. All that openeth the womb is Mine (34^{19}). V. Thou shalt observe the feast of weeks (34^{22a}). VI. <Thou shalt observe> the feast of ingathering at the year's end (34^{22c}). VII. Thou shalt not offer the blood of My sacrifice with leavened bread (34^{25a}). VIII. The fat of

INTRODUCTION

points in common with the Decalogue of Ex 20 as it stood in 900 B.C. before it was incorporated in E (see p. xliv sqq.). *The former betrays a relation of dependence on the latter.*—The Decalogue in Ex 34 is very far removed from that in Ex 20. The former Decalogue is preserved in 34¹¹⁻²⁶, but practically no two scholars agree as to what the ten Commandments were. According to Baentsch (*Das Bundesbuch*, p. 98), " The Decalogue in Ex 34 stands on the preprophetic stage of the Yahweh-Religion and so undoubtedly nearer to the Book of the Covenant than to the Decalogue in Ex 20." And again (p. 101): "in this its original form . . . the Decalogue in Ex 34 is older than the Book of the Covenant: in its revised form, on the other hand, in which it now lies before us, it bears manifestly the stamp of a later time." Baentsch

My feast shall not remain all night until the morning (34²⁵ᵇ). IX. The first of the first-fruits of thy ground thou shalt bring into the house of the Lord thy God (34²⁶ᵃ). X. Thou shalt not seethe a kid in its mother's milk (34²⁶ᵇ). So also Holzinger, *Ex.* 119. Stade (*Gesch.* i. 510) agrees with the above, save that for V. and VI. he reads as follows: V. Thou shalt keep the sabbath (34²¹). VI. Thou shalt observe the feast of weeks and the feast of the ingathering at the year's end (34²²). Kennett (*Deut.* p. 40 sq.) defines them as follows: I. Thou shalt worship no other god. II. The feast of unleavened bread thou shalt keep. III. All that open the matrix is Mine, and every firstling, etc. IV. Six days thou shalt work, but on the seventh day thou shalt rest. In the remaining six he agrees with Wellhausen. This Decalogue presupposes the settlement of Israel in Canaan. The nation has already abandoned the life of the nomad for that of the agriculturist. It celebrates three festivals, two of which are concerned with husbandry solely. But the Decalogue in Ex 20, when stripped of its later accretions, knows only of a weekly festival—a sabbath of rest for worship. This Decalogue is adapted to a nomadic people.

holds that the Decalogue in Ex 20 is the latest of the three documents in question. Holzinger's view (*Ex.* p. 120) is interesting. He concludes that the Decalogue in Ex 34, which is preserved by J, is older than that in Ex 20 preserved by E; but that this Decalogue in E shows traces of a groundwork which is older than the Decalogue of J.

In the preceding pages I have sought to show that the Decalogue in Ex 20 and D 5, when stripped of the accretions it received after 900 B.C., consisted of ten Commandments of one clause each, save in the case of III. (?), IV. and X. (see p. xliv sqq.), and also that the Book of the Covenant presupposes this Decalogue (see § 5).

If the Decalogue in Ex 20 stood in this relation to the Book of the Covenant, we have now to try and discover in what relation it stood to the Decalogue in Ex 34. The latter, as I hope to show, manifests in some degree its dependence on the former. Let us now compare the two Decalogues.

Ex 20, *c.* 900 B.C.	Ex 34, *c.* 900–850.
I. Ex 20³ "Thou shalt have none other gods before Me."	Ex 34¹⁴ "Thou shalt worship no other god."
II. Ex 20⁴ "Thou shalt not make unto thee a graven image"	Ex 34¹⁷ "Thou shalt make thee no molten gods." Molten images belong to a later period than graven images.

INTRODUCTION

IV. "Six days thou shalt work¹ . . . but² on the seventh day is a sabbath." Ex 34^{21} "Six days thou shalt work,¹ but on the seventh day thou shalt rest."

These correspondences are not coincidences. The one authority is dependent on the other. That Ex 34 in regard to the second Commandment is secondary to the form in Ex 20^4 there can be no question. Similarly, the first Commandment in Ex 34^{14} is secondary likewise. It is an interpretation or definition of Ex 20^4. If the fourth stood alone, it would not be decisive either way, but when taken in conjunction with the evidence of the first and second Commandments it not only attests the dependence of Ex 34 on the Mosaic Decalogue, but also the existence in that Decalogue of accretions in the fourth Commandment, before J (*i.e. c.* 850 B.C.) made use of the materials in Ex 34^{1-28}. Hence the Mosaic Decalogue with accretions in the fourth, most probably in the tenth³ and possibly in the third,⁴ existed in this form in 900 B.C. or earlier.

---

¹ Exactly the same Hebrew clause in each case.
² See footnote 3 on p. xli.
³ Seeing that the tenth Commandment in its original form must have been an occasion of great difficulty to the teachers of Israel, it is reasonable to assume that the addition to the original words, "thou shalt not covet," was made in it at an early date, *i.e.* 900 B.C. or earlier. For it was already in the Decalogue incorporated in E about 800–750 B.C. D, about 621 B.C. or rather earlier, recast this addition, as we have already seen.
⁴ The evidence of D 5^{11} throws back the date of the accretion in this Commandment to 621 B.C. at latest, while the joint evidence of D 5^{11} and Ex 20^7 presupposes a date anterior to 800–750 B.C., when E was composed of pre-existing materials.

§ 7. *Ex 34 has influenced the later form of the Decalogue in D 5 and thereby of the Decalogue in Ex 20.*—In § 4, p. xxxvii sqq., I have sought to show that

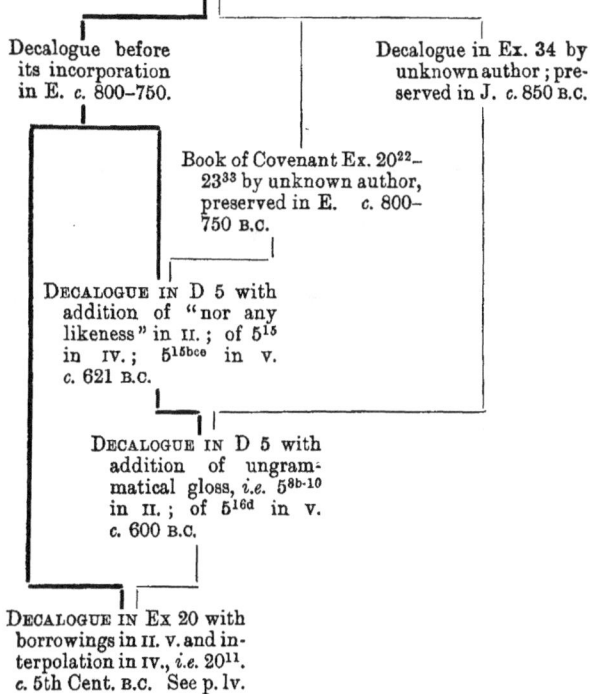

Mosaic Decalogue with additions in III. (?), IV. X. (see pp. xliv–xlviii). *c.* 900 B.C. or earlier.

Decalogue before its incorporation in E. *c.* 800–750.

Decalogue in Ex. 34 by unknown author; preserved in J. *c.* 850 B.C.

Book of Covenant Ex. 20^{22}–23^{33} by unknown author, preserved in E. *c.* 800–750 B.C.

DECALOGUE IN D 5 with addition of "nor any likeness" in II.; of 5^{15} in IV.; 5^{15bce} in V. *c.* 621 B.C.

DECALOGUE IN D 5 with addition of ungrammatical gloss, *i.e.* $5^{8b\text{-}10}$ in II.; of 5^{16d} in V. *c.* 600 B.C.

DECALOGUE IN Ex 20 with borrowings in II. V. and interpolation in IV., *i.e.* 20^{11}. *c.* 5th Cent. B.C. See p. lv.

N.B.—Heavy lines denote direct descent, light lines indirect descent.

D $5^{9\text{-}10}$ was originally a gloss based on Ex $34^{14,\,7}$. For the other sources of the gloss, see § 4. From D $5^{8b\text{-}10}$ this accretion passed over into the Ex $20^{4b\text{-}6}$.

INTRODUCTION

§ 8. *The relations of Ex 34 and the Book of the Covenant* ($Ex\ 20^{22}$–23^{33}): *the latter is later than the former.*—Into this question it is not the duty of the present writer to enter here. Baentsch and other scholars have arrived at the conclusion that Ex 34 (J) in its original form is older than Ex 20^{22}–23^{23} (E). Both documents, however, have suffered severely in the course of transmission and editing, so that Ex 34, which is the older document, contains elements which bear the stamp of a later period than Ex 20^{22}–23^{33}. See Baentsch, *Das Bundesbuch*, 97–103.

§ 9. *Relations of the Mosaic Decalogue to the Decalogue in Ex 34 and the Book of the Covenant*, i.e. *Ex* 20^{23}–23^{22}, *and later form of Mosaic Decalogue in Ex 20.* See previous page.

FIRST COMMANDMENT

" Thou shalt have none other gods beside Me."—Ex. xx. 3.

" The grace of our Lord Jesus Christ, and the love of God, and the communion of the Holy Spirit, be with you all."—2 COR. xiii. 14.

I HAVE chosen these two texts to indicate the development in the knowledge of God which man won through his spiritual experience in the course of some 1400 years. I propose to treat this development in the Old Testament at some length and to deal briefly with its consummation in the New Testament, a consummation which was desiderated or in part promised in the Old Testament.

You are aware, my brethren, that the Decalogue is preserved in two different forms, in the twentieth chapter of Exodus and the fifth chapter of Deuteronomy. Both have clearly undergone editorial changes.

An older form of the Decalogue is presupposed in the Book of the Covenant, while quite a different Decalogue is given in Ex. xxxiv. The relation of this last Code[1] to the other two just mentioned is still a matter of controversy. This third Code has not, however, been preserved accurately, and for our present purpose may be ignored.

[1] See Introduction, p. lix sqq.

2   THE DECALOGUE

The two codes we are considering are ascribed both in Exodus and in Deuteronomy to Moses. In some form, no doubt, they go back to him, but what the exact form was it is difficult now to determine with certainty.[1] In the Old Testament, as it was usual to attribute all the Wisdom books to Solomon and all the Psalms to David, so all Hebrew Law was universally ascribed to Moses—even the latest development of this law in the fifth century. Nevertheless, when we strip the Decalogue of obviously later accretions the essential element in each Commandment appears to be Mosaic.

There can be no valid ground alleged against the primitive Mosaic origin of the first Commandment: "Thou shalt have no other gods beside Me." Now let us weigh well these words. By the careless reader they are regarded as asserting that there is but one God. But that is exactly what the words do not assert. This first Commandment is not a formal declaration of Monotheism, that is, that there is only one God. For the words "Thou shalt have no other gods beside Me" did not require Israel to deny that other divinities existed. What they did require was that Israel should not worship any God but the God of Israel. The terms of this Commandment are perfectly consistent with the belief on the part of Israel that every nation had its own god, to whose protection it could trust, and whose sovereignty alone it was its duty to acknowledge. And as a matter of fact in the pre-prophetic times in Israel the existence of such independent deities outside Israel

[1] See Introduction, pp. xxxiv, xliv, xlvii.

was fully acknowledged by Israel. Each nation had its own god. Milcom was the god of Ammon, Ashtoreth of the Zidonians, and Chemosh of Moab. According to the belief of this period it was these gods that had given their respective peoples their territories, just as Yahweh had given Canaan to Israel. The divine name Yahweh may be unfamiliar to some of you, though you are all familiar with the shortened form "Yah" in the Psalms. Hence I would call the attention of such to the fact that the word Jehovah which is used in our English version in place of Yahweh is a *vox nulla*; that is, no real word at all. Taken at the best, it arises from a mispronunciation of the divine name. Such a pronunciation of the divine name was not introduced till A.D. 1520, or about 2800 years after the Mosaic legislation. This mispronunciation arose as follows. The name Yahweh was held so sacred by the later Jews that they avoided writing or pronouncing this name with its proper vowels and supplied its vocalisation from Adonai or Elohim. It is time that the use of this word should be abandoned. It is a fictitious form: it combines the consonants of the divine name with the vowels of one or other of two different divine names.

But let us return. We had observed that the various nations in the pre-prophetic period worshipped each its god. We find distinct reference to such beliefs in the Old Testament. Thus in the times of the Judges, say, about the end of the twelfth century B.C., Jephthah, who was leading Israel against the Ammonites, sends

4   THE DECALOGUE

the following message to the Ammonites (Judg. xi. 24):
" Wilt thou not possess that which † Chemosh †¹ thy
god giveth thee to possess ? So whomsoever Yahweh
our God hath dispossessed from before us, them will
we possess." Not only was the power of the national
deity conceived to be paramount within his own land,
but all who were resident in his country—even so-
journers or strangers—were regarded as in duty bound
to worship him. Hence one hundred years later David
complains to Saul that he had been driven forth from
his own land, and so had been compelled to abandon
the worship of Yahweh for the worship of the gods of
the land in which he was an exile. Thus in 1 Sam. xxvi.
19, David complains: "If it be Yahweh that hath
stirred thee up against me, let Him accept an offering;
but if it be the children of men, cursed be they before
Yahweh . . . in that they say, Go serve other gods."
Thus the sovereignty of the national deities was popu-
larly held to be coextensive and conterminous with the
bounds of their own lands and not to extend beyond
them. If an Israelite in those early days went into
the land of Moab, he would have felt it his duty, or
at all events he would have found it expedient, to
worship the god of that country, or if into the land of
Ammon, the god of Ammon. Indeed a man could not
worship a god in those days unless he was actually in
the country of that god, or was standing on the very
soil of that country. Thus about 850 B.C. Naaman the

¹ This is a primitive textual error. Chemosh was the god of
Moab.

FIRST COMMANDMENT 5

Syrian, after he had been cleansed of his leprosy, sought permission from Elisha the prophet to take home with him two mules' burden of earth. The object of this request was that he might offer sacrifices to Yahweh on Israelitish soil, that is, on the soil of Yahweh's own land. Otherwise he believed he could not have worshipped Yahweh. Since Elisha dismissed Naaman with the words " Go in peace," Elisha implicitly granted the request of Naaman. The inscription of Mesha, king of Moab, on what is called "the Moabite Stone," an inscription which belongs to the ninth century B.C., and is still preserved, and a copy of which you can see in the British Museum, the original being in Paris, confirms independently the account just given of the relation of the god of Moab, as intervening on behalf of his people and defeating Yahweh, the god of Israel, and this in very good Hebrew and in Biblical phraseology.

Now, if some of you are wondering why I have brought before you these primitive beliefs of ancient Israel and the neighbouring nations, there is no difficulty in furnishing the reason. For it is important that we should be acquainted with the early stages of God's divine education of Israel, and that we should recognise them as early stages, and that, accordingly, things that were permissible at such early stages were not permissible at later times.

At first the Israelites were practically Semitic heathens without intellectual culture, without spiritual attainment, only yesterday rescued from the land of Egypt, only yesterday emancipated from the house of bondage.

6   THE DECALOGUE

It was to such as these that God entrusted the truths which have been growing ever since in depth and fullness and which are slowly transforming the world. At this early stage God revealed Himself to Israel through the great lawgiver Moses, and claimed their undivided worship in the words: "Thou shalt have no other gods before Me."

This Commandment did not tell the Israelites that the gods of the neighbouring nations were non-existent: it only forbade them to worship them. The Israelites must worship Yahweh and Yahweh alone. Now this Commandment was good so far as it went. It required from these nomadic Hebrew tribes just as much as they could give at the time. If the Israelities obeyed it faithfully, all other gods would of necessity cease to exist for them. For a religious doctrine perishes, if it is not rooted inwardly in the heart and sustained outwardly by religious life and worship. Thus the belief in polytheism was ultimately doomed, if Israel were but faithful. We have already seen that such a claim extends only to those living in Yahveh's own land. Hence at this period there was no idea of Yahweh's jurisdiction extending to the next life. The beliefs with regard to the future life were throughout this early period purely heathen.

The primitive hope of the individual and his view of the future life were gloomy in the extreme. Sheol was the ultimate goal of all men. In Sheol a shadowy life prevailed, which faintly reflected the realities of the upper world. In Sheol, further, not moral but social distinctions were observed: a man enjoyed a position among the shades corresponding to the social position he had held in his earthly life. The poor man and the serf were a poor man and a serf still: the king and the noble a king and a noble still. In Isa. xiv. you find a survival of this belief. The shadowy kings on their shadowy thrones in Sheol rise up to greet the shade of the great King of Babylon when it enters Sheol, but it is with the derisive words which the prophet places in their mouth: "Art thou become weak as we? art thou become like unto us?" That such a realm was not under the sovereignty of Yahweh was to be expected, since Yahweh's jurisdiction was limited exclusively to the upper world, and in the upper world to His own nation and His own land. Thus a completely heathen view of the future life was not inconsistent with a genuine belief in Yahweh in its earliest stage. In other words, before the eighth century B.C. no conflict between Hebrew Theology and man's belief in the next world was possible, for their provinces were mutually exclusive.

The next stage of development appears in the eighth century. This was monotheistic. It was the work of the great eighth-century prophets—Isaiah, Hosea, Amos, Micah—and no doubt of many others whose names are lost to history. As opposed to the earlier teaching as it appears in the Decalogue, "Thou shalt have no other gods before Me," the teaching of monotheism from the close of the ninth century onwards was, "There are no other gods but Me."

THE DECALOGUE

Thus monotheism shows itself in the account of the creation in Gen. i., and in the addition to the fourth Commandment in Ex. xx. The God of Israel was now no longer worshipped as the God of a tribe, but as the one and only God who had created heaven and earth. Now, since the recognition of this great truth led to the recasting of the beliefs of Israel as to the beginnings of things, that is, as to the creation of heaven and earth and all that in them is, it ought to have led to the recasting of their heathen beliefs and expectations as to the final issues of this life in the world beyond the grave. But, as a matter of fact, these heathen expectations remained uninfluenced for 400 years or more, and it was not till 600 years later, *i.e.* in the second century B.C., that a belief in a blessed future life was accepted by a considerable body of the Jews. Even down to the fall of the Temple in A.D. 70 the powerful party of the Sadducees for the most part clung to the primitive beliefs of Israel in regard to the future life.

This startling fact cannot be too strongly emphasised. Though Israel possessed a monotheistic faith from the eighth century onwards, it did not for many centuries arrive at the obvious conclusion that, since God had created all things, the next world, just as much as this world, must be subject to His sovereignty, and that accordingly the heathen views of their forefathers as to the next world were quite impossible. Clearly the lesson we are to learn from this startling fact is that man learns his best lessons in religion not through the logical processes of the intellect, though these are

FIRST COMMANDMENT

indispensable in their right place, but through religious experience. Thus Israel ultimately learnt the fact of a blessed future life through the religious experience of its saints and psalmists, and therein arrived at a truth that is verifiable by all men should all men be willing to surrender themselves to like experiences. And so the Jews discovered for themselves, as every individual can discover for himself, that the only belief in a future life that can really endure, is that which men arrive at through the life of faith. All great spiritual truths must realise themselves in life before they can be clearly apprehended and defined by the intellect. God commits to life the best instruction in things divine.

After the eighth century the Jews themselves naturally interpreted the first Commandment from the standpoint of monotheism. Thereby the very roots of polytheism were destroyed. So far as the Israelites were obedient to the Commandment in the monotheistic sense they were freed from superstition, from belief in magic, spells and sorcery: from trust in amulets, which to the shame of Christendom reappeared under the form of mascots in the late war, and were accepted by large numbers of persons whose intelligence was not equal to the task of putting a bridle on their credulity and superstition.

He who believes in God will not trust in chance or luck, nor will he, Micawber-like, neglect his obvious duties and yet cherish the delusion that something will turn up. This early Commandment forbids oppor-

10   THE DECALOGUE

tunism and mere expediency in statecraft, which have
been the bane of all governments from the earliest ages,
and are the curse of most governments and most states-
men at the present day.

In the seventh century the writer of Deut. vi. 4, 5
gave a positive content to this Commandment, which
was accepted and repeated by our Lord. "Hear, O
Israel: the Lord our God is one Lord: and thou shalt
love the Lord thy God with all thy heart, and with all
thy soul, and with all thy might." If we Christians
fulfil this commandment of the Old Testament, we
shall fulfil all that is required of us in the New. For
the duty of man towards God cannot be more perfectly
expressed. Notwithstanding, there is a fuller revelation
of God in the New Testament.

There God is revealed by Christ first and foremost
as our Father, a term which the individual Israelite in
the Old Testament could not use in addressing God, but
only the nation as a whole.[1] It is true that about
seventy years after our Lord's ministry was closed this
term was introduced officially into the public and
private prayers of the Jews. It had been used occasionally by individual Jews at an earlier date. But
however this may be, the idea of God's Fatherhood has
never won in Judaism the central position which it has
occupied in Christianity from the first. For whilst we

[1] This term is used twice in Sirach. But its meaning is necessarily
limited by the Sadducean context in which it occurs. Moreover, in
xvii. 17, Israel is said to be God's portion ($\mu\epsilon\rho\acute{\iota}s$), whereas the
nations are put under the dominion of angels. It occurs also in
Test. Levi iv. 2 and Wis. ii. 16.

as Christians, alike in public and private worship, address God naturally and under all circumstances as "Our Father," the preponderating phrase in Jewish prayer books, even in the present day, is "O Lord our God, King of the universe." While the Christian phrase emphasises the nearness of God to His children, the phrase most commonly used in Jewish prayers expresses rather the vast gulf between God and the men whom He has created.

Now it is this fullest revelation of God's Fatherhood that we, His erring children, need. It is not enough for us to know that God loves them that love Him; for the best of us know that our love for Him is poor indeed: it is not enough for us to be assured that, like as a father pitieth his own children, so the Lord pitieth them that fear Him; for our fear and reverence are so fitful and ineffective: it is not enough to be told that the Lord heareth them that cry unto Him; for often, when we need Him most, we cry unto Him least. Nay, my brethren, the highest revelations of the Old Testament do not suffice. We need the knowledge that Christ gives us of the Fatherhood of God, who most reveals the Father when He goes forth after the lost masses of mankind; when He sitteth with publicans and sinners, and eateth with them; when He is gracious not only to those that love Him but to those who love Him not; when He follows the prodigal into the far country, and visits him with the chastenings of His love till he repent and return; when He leaves the ninety and nine in the wilderness and goes after the wandering sheep and seeketh it till He finds. This is the Fatherhood that Christ teaches us in the Gospel: this is the Fatherhood which alone can satisfy the hearts of men.

If, then, we would know God as the Father, we must do so through personal knowledge of the Son. In fact, it is only through Christ that we can have the ever-growing and fullest revelation of the Father. Through Him we learn that God is love: that man needs to be reconciled to God, not God to man: that God has been in Christ reconciling the world unto Himself, removing from man's heart the sin and wrongness that estrange him from God: that there is not, and never has been, unforgivingness in God: and that since God is supremely desirous to redeem man, all God's power is pledged to man's salvation, if only man will come unto Him through Christ.

But the revelation of God in the Father and the Son was not yet complete. So long as Christ was here on earth, His presence was limited by the conditions of time and space. Not till He had left this earth was He freed from the bonds of personal, local and national ties, and His presence become possible here and everywhere, now and at all times. And this fuller revelation has come through the manifestation of the Spirit of God, to whom we owe in ever greater fullness the further teachings of God and Christ. The Spirit of God had, it is true, been active throughout all the earlier ages, but with the day of Pentecost there was a manifestation of His influence hitherto inexperienced and unknown, and ever down the ages that influence had made itself felt in an increasing degree in the hearts of individuals and of Churches.

Such, in short, has been the historical manifestation of God as Father, Son, and Holy Spirit as revealed in the spiritual experience of man. With the metaphysical relations of the three Persons of the Godhead I have not the ability to deal; nay more, I do not believe that it is possible for the human intellect to define these, however often men may essay such a task, and essay it with all the audacity of an Athanasius, an Augustine, or a Thomas Aquinas.

SECOND COMMANDMENT

FIRST LECTURE

"Thou shalt not make unto thee a graven image, nor any likeness that is in heaven above, or that is in the earth beneath, or that is in the water under the earth: thou shalt not bow down thyself unto them, nor serve them: for I the Lord thy God am a jealous God, visiting the iniquity of the fathers upon the children, unto the third and fourth generation of them that hate Me; and showing mercy unto thousands of them that love Me, and keep My commandments."[1]—Ex. xx. 4–6.

THE first Commandment which we dealt with in the last lecture forbade the Hebrews to worship any other god than Yahweh: it did not deny the existence of other gods, but it required Israel to worship Yahweh alone. From the Captivity onwards, however, or rather from the eighth century B.C., the first Commandment was reinterpreted, not only as requiring Israel to worship Yahweh alone, but as implicitly denying the existence of all other gods but Yahweh.

It is in this sense that it was understood by the primitive Christian Church. From the standpoint of this later interpretation of the first Commandment we

[1] On the primitive form of this commandment and the forms it assumed in the different Decalogues, see pp. xxxv sq., xli.

can distinguish the first and second Commandments shortly as follows. The first forbids the worship of any but the one and true God : the second forbids the worship of the true God in a wrong way, that is, by means of images or the likeness of anything in heaven or earth.

Before we enter on the main subject of our sermon, I must draw your attention to the order of the Commandments as well as to the different numberings of the Commandments which prevail in Judaism and in the various Churches of Christendom since the fourth century. As regards the right order of the Commandments, most readers of the New Testament assume that in the three passages in the New Testament (Luke xviii. 20 ; Rom. xiii. 9 ; Jas. ii. 11) in which the seventh Commandment is placed before the sixth, this order is a purely accidental one, or added by the writer with the intention of enforcing his own immediate object. But this is not so. In the first centuries of the Christian era the seventh Commandment was generally placed before the sixth in works of Egyptian origin. Thus this order is found in the Hebrew Nash Papyrus, which is over seven hundred years older than any Hebrew MS of the Old Testament. It is found also in the first century B.C. in Philo (*De decem Oraculis*, 24–25), Clement of Alexandria (*Strom.* vi.), Augustine (*Sermo* ix. 7 (Paris, 1836, V. 79 A.B.) ; *c. Faustum*, xv. 4 (Paris, viii. 443c)) and other writers, as well as in the Codex B of Exodus, where the order is seventh, eighth, sixth ; and Deuteronomy, where the order is seventh, sixth, eighth. This is, in fact, the order that was most usual in Egypt. But the familiar order that we find in Exodus and Deuteronomy, Matt. v. 21, 27, xix. 18; Mark x. 19; Josephus (*Ant.* iii. 5. 5), the Didache (ii. 2, iii. 3), is the Palestinian,[1] and this may be accepted as the original.

Turning from the ordering to the numbering of the Commandments, we find that three distinct numberings have prevailed in Judaism and Christianity. (1) The first numbering is that of the Jewish Church. Thus the Talmud and the Jewish Prayer Books take the introductory words, "I am Yahweh, thy God that brought thee out of the land of Egypt, out of the house of bondmen," as constituting the first Commandment. Next in order, not to break with the traditional number ten, they put together the first and second Commandments and reckoned these two as the second Commandment. This usage prevails in Judaism to the present day.[2] (2) The second numbering is that adopted by the Roman and Lutheran [3] Churches, which follow the example of Augustine. Augustine merged

[1] Though the Palestinian order has the support of the MSS, the Samaritan text, the Targums of Onk. and Ps.-Jon., the Syriac and Vulgate versions, yet Dr. Peters (*Älteste Abschrift der zehn Gebote*, p. 33) regards it as a corruption of that which prevailed in Egypt. In the Book of the Dead the latter order is found (Brugsch, *Steininschrift und Bibelwort*, 1891, p. 260).

[2] This practice was followed for some time by the Greek Church also. Thus it is found in Syncellus (*c.* A.D. 790) and Cedrenus (1130). See Geffken, "Eintheilung des Dekalogs," 1838, quoted in *Encyc. Bib.* i. 1050 *n*. It is recognised in the margin of Codex B in Ex. xx. 2.

[3] But the Lutheran Church parts with the Roman Church by adopting the order in Ex. in the ninth and tenth Commandments.

SECOND COMMANDMENT

the first and second Commandments together [1] as one Commandment, and then in order to preserve the original number ten, divided the tenth Commandment into two, the ninth of which consists of "Thou shalt not covet thy neighbour's wife," and the tenth of "Thou shalt not covet thy neighbour's house.[2] (3) The third numbering is that adopted by the Church of England, which follows the precedents set by the ancient

---

[1] Augustine's division of the Commandments into groups of three and seven is due to dogmatic and arbitrary grounds. He deliberately rejected the division into groups of four and six—a division that had been adopted in the past by Philo, Josephus, Origen and the Early Christian Church, and has since the Reformation been observed by the Anglican, Greek and Reformed Churches generally. Having rejected this division, he divided the Commandments into groups of three and seven. The three referred to God, and indicated, according to Augustine's fanciful and extraordinary method of exposition, the Three Persons of the Trinity: *Epistolæ*, ii. 55. 20 (Paris, 1836, vol. ii., 202 B.C.): *Quæstiones in Exod.* 71 (III. 698 O.D.). It is not surprising that the grounds given here for this dogmatic exposition are inconsistent with those put forward in *Sermo* ccl. 3 (V. 1506 O.D.). Thus the division of the Commandments accepted from Augustine by the Mediæval Church and observed by the Roman Church rests on a groundless conceit. Augustine's methods of dealing with the Decalogue cannot be pronounced happy from the standpoint of modern research. The compression of the first four Commandments into three is implied in the margin of MS A, Ex xx. 9, 12, 15.

[2] This order is found in the LXX of Ex. xx. 17 (with the exception of some MSS) and Theod. and Symmachus. Hence Augustine had three of the Greek versions of Ex. and the Hebrew (but not Sam. T Sam.) of Deut. v. 21 in support of the order he adopted. Against this order in Ex. are M. Sam. T Sam. Syr. Onk. Aquila, Vulg. Luther follows the Roman Church in dividing the tenth Commandment. But he makes "Thou shalt not covet thy neighbour's house" as the ninth and the rest of the Commandment as the tenth. But Augustine is inconsistent; in *Sermo* ix. 7 (Paris, 1836, vol. i. 793), *Quæst. in Exod.* 71, we have the order given above in the text, but in *Sermo* ccl. 3 (V. 1507 C) this order is reversed.

Jewish writers, Philo and Josephus, by Origen and the Early Christian Church for the most part, by the later Greek Church, and the Reformed Churches generally.

1. Now as regards the Jewish division, it is enough to observe that the introductory words do not really form a Commandment at all. They simply state a fact, and are therefore in regard to form not homogeneous with the Commandments that follow.

2. In the next place, to the division adopted by the Roman and Lutheran Churches there is this strong objection. These Churches agree, as we have seen, in regarding the second Commandment as part of the first. This consolidation of the first and second Commandments into one has led to different modes of counting the remaining eight Commandments. Thus our third Commandment is the second in the Roman Church, our fourth their third, and so on, till our ninth corresponds with their eighth and our tenth with their ninth and tenth. Thus Augustine and his followers were forced to divide the tenth Commandment into two in order to get the number ten. Hence it comes to pass that the ninth Commandment in the Roman Church is "Thou shalt not covet thy neighbour's wife, and the tenth "Thou shalt not desire thy neighbour's house, his field, or his manservant, his ox, or his ass, or any thing that is thy neighbour's."

But this division of the tenth Commandment is unjustifiable. That it is one Commandment is manifest from the essential unity of its subject. It deals with one and the same sin, that of coveting. The Decalogue

SECOND COMMANDMENT

devotes to the sin of coveting one Commandment, and not two, and thereby follows the same principle that it has done throughout by assigning one Commandment to one subject. Again, if we compare this Commandment in Ex. xx. 17 and Deut. v. 21 we find that the order of the first two clauses in Ex. are transposed in Deut., and that, whereas the neighbour's house is put before the neighbour's wife in Ex., the neighbour's wife is put before the neighbour's house in Deut. Since both these clauses belong to the same Commandment according to the numbering of the Jewish, English and most other Christian Churches, this transference does not affect them. But the effect is disconcerting for the Roman Church: for what is the ninth Commandment in Ex. becomes according to the Roman Church the tenth according to Deut.

But this is not all. Ex. furnishes us with the earliest recension:[1] yet the Roman Church adopts the recension in Deut., which in this respect is probably two hundred years later.

At the outset it may be well to indicate that we shall interpret this Commandment as forbidding the worship of God alike through images and unfigured symbols, as it was in Judaism from the Captivity onwards. The images were iconic; that is, were likenesses of some deity in the form of pictures or statues: the unfigured symbols, which were sacred stones, pillars, trees and the like, were aniconic; that is, they were not the like-

[1] So M. Sam. Syr. Vulg. But the LXX. Sym. and Theod. give the same order as in Deut.

nesses of any god, but a god was believed to dwell or manifest himself in them.

The wide diffusion of idolatry in ancient Israel is to be inferred from the wide range of the objects, natural and manufactured, that were worshipped. The Hebrews had quite a dozen of words for various kinds of idols. But the subject is so vast that we cannot enter into it here. All we conclude from the second Commandment is that men were not to use any objects, whether iconic or aniconic, in the worship of Yahweh. The difference between these two terms should be carefully borne in mind. The aniconic worship [1] of stones, trees and other substances, which is often designated fetishism, is the older, but it has not been dislodged by the iconic or the worship of images. The worship of images arose with the birth of art, and belongs to a comparatively advanced stage of religion. These two stages coexist, as will be shown in a later lecture in modern Christianity.

The second Commandment presents many difficulties in connection with the history of Israel and Christianity, whether we study this Commandment in its original context, in the interpretations assigned to it at various times by the Jewish and Christian Churches, or in the unjustifiable abuses it has suffered from the eighth century down to the present day in the Councils and Catechisms of the Mediæval and Roman Churches.

The first problem that confronts us is set forth by a strong body of scholars who maintain that the second,

[1] Strictly speaking, aniconic worship does not come under this Commandment.

SECOND COMMANDMENT

fourth and tenth Commandments were later additions to the Decalogue.[1] With the fourth and tenth we are not at present concerned. For the thesis that the second Commandment was not earlier than the eighth or ninth century B.C. there is certainly evidence in the Old Testament. During the preceding centuries the Israelites appear to have combined image worship with the worship of Yahweh, and that without any consciousness of wrongdoing. Thus in Judg. xvii.-xviii. the priest who conducted the worship of Yahweh in Micah's house was Jonathan, a grandson of Moses. The rites connected with this worship were certainly of an idolatrous character, and yet of this idolatrous worship there is no sign of disapproval in the text. The idolatrous images used were the ephod[2] and teraphim. The teraphim was an idol or image in a human form. David, the champion of Yahwism, kept such images in his house (1 Sam. xix. 13-16). Now the teraphim of Micah, which was a graven image, was transferred to the great sanctuary at Dan, and the Book of Judges (xviii. 30) records

---

[1] So Kautzsch *HDB* v. 634[b], following Eerdmans.

[2] This word appears originally to have had two meanings: (1) the garment worn by the priest; (2) some symbol of the divinity—probably some kind of statue. See, however, Burney, *Judges*, pp. 236-243, who concludes that the ephod was never an idol, but only "the ordinary priestly vestment which was employed in obtaining an oracle." Lotz, Foote and Sellin take the same view, but most scholars are of opinion that the word had two distinct meanings. See Nowack, *Hebräische Archaologie*, ii. 21 sq.; Marti, *Gesch. der Israelit. Religion*, 29, 30; Stade, *Gesch.* i. 466; Budde, *Richter and Samuel*, 115 *n.*; Moore in *Encyc. Bib.* ii. 1306 sqq.; Kautzsch, *Die heilige Schrift*, i. p. 264.

that Jonathan, the grandson of Moses, and his sons after him were priests at Dan till the time of the Captivity.[1]

At Bethel and Dan, Yahweh was worshipped under the form of golden Bulls—called calves in the Old Testament in the way of derision—a form of worship quite in keeping with the conception of Yahwism in the tenth century B.C.

Yet according to the author of the Book of Kings, written towards the close of the seventh century, Jeroboam (933–912 B.C.) is represented as being the first to introduce this worship into the Northern Kingdom. But it is hardly credible that, when Jeroboam rebelled against the dynasty of David, he would have been so imprudent as to endanger his own position and that of his successors by setting up strange and alien images in the great sanctuaries of the Northern Kingdom. There is nothing so perilous as for a king or dynasty to interfere forcibly with the traditional beliefs of a vigorous race. In fact, the truth lies the other way. Jeroboam came forward as the champion of the traditional faith of Northern Israel over against the heathen innovations introduced by Solomon in the Southern Kingdom, which were breaches of the first Commandment, such as the worship of Ashtoreth, Chemosh and Molech (1 Kings xi. 1–8), and by Rehoboam, who sanctioned the consecration of prosti-

[1] But the text here seems uncertain. Houbigant, followed by Burney, emends the text so that it reads " until the day of the captivity of the ark," instead of " until the day of the captivity of the land." But the emendation is unconvincing.

SECOND COMMANDMENT

tutes to serve in sacred worship (1 Kings xiv. 23, 24).[1] Jeroboam, therefore, rallied to his standard the upholders of the older traditional elements in the Hebrew religion—in other words, he rallied to his standard the religious conservative party in the Northern Kingdom, and thereby strengthened his position over against the Southern Kingdom, in which the reaction to heathenism initiated by Solomon persisted to the reign of Asa, 913–873 B.C. (1 Kings xv. 12, 13).

Again, that the worship of Yahweh was associated with the worship of the golden calves long before the reign of Jeroboam, is to be inferred from the fact that Elijah uttered no word of protest against the worship of Yahweh through the golden calves at Dan, Bethel and Samaria.

And yet Elijah [2] was the chief prophet of the Northern

---

[1] These "Temple prostitutes" were a standing feature of the Canaanite sanctuaries. Deut. xxiii. 17 forbids their introduction into Israel. Asa (1 Kings xv. 12) and Jehoshaphat (xxii. 46) banished them from Judah. Josiah destroyed the houses of these persons, which during Manasseh's reign had been built in the Temple precincts (2 Kings xxiii. 7).

[2] There were, it is true, two distinct schools of the prophets in the Northern Kingdom, and both upholders of Yahwism. One school came to terms apparently with the foreign influences that were active under Ahab and so escaped persecution, but the other school opposed them to the death. To the former belong the 400 prophets under Zedekiah mentioned in 1 Kings xxii. These supported Ahab against Micaiah. When first consulted they spoke of God as Adonai (xxii. 6), and only later when pressed by Jehoshaphat did they give Him the name Yahweh (xxii. 12). It is not likely that Jezebel took active measures against this temporising school as she did against the other school (1 Kings xviii. 4, xix. 10-14 ; 2 Kings ix. 7). To this other school belonged the 7000 prophets, who were no doubt in sympathy with Elijah (1 Kings xix. 18). But *neither school took any objection to the worship of Yahweh through the symbols of the golden calves.*

Kingdom in the ninth century and destroyed the worship and priests of Baal, since Baal was a false god and his worship a direct breach of the first Commandment. No more did his great disciple Elisha protest against this worship, nor seemingly the far greater prophet Amos in his terrible indictment of the morals and worship of the Northern Kingdom. These facts imply that these prophets were acquainted with the first Commandment, but that either they knew nothing of the second or regarded the second as in abeyance.

But before we proceed further in this investigation, we should bear in mind that the use of the golden calves at these sanctuaries of the Northern Kingdom was mainly symbolic. They were not identified with Yahweh: they were to the intelligent worshipper symbols of Yahweh: Yahweh was worshipped through them, and the festival celebrated in their honour was a festival of Yahweh. But to the unintelligent, that is, to the people generally, they were, no doubt, actual idols. Such worship in Northern Israel was, therefore, in reality the *survival*, and not, as it is generally represented, the *revival* of a more primitive and lower phase of worship. But, though the three prophets [1] of the ninth and eighth centuries just mentioned did not impeach the worship of the golden calves, Hosea, the

[1] Amos, of course, was a prophet of the Southern Kingdom, but his prophecies dealt largely with the Northern. Amos may include under "the sin of Samaria" (viii. 14) the cult of the golden calves, but he nowhere expressly mentions this cult; for the worship of the calves was expressly the sin of Dan and Bethel, and not distinctively that of Samaria. But both text and interpretation are doubtful.

younger contemporary of Amos in the Northern Kingdom, denounced every form of idolatry, and that in the most scathing terms, declaring that these their idols would be shattered, and that, as Israel has sown the wind, it should reap the whirlwind (Hos. viii. 4–6, x. 5, xiii. 1–3). But in the Southern Kingdom the revolt against idolatry had begun at least a century earlier under King Asa (913–873), who, we read, removed all the idols that his father had made (1 Kings xv. 12–13). In the so-called older Decalogue in Ex. xxxiv. 17, which many scholars assign to this period, only the worship of molten images, not of graven, was forbidden—a point of view which may be reflected in the story of Aaron's making the golden calf, and which may form from a later standpoint a repudiation of the religion of Northern Israel.

Isaiah forbade the use of idols of silver and gold (ii. 8, 20).[1] It was in all likelihood Isaiah who prevailed on Hezekiah to destroy the brazen Serpent [2] which received divine honours in the Temple in Jerusalem. This brings us to the close of the eighth century, the date at which the second Commandment either first took its place in the now completed Decalogue, or rather, since we recognise its origin as Mosaic, came to exercise its legitimate force. The fact that it lay in

[1] Scholars are divided as to the meaning of Isa. xix. 19, some holding that Isaiah in this passage condoned the use of the pillar in connection with divine worship.

[2] That the worship (2 Kings xviii. 4) offered to the brazen serpent was a breach of the second Commandment cannot be explained away.

abeyance from 400 to 600 years in Palestine need cause no difficulty, seeing that it was deliberately explained away or ignored by *the entire Christian Church* despite the unmistakable and universal condemnation of the worship of images in the New Testament from the seventh century to the sixteenth, that is, for 800 years; while the Roman and, in part, the Eastern Churches have treated it as null and void from the seventh General Council to the present day, that is, for over 1100 years.

Hence we can see no reasonable objection to the acceptance of the second Commandment as Mosaic in origin, though it long failed to become effective in Palestine.

For a similar declension from the purity and truth of primitive teaching we have only to turn to Buddhism in India. Its founder was born in the sixth century B.C. (*circa* 586). Ethically Buddhism was unsurpassed even by the Judaism of the time. It rejected sacrifice and taught the Noble Eightfold Path. But it, too, declined from its lofty ideals and approximated more and more with each century to the popular superstitions and the degraded religions which surrounded it. Its most striking outward success, in securing the conversion of Asoka in the third century B.C. and the support of this powerful prince, only hastened its decline, as the conversion of Constantine contributed to the paganising of Christianity. In both cases thousands, nay millions, of nominal converts followed the safe and fashionable line of least resistance, and their adhesion corrupted the faith they had joined: they introduced into the religions they severally adopted the very superstitions,

SECOND COMMANDMENT

idolatries and abominations which these religions condemned as anathema.

After this period the prophetic elements of the nation advance steadily towards the conception of a non-idolatrous worship of God. The motive for such worship is given in Deut. iv. 12 : "The Lord spake unto you out of the midst of the fire : ye heard the voice of words, but ye saw no form." In this book it is ordained that not only is the idolater to be put to death (xvii. 2 sqq.), but also the man who entices another into this sin (xiii. 6–9).

And yet as late as the reign of Josiah (639–608) there were asherim standing by the altar of Yahweh, not only in Samaria (2 Kings xiii. 6) and Bethel (2 Kings xxiii. 15), but even in the temple in Jerusalem (2 Kings xxiii. 6).

In the seventh century and later we find the prophets treating the gods of the heathen with the utmost contempt and identifying them with idols, while the writers of the sixth and later centuries assail with trenchant satire the makers of gods of gold and silver, of wood and stone (Isa. xl. 18–20, xli. 6 sqq., xliv. 9–20, xlvi. 6 sq. ; Jer. x. 2–5, 9, 14 sq.).

When we reach the second century the propaganda against idolatry has become so relentless and to a certain extent extravagant and irrational, that the second Commandment is interpreted as forbidding not only the manufacture of images *for worship*, but the manufacture of any kind of image, picture or likeness, even when these were not intended for worship at all (Wis. xiv.

12–21). This unjustifiable interpretation shows itself in an embittered form in later Judaism.[1] Thus, whereas we know that Solomon's Temple contained representations of many natural objects, animal and other, in the later Temple no image of any kind was allowed; and a wild storm of indignation burst forth against Herod when he set a large golden eagle above the great gate of the Temple (Jos. *Ant.* xvii. 6. 2–4; *B.J.* i. 33. 2–4; *Vita*, 12). Still later the same extreme party succeeded in thwarting Pilate's attempt to introduce the Roman legions into Jerusalem, because their ensigns bore the image of Cæsar (*Ant.* xviii. 3. 1; *B.J.* ii. 9. 2 sq.). The impression that the Jews made on the Romans is rightly represented by the Roman historian Tacitus (*Hist.* v. 5), who writes: "The Jews worship one God in their minds only . . . therefore they allow no image in their cities much less in their temples." This was the law in Palestine; but at Palmyra, Rome, Carthage and elsewhere there are carvings of human and other figures on the Jewish tombs.

This usage of the Jews of the Dispersion shows a more rational interpretation of the second Commandment. To resume our conclusions, therefore, we observe that the tendency of the best religious elements in

[1] Even Philo so interpreted the second Commandment; see p. 29 *n*. Also Josephus, who writes thus: "The second Commandment forbids us to make the image of any living thing and worship it" (ὁ δὲ δεύτερος κελεύει μηδενὸς εἰκόνα ζῴου ποιήσαντας προσκυνεῖν, *Ant.* iii. 5. 5). These words might, of course, be interpreted in two ways, but there is no doubt as to Josephus' view; for he condemns Solomon for making the brazen oxen (*Ant.* viii. 7. 5). See also xvii. 6. 2, xviii. 3. 1; *B.J.* i. 33. 2, ii. 9. 2, 10. 4.

Judaism from the seventh century B.C. was to lay an increasing emphasis on the second Commandment,[1] which forbade the use of any kind of image in order to worship God through it. In remarkable contrast with this fact we shall have to call attention to the contrary tendency in Christianity from the sixth century of the Christian era onwards, which either by explaining away the second Commandment or by suppressing it altogether, put its claims out of court and introduced image worship into the Christian Church. The Jewish tendency led to the destruction of art in worship: the Christian tendency leads to the destruction of religion itself.

It is needless to controvert the narrow Jewish misinterpretation of the second Commandment to which we have above referred. But we may well wonder why the enforcement of this Commandment was adjourned

[1] Philo's (*De decem Orac.* xv., xvi., xxix.; *De Vita Contemplativa*, i.–ii.) condemnation of images is expressed in vigorous terms. The worshippers of images are greater sinners than polytheists (*De decem Orac.* xiv.). Philo even condemns art under this commandment. He anticipates the Christian objection of later times, that it would have been more proper to deify the artists rather than the things they had created. Καὶ δέον, εἴπερ ἄρα ἐξημάρτανον, τοὺς ζωγράφους αὐτοὺς καὶ ἀνδριαντοποιοὺς ὑπερβολαῖς τιμῶν ἐκτεθειωκέναι, τοὺς μὲν εἴασαν ἀφανεῖς οὐδὲν πλέον παρασχόντες, τὰ δ' ὑπ' ἐκείνων δημιουργηθέντα πλάσματα καὶ ζωγραφήματα θεοὺς ἐνόμισαν (*op. cit.* 14). Philo, as he proceeds, presses this argument in an intensely ironical vein: " I have known that some of the men who made the idolatrous images both pray and offer sacrifices to the very things they had themselves made. Now for these it would have been much better to worship their own hands severally; but, in case they shunned the reproach of self-conceit . . . at all events to worship their anvils, and hammers and graving tools . . . by means of which the materials took their shape."

to the eighth century B.C. in the history of Israel. The answer shortly is that it is in keeping with the rest of God's education of man. This education is adapted to the capacities of the pupil, and yet is always in advance of the pupil's attainments. It is no greater difficulty than the facts that God was worshipped by Israel as one God amongst many for several centuries, and that a belief in a blessed future life was not arrived at by Israel till the third or second century before the Christian era. Hence this semi-idolatrous period in the history of Israel had its part in the education of mankind. That in the childhood of the race God should be conceived as a Being with certain human passions of a not wholly desirable kind, and that He should be worshipped through symbols and images is not unnatural. Pious souls have risen in such periods and with such imperfect means of worship to faith and hope and holiness—even to a real communion with God. But though all this be admitted, it must at the same time be maintained that such imperfect worship can only rightly belong to the childhood of the race, and that, so far as a man worships God through images, he thereby makes it evident that he has not yet put away childish things from him, nor as yet come into the prerogatives that belong to his spiritual manhood. Furthermore, where, as in Christianity, the principles of spiritual worship are laid down from the outset, the tolerance, much more the teaching of an idolatrous worship of God, calls for the strongest reprobation. When such primitive worship of God by means of images or unfigured forms—permissible in the early childhood of the race—is deliberately introduced into or tolerated in Christianity, it is nothing less than gross idolatry.

That such idolatry is practised in the Christian Church is undeniable, if we compare the idolatrous rites, which the Hebrew prophets denounced, with the rites that have prevailed in many Christian Churches for the past 1400 years. In fact, the Christian Church from the fourth century A.D. onwards began to revive the very rites explicitly condemned by the Hebrew prophets as idolatrous. Thus the prophets brand as idolatrous the following practices: the custom of kissing idols or images (Hos. xiii. 2; 1 Kings xix. 18); of clothing them in costly garments (Ezek. xvi. 18; Jer. x. 9); of offering incense to them (Ezek. viii. 11); of making genuflexions and prostrations before them (Isa. xliv. 15; Ep. Jer. 6); of embracing, anointing or washing them (Sanh. vii. 6); of carrying them in procession (Isa. xlvi. 1, 7; Jer. x. 5; Ep. Jer. 4, 26); of lighting candles before them (Ep. Jer. 19).[1] That these idolatrous practices of Judaism and the idolatrous practices of Christianity are practically one and the same, is clear even to the most superficial observer.

But image worship has had in all ages its defenders. Christians who maintain the value of images in worship urge first of all that no one supposes that the

[1] Lactantius (*Institut.* vi. 2) speaks ironically of this practice: " They kindle lights as for one who is in the dark " (" accendunt lumina velut in tenebris agenti "), and asks if the worshipper who offers such a gift is " in his right senses " (*mentis suæ compos*).

figured or unfigured block of wood or stone or gold is the real god : they contend that it is only a symbol of the unseen Being to whom the worship is really offered.

Further, they contend that even those who condemn material images of God do themselves form an intellectual image of God, and by means of such an image offer to God their worship; and wherein, they ask, does worship offered by means of a material image differ from worship rendered by means of an intellectual image ? In both cases the representation is far removed from the Divine Original it stands for, and in both cases the symbol is of our own creation. If the one is a material idol, it follows that the other is a mental idol.

But, however forcible this reasoning may appear at first sight, we feel instinctively that it is not valid. For all history teaches that the curse, pronounced on those who change the glory of the invisible into the visible, of the spiritual into the material, has been fulfilled in the case of every nation upon earth ; and that the Church or people which degrades the conception of God inevitably brings about its own degradation.

But to deal with this argument more definitely. It is not true that intellectual images are as hurtful as material. It is not true that it is just as dangerous to the race to form a mental image of God in our minds as to make an external and material image of Him. Both even at their best are confessedly inadequate, but material images are more hurtful than intellectual, and for this reason. The mental image is capable of being improved : it can grow in purity with the man's spiritual growth, whereas the material image is fixed, crystallised and incapable of growth, and thus becomes a reactionary element in religion and cannot fail to degrade the worship of such as avail themselves of its services. The growth of the conception of God is manifest in the history of the Jewish people. Their Scriptures, while representing God as a Spiritual Personal Power, assigned to Him in earlier days many an attribute that was wholly unworthy of the Deity. But so far as Israel was faithful to the truth they had, nobler and diviner truths were revealed to them, and so they reached more adequate conceptions of God, who, if He is to be worshipped at all, must be conceived as infinitely better than the best conceivable by us.

Since, then, images are the embodiment of an utterly inadequate and likewise a degrading conception of God, and can never represent the invisible God, Israel was forbidden their use in worship. If it was God's purpose to reveal to Israel, and through Israel to the whole world, some of the highest and truest conceptions of the Divine attainable by man, the prohibition of image worship was inevitable at some period in the course of the Divine education of Israel. For, so far as religion makes use of images, it anchors itself inevitably to a pagan level.

At this stage, for the sake of avoiding confused thought, let us distinguish *images* of God, whether material or mental, the essential element of which is their form, from *conceptions* of God which are purely mental and formless. In religious worship the use of images, whether material or mental, was absolutely forbidden by the later Old Testament prophets. This prohibition, however, was not extended in the Decalogue to intellectual conceptions of deity which are mental and formless. But, since such conceptions, though formless, might be either good or bad, to cherish wrong or degrading conceptions of God came in due time to be denounced by Hebrew prophecy as idolatry—a mental idolatry independent wholly of the use of images. Thus Ezekiel (xiv. 3) declares, " Son of man, these men have taken their idols into their hearts," and the Psalmist (l. 21), " Thou thoughtest that I was altogether such an one as thyself." Through such mental idolatry men become the worshippers and the slaves of the idols of their own hearts—either of lawless ambitions or ungovernable passions, of greed or malice, of lying, hate or lust, whether as embodied in, or suggested by outward idols or not. Hence over against such idols, material or mental, formed or formless, with all their evil qualities the Bible proclaims the God of Israel as " The Lord God compassionate and gracious, long-suffering and abundant in mercy and truth " (Ex. xxxiv. 6), " forgiving iniquity and transgression, and that will by no means clear the guilty " (Num. xiv. 18). Or again, " Thus saith the High and Lofty One that inhabiteth eternity, whose name is holy : I dwell in the high and holy place, with him also that is of a contrite and humble spirit "

(Isa. lvii. 15). Now to such a conception of God we can attach no form. No more can we attach any form to such individual attributes of God as His truth, or His righteousness, His purity or mercy, His Omnipresence or His eternal years. In the New Testament the same teaching is enforced and developed. Thus in the Fourth Gospel we read, " Ye have neither heard His voice at any time nor seen His shape " (John v. 37); and in an earlier chapter, " the hour cometh, and now is, when the true worshippers shall worship the Father in spirit and in truth : for the Father seeketh such to worship Him. God is Spirit : and they that worship Him must worship Him in spirit and in truth " (iv. 23, 24); and again, if we turn to the Johannine Epistles we find the two crowning definitions of the Deity, the first being " God is light, and in Him is no darkness at all " (1 John i. 5), and the second and greatest of all, " God is love " (iv. 8). Such conceptions cannot be visualised. Hence in Christianity from the very outset the prohibition of idolatrous images and conceptions is inevitable, not only of images material and mental, but also of all unworthy conceptions of God. A degraded conception of God is an idol. Hence the Fourth Evangelist in his first Epistle is never tired of repeating : " Little children, keep yourselves from idols."

SECOND COMMANDMENT

SECOND LECTURE

"Thou shalt not make unto thee any graven image, nor any likeness that is in heaven above, or that is in the earth beneath, or that is in the water under the earth. Thou shalt not bow down unto them, nor serve them."—Ex. xx. 4, 5.

"God is Spirit: and they that worship Him must worship Him in spirit and in truth."—JOHN iv. 24.

IN my first lecture on the second Commandment I dealt with this Commandment as promulgated and enforced in the Old Testament, and accepted and still further developed in the New Testament. This morning we have to inquire how far the Christian Church has been faithful to the teaching which the prophets of the Old Testament gave on the true worship of God, and which culminated in that of the New Testament—" God is Spirit : and they that worship Him must worship Him in spirit and in truth." The chief writers in the Early Church were faithful to all that was best in the past. Apparently in the first two centuries there were no attempts at image worship within the Church. In these centuries the Christian apologists directed their attacks against idolatry outside the Church in the pagan world; but in the third century, not only against

SECOND COMMANDMENT 37

idolatry in the pagan world, but in its beginnings in Christianity. Thus in the first half of the second century Justin Martyr denounces the infatuation of heathen idolatry,[1] and attacks the Greeks for making images of God in the likeness of men.[2] Tatian[3] follows in the footsteps of Justin. Later in the same century Athenagoras[4] maintains that the heathen gods are of recent origin, and their images only of yesterday. His contemporary, Melito of Sardis, condemns the worship of idols wrought in stone and other materials.[5] About the same date Theophilus,[6] sixth Bishop of Antioch, inveighs against the gods of the heathen as the work of men's hands and made of stone or brass or wood or other material, and in still more vigorous terms the anonymous *Epistle to Diognetus*, ii. Irenæus (*flor.* 180) attributes the first use of images to heretics, namely, to the Gnostics, who claimed that a likeness of Christ had been made by Pilate.[7]

Early in the third century Tertullian (A.D. 155–222) maintains that the artificer of an idol is as guilty of idolatry as its worshipper;[8] while a few decades later

[1] *Apol.* i. 9.
[2] *Cohort. ad Gentiles*, xxxiv.
[3] *Ad Græcos*, iv.
[4] *Legatio pro Christo*, xv.–xvii.
[5] *Chronicon Paschale*, ed. Dindorf, p. 483.
[6] *Ad Autolycum*, ii. 2.
[7] *Hær.* i. 25. 6.
[8] *De Idol.* i. 3, 4. In this treatise Tertullian charges Christians with idolatry on the ground that they had manufactured idols for their heathen neighbours, made contracts in their names and taken part in their festivals.

38 THE DECALOGUE

Minucius Felix [1] (c. A.D. 234) holds up to derision the idols of the heathen gods, and states [2] that the charge brought against the Christians was that they had no images. Celsus [3] states that the Christians "could not tolerate either temples, altars or images"; and Origen replies that it is on the ground of the second Commandment that Christians abhor all worship or use of images,[4] and adds that "It is not possible at the same time to know God and to address prayers to images."[5] Cyprian (200–258)[6] maintains that evil spirits have their habitation in heathen idols, and that the heathen take them to be gods.[7]

In Canon xxxvi. of the Synod of Elvira (c. A.D. 300) we read : " It is ordained that pictures are not to be placed in the churches, nor is that which is worshipped and adored to be painted on the walls." Lactantius (260–340) directs the shafts of his wit against idolaters bowing down before the work of their own hands. " These most foolish beings," he writes, " do not understand that, if their images had been endowed with sense and motion, they would have taken the initiative and adored the artist to whom they owe their creation." [8] Eusebius (ob. 340) calls representations of Christ and

---

[1] *Octavius*, 23.
[2] *Op. cit.* 10.
[3] Origen (185–254), c. *Celsum*, vii. 62.
[4] *Op. cit.* vii. 64.
[5] *Op. cit.* vii. 65.
[6] *De Idolorum vanitate*, vii.
[7] *Testimonia*, 51.
[8] *Div. Instit.* II. 2: "Ultro adoraturi hominem a quo sunt expolita." See note on Philo's view, p. 29 n.

SECOND COMMANDMENT

His Apostles in pictures "a heathen custom";[1] and Epiphanius of Salamis (ob. A.D. 403) tore down a curtain in a Palestinian church because it had a picture of Christ or a saint upon it.[2]

St. Augustine, in condemning heathen idolatry, condemns implicitly the use of images in Christian worship. The heathen, he writes, alleges in defence of his worship: "I worship not the image, but what the images signify"; but Augustine will have none of this, and brands such worship as sheer idolatry: "He who worships an image turns the truth of God into a lie."[3] In support of his attack on heathen idolatry, Augustine enforces his arguments by quoting even a heathen author, namely, Varro, on this subject. Varro, he informs us, maintained that worship was holier and purer (castius) when dissociated from images; and Varro supported this contention by actually adducing the example of Jewish worship.[4] Augustine adduces Seneca also as reprobating the use of images.[5] If Augustine denounces so strongly image worship even amongst the heathen, how unsparing must have been his condemnation of image worship amongst Christians; and yet to his great

[1] *H.E.* vii. 18 : ἐθνικὴ συνηθεία. Eusebius says in this passage that there were such paintings in his time (εἰκόνας . . . διὰ χρωμάτων ἐν γραφαῖς σωζομένας). Here also he states that he saw in Cæsarea Philippi a bronze relief (ἐκτύπωμα χάλκεον) which was said to be of Christ healing the woman with an issue of blood.

[2] Epiphanius, *Ep. ad Joann. Hieros.*

[3] *Sermo* cxvii. (Paris), vol. v. 1313 A : "Non simulacrum colo sed quod significant simulacra . . . qui simulacrum colit convertit veritatem Dei in mendacium."

[4] August. *De civ. Dei*, iv. 31. 2 (vol. vii. 182 C).

[5] *De civ. Dei*, vi. 10. 1 (vol. vii. 256 C).

sorrow he was obliged to confess that there were already many idolaters in the Christian Church.[1]

From the above evidence, which could be largely increased, it is clear that images were not used in the earliest days of the Christian Church; but that, though sporadic attempts were made to introduce them from the close of the second century onward, yet the greatest thinkers, apologists, writers and bishops of the first four centuries protested against any use of images in the Christian Church. This attitude of the Church to image worship is very intelligible; for before the time of Constantine the Church had been engaged in a mortal struggle against an idolatrous Empire and an idolatrous world. Accordingly, to its converts from heathenism the use of images was absolutely forbidden; but, with the so-called conversion of the Empire, the bulk of its heathen subjects, lightly relinquishing their old faith and as lightly embracing the new, carried over with them into Christianity their idolatrous tendencies and practices.[2]

[1] *De Mor. eccles. cath.* i. 75, vol. i. 1153.
[2] Cumont (*Oriental Religions in Roman Paganism*, p. xxiv, 1911, trans. from the French) speaks of the invaluable contributions of the Oriental cults towards preparing the way for Christianity. He writes: " As the religious history of the Empire is studied more closely the triumph of the Church will, in our opinion, appear more and more as the culmination of a long evolution of beliefs. We can understand the Christianity of the fifth century with its greatnesses and its weaknesses, its spiritual exaltation and its puerile superstitions, if we know the moral antecedents of the world in which it developed." Amongst the most puerile but most dangerous of these superstitions may be reckoned the idolatrous elements in these Oriental Cults.

SECOND COMMANDMENT 41

Furthermore, with this conversion of the Empire to Christianity in the beginning of the fourth century, the arts came to be cultivated by Christians, and the services of painting and sculpture were increasingly made use of in worship, apparently without the sanction of any regular ecclesiastical authority. Image worship, moreover, followed naturally in the wake of the worship of the saints. The honours of the original were inevitably transferred to their images.[1]

For a time the Church resisted this pressure of heathenism from without; but the evil leaven went on steadily, leavening the Church at large, and that so successfully, that in the sixth and seventh and eighth centuries the grossest idolatry was practised throughout the greater part of Christendom. This abuse naturally led to a reaction, which culminated in the Iconoclastic controversy in the eighth and ninth centuries.

But before we touch on this controversy let us ask archæology what report it has to make on the date of the introduction and use of images in the Christian Church. No images of any kind were apparently used for some generations after the foundation of the Christian Church. In the Catacombs,[2] Christ is represented on

[1] The assertion of this astounding obliquity of thought does not appear first in Basil the Great, as it is generally maintained. We shall return to this subject later.

[2] The Catacombs were discovered by an accident on May 31, 1578. They contain little that can be called sculpture. Pope Damasus (A.D. 366–384) employed an engraver, Furius Philocalus, to restore the works of art on the walls. This gave rise to extensive alterations which have much lessened their value as authentic memorials of the second and third centuries.

a bas-relief as the Good Shepherd,[1] or as seated before figures of saints, and once as crowned with thorns in the Catacomb of Prætextatus on the Appian Way.[2] But there is not a single picture of the Crucifixion in any of the Catacombs, and yet Christians were buried there down to the sack of Rome in A.D. 410. The only representation of the Crucifixion of an early date is a caricature scratched in derision by a pagan soldier in the Palatine Barracks.[3] From the fourth to the seventh century in countless churches Christ is represented in the apse of the church as triumphant and not as crucified. The cross, it is true, was treated as an honoured symbol from the middle of the second century onwards. Justin Martyr (*Dial. c. Tryph.* 91) attempts to discover its symbolism in various events in the Old Testament, and Tertullian states that the heathen charged Christians with being "priests of the cross."[4] But the reverence with which the cross was treated was a thing wholly apart from image worship. Yet even in the Catacombs it is portrayed in a veiled and hesitating manner.

In keeping with the information we have elicited from the Catacombs, is the further truth that in Christian worship the use of the crucifix was unknown till the

---

[1] There is a statue of Christ as the Good Shepherd in the Lateran Museum. The Vatican possesses a statue of this character said to be derived from the earliest part of the third century (Kraus, *Gesch. d. christl. Kunst*, i. 227; 1896, Freiburg. See *Catholic Encyc.* vii. 666.

[2] Leclercq, *Manuel d'Archéologie Chrétienne*, i. 542; Paris, 1907 (quoted in the *Catholic Encyc.* vii. 666).

[3] Kraus, *Gesch. d. christlichen Kunst*, i. 173; Freiburg, 1896 (quoted in *Catholic Encyc.* vii. 666).

[4] Antistites crucis. *Adv. Nationes*, i. 12.

SECOND COMMANDMENT 43

sixth century. The earliest representations have been found at Gaza, Tours and Narbonne.[1] Now it is a remarkable fact that crucifixes were unknown during the first five centuries of the Christian Church : it is, moreover, an impressive fact that the use of crucifixes form part and parcel of the idolatrous development that reached its climax in the ninth and later centuries.

This development we shall deal with presently, but let us for a few minutes pause and consider the growing use of the crucifix in the present day. Is it also part and parcel of a similar movement towards idolatry as that which occurred between the sixth and ninth centuries ? Is this use of the crucifix salutary or strengthening ? Now it must be acknowledged that the image of Christ in His dying agony, His face strained with suffering, His hands and His feet nailed to the cross, may make a strong appeal to the heart and imagination, and awake such anguish and grief as may lead

[1] The worship of the crucifix was introduced into the West by the Syrian Church : cf. Bréhier, *Les Origines du crucifix dans l'art religieux*, 1904 ; Cumont, *Oriental Religions in Roman Paganism* (translated 1911), p. 109: " During the first five centuries Christians felt an unconquerable repugnance to the representation of the Saviour of the world nailed to an instrument of punishment. . . . The Syrians were the first to substitute reality in all its pathetic horror for a vague symbolism." Gregory of Tours (*ob.* 595), *De gloria Martyrum*, i. 23, describes the crucifix in Narbonne. But since this crucifix gave offence, it was veiled by order of the Bishop and only uncovered on special occasions. Bede (iv. 376, ed. Giles) relates that a crucifix was brought from Rome to the British cloister at Weremouth in 686. The crucifix was first officially authorised at the Council of Constantinople, A.D. 692. " Hereafter instead of the Lamb the human figure of Christ shall be set up on the images." As early as the fifth century the figure of the Lamb was attached to the cross, sometimes at the top, sometimes at the bottom.

44 THE DECALOGUE

to a reformation of life. It is on the strength of such impressions that those who use this symbol as a means of worship base their justification of its use. But, on the other hand, there are not a few weighty objections. The very same arguments could have been alleged in defence of the golden calf, which, according to the Pentateuch, Aaron made to satisfy the sensuous longings of the people for a visible symbol of Yahweh. Though the sight of the golden calf made Yahweh's presence more vivid and real to His people, were they really brought nearer in their sensuous worship to Him than they had been before ? The golden calves in Dan, Bethel and Samaria were treated as outward symbols of Deity and not as Deity itself, and had just as valid claims to be used in the religion of Israel as the crucifix and other images in Christianity. Though a few may use such symbols safely as suggestive of the claims of Christ on their obedience and not as images through which to offer Him worship, by the inevitable laws of association such symbols cannot but become a danger to the many. The symbols may be at first symbols and nothing more : they may stir and quicken thought, but inevitably they gather round them associations of sacredness and reverence, which are of the essence of idolatry when directed to anything short of God Himself.

In such worship also the sensuous feelings and sympathies which are stirred into activity, are wrongly identified by the worshippers with the spiritual faith which addresses itself direct to nothing less than God Himself as revealed in Christ. Such feelings are much

SECOND COMMANDMENT

more easily aroused by influences coming from below than by influences which make their appeal from above; and when men, and especially women, have once yielded to the hypnotic spell of the sensuous in religion, the still small voice of God's Spirit in the conscience and the understanding has but a slender chance of being heard.

Ruskin denounces in the strongest language the evil effects of realistic art on the religious mind of Europe. He admits that such realistic art in its higher branches may touch the most sincere religious minds, but that "in its lowest it addresses itself not only to the most vulgar desires for religious excitement, but to the mere thirst for sensation of horror which characterises the uneducated orders of partially civilised countries; nor merely to the thirst for horror, but to the strange love of death, as such, which has sometimes in Catholic churches showed itself peculiarly by the endeavour to paint the images in the chapels of the Sepulchre to look . . . like corpses. The same morbid interest has affected the minds of many among the more imaginative and powerful artists with a feverish gloom, which distorts their finest work, and, lastly . . . it has occupied the sensibility of Christian women, universally, in lamenting the sufferings of Christ, instead of preventing those of His people." [1]

And what holds true of the use of images generally is true in a wholly exceptional degree of the use of the crucifix. The representation of physical anguish, torture and agony is a thing that the Eastern religions,

[1] *Lectures on Art*, p. 53 sq.

46   THE DECALOGUE

such as Hinduism, delight in. Devotion to such horrors is characteristic of lower types of civilisation. In the West it is characteristic of women more than of men, and amongst men it is a sign of the morbid and less sound and healthy types.[1]

Furthermore, what must we think of such representations as that of the crucifix, if contemplated from the Divine side ? Christ's appeal throughout the Gospels is practically first and last to man's conscience, thought and will. Devotion based *simply on the emotions* He rejects in the most scathing terms, as in the case of Peter. And yet in the crucifix the appeal is first and mainly to the emotions, and to those elements that are paramount in men and women that are most lacking in self-control and self-respect. In fact, the crucifix is a crowning exhibition of self-pity, an unblushing proclamation to all and sundry of the physical sufferings sustained by Christ for the sons of men, and a demand, clamant though unvoiced, for their due recognition. Homeric heroes and North American braves were in olden days accustomed to acclaim their own doughty and heroic deeds ; but no real disciple of Christ, no true

[1] " When any of you next go abroad, observe and consider the meaning of the sculptures and paintings which, of every rank in art, and in every chapel and cathedral, and by every mountain path, recall the hours, and represent the agonies, of the Passion of Christ : and try to form some estimate of the efforts that have been made by the four arts of eloquence, music, painting and sculpture, since the twelfth century, to wring out of the hearts of women the last drops of pity that could be excited for this merely physical agony : for the art nearly always dwells on the physical wounds or exhaustion chiefly, and degrades, far more than it animates, the conception of pain " (Ruskin, *op. cit.* p. 54).

SECOND COMMANDMENT

Christian martyr or child of God, can follow in their footsteps; and least of all can such conduct be ascribed to, or admitted as possible in, Him who is the manifestation of God, and the supreme Exemplar of that to which all that is best and noblest in man responds by virtue of an inherent and divine necessity. The last words that were spoken by Christ to the women that followed Him as He bare the cross to Golgotha, "Daughters of Jerusalem, weep not for Me, but weep for yourselves, and for your children" (Luke xxiii. 28), ought to have made the horrors of the crucifix an impossibility, and taught His disciples the true character of the Christ, who is the most self-forgetful and unselfconscious figure in all history, and not a sentimental being, full of the weak self-consciousness and self-pity which the combined evil ministeries of art and religion have represented Him for over 1200 years.[1]

It should here be added that the Sermon, which makes its sole appeal to the emotions, comes under the same condemnation.

Preachers have often laid the main emphasis on the physical sufferings of Christ—on the bloody sweat in the garden, on the scourging in the governor's palace,

---

[1] Ruskin (*op. cit.* p. 56) in this connection speaks of "the deadly function of art in its ministry to what, whether in heathen or Christian lands, and whether in the pageantry of words, or colours, or fair forms, is truly, and in the deep sense, to be called idolatry—the serving with the best of our hearts and minds, some dear or sad phantasy which we have made for ourselves, while we disobey the present call of the Master, *who is not dead, and who is not now fainting under His cross, but requiring us to take up ours.*" The italics are mine.

on the overwhelming weight of the cross, on the jeering multitudes, on the horrors of the crucifixion, and described these in such rhetorical and passionate terms that even strong men, and not merely women and children, have broken down in an agony of weeping and of tears. But in such experiences the vehemence of human passion has been wrongly taken to be the expression of a living faith. If our religious feelings have been aroused while our conscience and will have remained quiescent, then every such right feeling that has been aroused and not been forthwith translated into action is so much waste of the spiritual nature, and tends to degrade the life it was designed to transform and strengthen.

With such sensuous appeals to the emotions, either through images or through words, contrast the calm accounts of the Evangelists. With what a severe reticence, with what an austere self-control, the Evangelists tell in simple and inimitable words the story of the cross. Their appeal is addressed primarily, not to man's emotions through dwelling on the natural horrors inspired by human agony, but first and foremost to man's conscience and thought, and then to his will and affections through this crowning manifestation of the love of God in Christ.

Let us now return to the history of image worship in the Church. To Basil the Great has been attributed the statement : " I honour and kiss the features of their images " (*i.e.* of Christ, the Virgin, Apostles, etc.), " inasmuch as they were handed down from the holy

SECOND COMMANDMENT

apostles" (*Ep.* ccclx.). But the Epistle in which these words occur is now rejected as spurious on the ground that the vocabulary and style are unlike those of Basil.[1] I have found it further ascribed to Basil that he maintained in regard to images, that "the honour paid to an image passes on to the prototype." But these words have been wrested from their context and given a meaning and comprehension they were never intended to bear. This relation of the image to its prototype Basil uses only in reference to God.[2] His brother, Gregory of Nyssa (*ob.* 395), held that much good was done by paintings on sacred subjects; and

---

[1] Maran (*Vita Bas.* xxxix.), quoted in footnote on *Basil*, p. 326 (Nicene and Post-Nicene Fathers).

[2] *De Spiritu Sancto*, xviii. (Migne, *PG* xxxii. 149). The words in inverted commas are used by Basil in reference to Christ as the image of the Father—not to an image of Christ. The Greek is: ἡ τῆς εἰκόνος τιμὴ ἐπὶ τὸ πρωτότυπον διαβαίνει. These words are immediately followed by a clause that defines their application: ὃ οὖν ἐστιν ἐνταῦθα μιμητικῶς ἡ εἰκών, τοῦτο ἐκεῖ φυσικῶς ὁ υἱός: *i.e.* "What value therefore the image has here by force of outward likeness, there the Son has by (His) essential nature." These words of Basil were later unjustifiably extended to images of every description. Again, in the same treatise, Basil (ch. ix. (Migne, *PG* xxxii. 109)) speaks of Christ as τὴν εἰκόνα τοῦ ἀοράτου. For the universal application of these words, see John of Damascus, *De fide orthodoxa*, iv. 16, "the honour rendered to the image passes to the prototype." Basil's words, it is true, lend themselves easily to this abuse. But I cannot find any real instance of it in Basil himself. The relation of the image to its prototype seems to be limited to the Divine Being. Thus in his *Comm. in Esaiam*, cap. xiii. 267 (vol. i. 583; Paris, 1721, ed. Garnier) he states that those who "treat the temple with insolence, treat with insolence also something connected with the image of the Creator" (ἐξυβρίζουσι . . . καὶ εἰς τὸ κατὰ εἰκόνα τοῦ κτίσαντος). These words are followed by a similar phrase to that given above: "Through the image the insolence passes to the Creator" (διὰ τῆς εἰκόνος ἡ ὕβρις ἀναβαίνει ἐπὶ τὸν κτίσαντα).

Paulinus of Nola (*ob.* 409) thought that the uneducated rustic was influenced for good and restrained from evil by such representations.[1] St. Augustine (*ob.* 435) laments that among the Christian masses there were many image worshippers,[2] but treats these as merely nominal members of the Church and as lacking in the essence of the Christian faith. Leontius, bishop of Neapolis, in Cyprus (*fl.* 582–602), wrote a defence of Christianity against the Jews, and maintained rightly that the law of Moses was not directed unconditionally against the use of religious images, but against the worship of them, and that sinners were daily moved to contrition and led to renounce their sins by a look at the Cross of Christ. It is clear, however, that idolatry combined with imposture had already made great strides in connection with image worship; for this bishop ingenuously maintains that blood flowed miraculously in his day from many of the images.[3] In his letter to Severus, Pope Gregory I. (*ob.* 604) defends the use of images and describes them as the books of the unlearned. Image worship at this time had become to the mass of the people the worship of the material

---

[1] *Carmen,* ix. and x. *de S. Felicis natali.*

[2] *Novi multos esse . . . picturarum adoratores* (*De Mor. Eccles. Cath.* (i.) 75). Adorare in its technical sense = worship of God Himself. That the uninstructed, if not many of the instructed, have lapsed since Augustine's time to the present day into the belief that the picture and image are not merely such things in themselves, but are tenements and vehicles of Deity and so possessed of divine powers, is manifest to the student of history.

[3] πολλάκις αἱμάτων ῥύσεις ἐξ εἰκόνων γεγόνασιν. See the fragments of this *Apology* in the fourth Act of the Second Council of Nicæa.

present image rather than of the spiritual power it symbolised. The Church's leaders might continue to draw fine distinctions between images as objects of reverence and images as objects of adoration, but the vulgar neither understood nor paid heed to them.

This wholesale reversion to idolatry called forth the opposition of several of the Byzantine Emperors, who strove to destroy all images throughout the Christian world. But the evil was too deeply rooted to be destroyed by the State. Moreover, the Church was already in a large measure committed to it. Three champions of image worship came forward in the persons of the Patriarch of Constantinople, Pope Gregory II. and John of Damascus in the eighth century. We shall consider only the latter two. Pope Gregory in the year 729 wrote two letters to the Iconoclastic Emperor Leo. The first letter is an astonishing production for an occupant of the Papal See—astonishing alike for its lack of dignity, its dogmatism, its arrogance and its ignorance. Gregory asserts that David placed the brazen serpent in the Temple. Now we do not require the erudition of Macaulay's schoolboy to be assured that David was dead before the foundation of the Temple was laid. Gregory takes Hezekiah, who destroyed the brazen serpent, to have been the same man with his grandfather Uzziah, who wished to exercise the priest's office, though he began to reign eighty-four years before Hezekiah.[1] He maintains that images were made of Christ and of the apostles and

[1] Cf. 2 Chron. xxvi. 16 and 2 Kings xviii. 4.

disseminated throughout the world in the first half of the first century. For this extraordinary statement he finds the evidence in a still more extraordinary interpretation of certain words of Christ : " Where the body is, there will the eagles be gathered together." " The body," says Pope Gregory, " is Christ, and the eagles are the religious men who flew from all quarters to behold Him. When they beheld Him, they made a picture of Him. But not of Him only, but also of James the brother of the Lord, of Stephen and of all the martyrs." Gregory denies that Christians adore the images as gods: they only use them as reminders, and invoke their intercession. But the fact that the worshipper invokes the intercession of the image invests it with supernatural associations. Hence when Gregory speaks of the statue of St. Peter at Rome, we are not surprised that he describes it as one "which all the kingdoms of the West esteem as a god upon earth." [1] These words surely have a thoroughly idolatrous ring about them. In his second letter he answers Leo's question : " Why have not the Councils commanded image worship ? " with the counter-question, " Why have they not commanded us to eat and drink ? " It thus appears that Gregory considered images as indispensable to the spiritual life as food is to the bodily life. Furthermore, Gregory asserts that " no religious man goes on a pilgrimage without an image."

But the strongest champion of image worship was John of Damascus, whose life extends over the greater

[1] Quam omnia Occidentis regna velut Deum terrestrem habent.

SECOND COMMANDMENT

part of the eighth century. In his three famous orations he expresses the ordinary arguments of the day with greater ingenuity and in more vigorous style than any of his contemporaries. He was a man of great learning and high character. I state this fact in order to make clear the grip which image worship had won on the leading men of the time, and the havoc such worship had wrought on their mental and ethical outlook. Only reflect to what depths of mental degradation such men had sunk, when John of Damascus could quote the following story as supporting the duty of image worship. John tells how a certain recluse [1] on the Mount of Olives

---

[1] The monk's name is said to have been John Moschus (*ob.* 620). The story is told in the Νέος Παράδεισος attributed to him and translated into Latin under the title *Pratum spirituale*. It is recounted in full by John of Damascus, *De imaginibus oratio*, i. 328 (Migne, *PG* xciv. col. 1280):

ἐκ τοῦ Λειμωναρίου τοῦ ἁγίου πατρὸς
ἡμῶν Σωφρονίου ἀρχιεπισκόπου Ἱεροσολύμων.

"Ἔλεγεν ὁ ἀββᾶς Θεόδωρος ὁ Αἰλιώτης, ὅτι ἦν τις ἔγκλειστος ἐν τῷ ὄρει τῶν Ἐλαιῶν, ἀγωνιστὴς πάνυ· ἐπολέμει δὲ αὐτῷ ὁ δαίμων τῆς πορνείας. Ἐν μιᾷ οὖν, ὡς ἐπέκειτο αὐτῷ σφοδρῶς, ἤρξατο ὁ γέρων ἀποδύρεσθαι, καὶ λέγει τῷ δαίμονι· Ἕως πότε οὐκ ἐνδίδως μοι; ἀπόστα λοιπὸν ἀπ' ἐμοῦ. Συνεγήρασάς μοι. Φαίνεται αὐτῷ ὁ δαίμων ὀφθαλμοφανῶς, λέγων· Ὅμοσόν μοι ὅτι οὐδενὶ λέγεις ὃ μέλλω λέγειν σοι, καὶ οὐκέτι σοι πολεμῶ. Καὶ ὤμοσεν αὐτῷ ὁ γέρων, ὅτι μὰ τὸν ἐνοικοῦντα ἐν τοῖς ὑψίστοις. Οὐκ εἴπω τινί, ὅπερ λέγεις μοι. Τότε λέγει αὐτῷ ὁ δαίμων· Μὴ προσκυνήσῃς ταύτῃ τῇ εἰκόνι, καὶ οὐκέτι σοι πολεμῶ· Εἶχε δὲ ἡ εἰκὼν ἐκτύπωμα τῆς Δεσποίνης ἡμῶν τῆς ἁγίας Μαρίας ... Λέγει ὁ ἔγκλειστος τῷ δαίμονι. Ἄφες, σκέψομαι. Τῇ οὖν ἐπαύριον δηλοῖ τῷ ἀββᾷ Θεοδώρῳ ... οἰκοῦντι τότε ἐν τῇ λαύρᾳ Φαρών, καὶ ἦλθε, καὶ διηγεῖται αὐτῷ ἅπαντα. Ὁ δὲ γέρων λέγει τῷ ἐγκλείστῳ ὄντως ἀββᾷ· Ἐνεπαίχθης, ὅτι ὤμοσας τῷ δαίμονι· πλὴν καλῶς ἐποίησας ἐξειπών· συμφέρει δέ σοι, μὴ ἐᾶσαι εἰς τὴν πόλιν ταύτην πόρνην (? πορνεῖον) εἰς ὃ μὴ εἰσέρχῃ, ἢ ἵνα ἀρνήσῃ τὸ προσκυνεῖν τῷ κυρίῳ καὶ θεῷ ἡμῶν Ἰησοῦ Χριστῷ μετὰ τῆς ἰδίας αὐτοῦ μητρός.

was tempted by a demon of uncleanness. One day the demon appeared to him and offered to discontinue his assaults, if the monk would but cease to worship an image of the Virgin and the Infant Christ which hung in his cell. In his weakness the monk consented, but, later, conscience-smitten, he disclosed his rash vow to his spiritual adviser, a well-known abbot. " Better," said the abbot, " that you should visit every brothel in Jerusalem, than abandon this worship." That such a story should be approved by the highest authorities in the Church of the time shows how the moral sense can be destroyed in an ecstatic devotion to sensuous symbols. Hence adultery and perjury were regarded by the leaders of the Church as venial offences compared with the mortal sin of refusing to worship a brazen or other image.

Notwithstanding the universal trend of the Empire to image worship, the Emperor Constantine succeeded in convening a Council against this worship at Constantinople in 754. This Council appealed first and last to the second Commandment in its strict sense as interpreted by the Jews and Early Christians, and it denounced, accordingly, image worship as a relapse into heathen idolatry. But the iconoclastic party were profoundly and hopelessly inconsistent. They rejected the worship of images and at the same time clung to the worship of the saints. And yet the latter superstition is the parent of the former. In the gathering darkness, which had been deepening in intensity since the reign of Constantine the Great, the Church had lost

SECOND COMMANDMENT

its way and could not unravel the mazes of the labyrinth into which it had wandered. Accordingly this partial reaction in the direction of a purer worship could only be of a negative character and of no real spiritual value. It is, therefore, not surprising that in 787 another Council was called under the Empress Irene at Nicæa, a Council afterwards known as the Second Council of Nicæa or Seventh General Council. At this Council the shocking story of the monk which I have just quoted to you from John of Damascus was twice read with approval, as well as the spurious Epistle of Basil above referred to. At its Seventh Session it was enacted—
" that both the figures of the sacred and life-giving cross, as also the venerated and holy images, whether in colours or mosaic or other materials, are to be placed in the holy churches of God, on sacred vessels and vestments, on walls and pictures, in houses and by roads . . . that people may kiss them and do them honourable reverence ($\dot{a}\sigma\pi a\sigma\mu\grave{o}\nu$ καὶ τιμητικὴν προσκύνησιν) but not real adoration ($\dot{a}\lambda\eta\theta\iota\nu\grave{\eta}\nu$ λατρείαν).[1] . . . Offerings of incense and lights are to be given unto the images. For honour paid to an image passes on to its prototype.[2] He who worships (ὁ προσκυνῶν) an

---

[1] λατρεία (=*adoratio*) is the worship addressed to God. προσκύνησις or δουλεία (=*veneratio* and *cultus*) is relative as distinguished from absolute worship, and could be addressed to images. In honouring the sign we honour the prototype according to this theory. This worship is paid with prostrations, genuflexions, kisses, incense and crowns. But this distinction does not relieve image worship of its idolatrous character.

[2] ἡ γὰρ τῆς εἰκόνος τιμὴ ἐπὶ τὸ πρωτότυπον διαβαίνει. This view is wrongly ascribed to Basil the Great ; see p. 49 *n*.

image worships the reality of him who is painted on it." Only paintings and other representations on a flat surface were sanctioned at this Council.[1] Statues were not sanctioned as they were subsequently by the Roman Church. To this law the Greek Church has ever since adhered.

I must now conclude, but I cannot do so without drawing attention to the character of the Empress who thus succeeded in degrading the worship of the Christian Church.

The Empress Irene, who convened this Council and acted as the sponsor for image worship, has left behind her an unsavoury record. A devoted image worshipper all her life, she concealed this fact from her iconoclastic husband, Leo IV., and on his death reversed all his legislation on this question. Acclaimed by the Council of Nicæa as a model of Christian virtue and devotion, this woman, with a view to getting the supreme power of the Empire into her own hands, deliberately encouraged her son Constantine in vicious habits: she also persuaded him to blind and mutilate his uncles, and five years later procured the murder of this son in the very bedchamber in which she had given him birth. Is it strange that the Church plunged

[1] Though this Council settled the iconoclastic controversy for the Eastern Church, the conflict of the two parties was renewed and carried on with varying fortunes till it was finally brought to a close by a Synod at Constantinople in 842. The chief advocate for image worship during this period was Theodore of Studium. It is noteworthy that εἰκών, which in earlier days could mean either a picture or statue, was henceforth used only in the former sense.

into still grosser idolatries in the centuries that followed ?

Romanists, it is true, maintain that, since prostrations and kisses were the customary ways of showing honour to civil and social superiors, the early Christians after Constantine came naturally to treat symbols in the same way, paying to them the honour that was meant really for their prototypes. But to bow to or kiss a friend is an act inherently different from a like act in connection with an image, seeing that, according to the Roman view, it is of the essence of the latter act that it is conceived as passing on automatically to the prototype. The one is a purely social act, the other, according to the presupposition of the image worshippers, a supernatural one.

This argument holds still more strongly in the case of incense. Incense implied the presence of deity in some form. These and similar acts of worship in connection with images are, as I have shown, denounced in the Old Testament and in the Talmud as idolatrous in essence, and have sooner or later always issued in idolatry in practice.

In the *Catholic Encyclopædia*, vii. 618, it is practically conceded that worship was addressed actually to the images in the seventh and eighth centuries. God worked miracles through images. They were crowned with garlands, they were kissed, they were censed and carried about in processions. Hymns were sung in their honour. They were held to possess magical powers, and placed in the face of menacing floods and fires to bar their progress.[1] Personality of a certain kind was ascribed to them; for Theodore of Studium (*ob.* 823), the leading protagonist of image worship in the ninth century, congratulates an official of the Court for choosing a holy image as godfather for his son (Migne, *PG* xcix. 962-963). Still later these images were accredited with powers of physical movement. Thus even to the present day there are in plastic form winking Madonnas and weeping saints.

[1] Since this lecture was delivered history has repeated itself in the case of Southern Italy, where the images were used to withstand the rivers of lava from Etna, and different towns came into conflict in support of their respective images and idols. Superstition dies hard in the Roman Church—if it can die at all.

SECOND COMMANDMENT

THIRD LECTURE

"Thou shalt not make unto thee any graven image, nor any likeness that is in heaven above, or that is in the earth beneath, or that is in the water under the earth; thou shalt not bow down thyself unto them, nor serve them."—Ex. xx. 4–5.

IN my last lecture on the second Commandment I set before you at some length the hostile and uncompromising attitude adopted by the Christian Church towards image worship in the first four centuries, and then the slow but steady declension of the Church from its high ideals during the next four centuries, till at last image worship received the sanction of the Seventh General Council.

Now it may be helpful to recall to your recollection certain salient facts in this reversion to a heathen type of worship. First of all we found that Irenæus attributed the introduction of image worship to heretics; next, that the chief Fathers of the first four centuries denounced in the most scathing terms every form of image worship; and amongst these Fathers were the greatest thinkers, teachers and saints of the Christian Church—such as Justin Martyr, Irenæus, Tertullian,

Origen, Cyprian, Lactantius and Augustine. By the Church of the first four centuries, then, image worship was condemned as an evil thing—derived from an evil origin. But with the conversion of the Roman Empire under Constantine a change set in. The Church was forthwith deluged by crowds of half-converted heathens, and not unnaturally these new converts brought with them many of their heathen practices into their newly adopted faith.[1] Amongst these was image worship. Thus it came about that the worship of images at first took root without the sanction of any regular ecclesiastical authority. It began with the more ignorant and more or less heathen elements in the Church. Notwithstanding, this degenerate element in religion made steady progress in illicit and unauthorised ways during the fourth and fifth centuries. And yet the progress was slow; for we find that even the crucifix was wholly unknown till the sixth century.

But from the sixth century onwards the degradation of religion grew apace, till at last image worship was all but wholly in the ascendant, and Christians began to justify this worship by the very same arguments that the heathen themselves had used centuries earlier in its defence.[2] This leavening of the Christian Church

---

[1] Jerome (on Ezek. xliv., Migne, *PL* xxv.; Jerome, v. 437), writing about A.D. 410–414, protests against the introduction of the heathen practice of the tonsure. "By this it is clear that we ought not to have shaven heads (*rasis capitibus*) like the priests and worshippers of Isis and Serapis": . . . "shaven heads belong to heathen superstition" (rasa capita habet superstitio gentilis), v. 548.

[2] See pp. 65 sqq., 37 sqq.

SECOND COMMANDMENT

with an idolatrous spirit having begun with the masses, at last got hold of the leaders of the Eastern Churches and of the Church in Rome, though not for several generations later of the Churches of France, Germany and England. Hence in the eighth century the Seventh General Council (A.D. 787) enacted that " the venerated and holy images . . . should be placed in the holy Churches of God . . . that they should receive honourable worship . . . that offerings of incense and lights should be made to them; for that any honour paid to an image passed on to its prototype."

The Empress Irene, who summoned this Council, was a person of infamous character, and some of the grounds advanced for the acceptance of image worship were as infamous as was the Empress herself.

Though derived from such a source, Pope Hadrian I. (*ob*. 795) gave his sanction to the decrees of this Council. Notwithstanding this action of the Papacy it failed to secure for nearly two hundred years the general acceptance of image worship by the French, German and English Churches. Amongst the earliest and most notable opponents of the Seventh General Council was Charlemagne.

Charlemagne, with the aid of French theologians and, above all, of the English scholar Alcuin,[1] published in 790 an important work on image worship entitled *The*

---

[1] Some writers have questioned Alcuin's share in the composition of the Caroline Books; but, as Dr. Stubbs (*DCB* i. 76) states, these objections are based on late authorities and are futile.

62 THE DECALOGUE

Four Caroline Books.[1] In this work the worship of images is condemned, and the Second Council of Nicæa —*i.e.* the Seventh General Council—is denounced as a conclave of fools.[2] This work maintained that to salute, bow, or kneel before images, to kiss them, to strew incense or light candles before them, is superstitious and idolatrous. Images, it conceded, may be used to adorn the Churches or to perpetuate the memory of the persons they represent. Yet even this concession it urged was unnecessary; for without such sensuous means Christians ought to be able to ascend to the fount of eternal light.

The Synod of Frankfort, which met in A.D. 794,[3] and represented the Churches of France and Germany, and also of England through Alcuin and other English scholars, endorsed the conclusions of the *Caroline Books*, and in the presence of two Papal legates this Synod condemned without a dissentient voice every form of

[1] *Quatuor libri Carolini*. Baronius, Bellarmine and other Romanists denied the genuineness of this work, and ascribed it to heretics of the time of Charlemagne; others, to Carlstadt of the Reformation period! But in 1866 a tenth-century MS was discovered in the Vatican. The genuineness of this work is no longer questioned. The best edition is that of Heumann, Hanover, 1731, under the title *Augusta Concilii Nicæni II. Censera*, i.e. *Caroli Magni de impio imaginum cultu libri IV*. Migne unfortunately reprinted the earlier and less truthworthy edition of *Elias Philyra* (*i.e.* Jean du Tillet, Paris, 1549).

[2] The words are *Synodus ineptissima*.

[3] This Synod made some mistakes. Thus it supposed that the Second Nicene Council sat at Constantinople. Also owing to the mistranslation of προσκύνησις by *adoratio* in the Latin version before them, Roman controversialists claim that it made this Nicene Council authorise the adoration of images. See, however, next note. In any case this Synod condemned every form of image worship.

SECOND COMMANDMENT 63

image worship, and rejected the Seventh General Council.[1] This was the last great attempt for over six centuries to stem the growing idolatry of Christian worship. There were, it is true, sporadic efforts to recover a more enlightened faith, such as that of the Conference of French Bishops at Paris in 825. This Conference adopted practically the same attitude on the question as the Synod of Frankfort, but their efforts produced no effect at the Vatican. Notwithstanding, down to the eleventh century here and there were heard voices in the wilderness raised in denunciation of image worship.[2] But, as we are aware, Rome succeeded in silencing these occasional protests, and secured the acceptance of image worship throughout the Church till the era of the Reformation.

The Western Church, however, had not as yet pronounced authoritatively on image worship through a General Council; and when, in the sixteenth century,

---

[1] See Mansi, *Concilia*, xiii. 909 : " Sanctissimi Patres nostri omnimodis et adorationem et servitutem (imaginibus sanctorum) renuentes contempserunt atque consentientes condemnaverunt." The Latin versions of the decrees of Nicæa II. (in Seventh General Council) which the Pope sent to Charlemagne, rendered προσκύνησις by *adoratio*, and Anastasius, the Papal librarian, did so also in the revised translation. The word *servitus* in the preceding note is the rendering of δουλεία in the worship of images.

[2] English Churchmen of a later age, and a less virile type than Alcuin, justified image worship on the ground that the prohibition of the use of images in the Old Testament was but a temporary matter, and that the second Commandment was abrogated by the Incarnation (cf. Lyndwood's *Provinciale*, p. 252). " Nil obstat Ex. xx. ubi dicitur, *Non facies tibi imaginem nec sculptam similitudinem*, quia illud pro eo tempore erat prohibitum, quo Deus humanam naturam non assumpserat."

the Council of Trent addressed itself officially to this subject, the Western Church was already broken up into the Anglican Church, the other Reformed Churches, and the Church of Rome.

The Church of England made its authoritative pronouncement on this question in 1562 in the Twenty-second Article, and declared that " the Romish Doctrine . . . of images as of reliques and also invocation of Saints is a fond thing vainly invented and . . . repugnant to the word of God." The other Reformed Churches had already denounced all such worship as idolatrous.

In the year 1563 the Roman Church made at last its *ex cathedra* decrees on this question through the Council of Trent. This Council (*Sessio* xxv., 1563) sanctions, together with the worship of saints and relics, also the use of images in the following terms. It ordained that " the images of Christ, of the Virgin Mother of God, and of other saints, are to be had and retained, particularly in temples, and that due honour and veneration are to be given to them ; not that any divinity or virtue is believed to be in them, on account of which they are to be worshipped ; or that anything is to be asked of them ; or that trust is to be reposed in images, as was of old done by the Gentiles, who placed their hope in idols ; but because the honour which is shown to them is referred to the prototypes which those images represent ; in such wise that by the images which we kiss, and before which we uncover the head and prostrate ourselves, we adore Christ and we venerate the saints,

SECOND COMMANDMENT 65

whose similitude they bear; even as it has been defined by the decrees of Councils, especially, indeed, of the second Synod of Nicæa, against the opponents of images." The Roman Church goes beyond the Second Council of Nicæa in that it sanctions the use of statues as well as of pictures or flat images.

This Council, it will be observed, strives to defend itself against the charge of idolatry, but the attempt cannot be regarded as successful. For it authorises the idolatrous rites of kissing, and of making genuflexions and prostrations before these images—rites which are condemned explicitly in the Old Testament, implicitly in the New Testament, and in the strongest terms in the chief Fathers of the early centuries of the Church. But this is not all. The very arguments used in defence of image worship by the Roman Church could have been used as legitimately by the worshippers of the golden calves in Israel, and were actually used by heathen writers in defence of their worship of images during the first four centuries of the Christian era. Thus Maximus of Tyre (*Dissertatio*, viii. 2) in the first century argues that the weakness of men requires images, and that by such outward things we should seek to win some understanding of Him who is the Father and Maker of all things.

Porphyry (3rd Century: Eusebius, *Præp. Evang.* iii. 7) speaks of men "indicating God or God's powers by images" and "sketching invisible things by visible forms."

Dio Chrysostom (c. A.D. 40–115; *Orat.* xii. 407, ed.

Reiske) defends the use of images as a help in the worship of the gods; while Plotinus (*ob.* 269; *Ennead.* iv. 3. 11) ascribes the making of images to the wise men of old. Origen (*c. Celsum*, vii. 66) declares that Christians refrain from doing homage to (τιμᾶν) images lest they should be supposed to regard them as gods. He condemns Celsus and other heathens who, though admitting that the images are not gods, yet render them homage (τιμή). Arnobius (*fl.* 303; *Adv. Nationes*, vi. 8, 9) represents the views of the cultured heathens of his time in regard to idols in the following question: "Do you perchance maintain, that under these images the deities display in a manner their presence to you, and that, because you are not endowed with power to see the gods, you worship them in this fashion and render (them) the services that are their due?" Arnobius emphasises the unreasonableness of such worship in these words: "If you are certain that these supposed gods exist . . . what ground, what reason is there for fashioning these images, when ye have true beings to whom ye can pray and address your requests for help in time of need?" And again he urges with deep irony: "Are these gods not aware that worship is being offered to them unless through the mediation of such images?" "If they are aware," he retorts on these image worshippers, "what greater injury, contumely, or shamelessness can there be than to acknowledge a deity who is essentially of one nature and to pray for help to a thing essentially of another?" St. Augustine represents the pagans of his time as defending their use of idols in these words: "Some heathen controversialist . . . says: 'I do not worship that stone or that senseless image . . . but I serve him whom I see not.' 'Who is that?'" asks Augustine. The heathen replies: "'A certain invisible divinity who presides over the image.'"[1] This is exactly the modern Roman defence of image worship, and this worship Augustine calls idolatry. Again in commenting on Ps. cxiii. (*i.e.* cxiv.) 4, Augustine quotes another heathen as asserting: "I do not worship the image, but I regard the material effigy as a sign of the thing which I ought to worship." The pagans have anticipated every argument of the Roman Church in defence of image worship.

I have now shown at sufficient length that the worshippers of images in the Roman and Eastern Churches employ exactly the same arguments in defence of their idolatry as the heathen worshippers employed of old when confronted by the early Christian Apologists. Surely the Church that is obliged to defend its worship of images with arguments that are common to the idolaters of all ages cannot escape the guilt of idolatry itself.

From this point we pass on to the next. Although the image worshippers in the Christian Church have always maintained that their worship was not idolatrous, they betray a troubled consciousness that their worship

[1] *In Psalmum*, xcvi. 7 (vol. iv., 1495 C.D.): "Existit nescio quis disputator qui . . . ait: Non ego illum lapidem colo, nec illud simulacrum quod est sine sensu . . . sed . . . servio ei quem non video. Quis est iste? Numen quoddam, inquit, invisibile quod præsidet illi simulacro."

is not as legitimate as they assert it to be. Otherwise why do they adopt three illegitimate measures in order to conceal their untenable position? These measures were taken when the Churches of the East and West were forced to meet the challenge of the second Commandment. The second Commandment was a stumbling-stone and rock of offence. Hence they either retained it in the text but explained it away in the notes; or, secondly, they removed it from the text and relegated it wholly to the notes; or, thirdly, they excluded it altogether from the Decalogue. The Eastern Church was never guilty of the second or third offences. This Church has always held fast to the second Commandment, and obeyed literally the first part of it which forbade the making of graven images: though they ran counter to the spirit of the Commandment in authorising the worship of pictures and icons.

But since the Eastern Church has not been guilty of removing the second Commandment from the text to the notes or of omitting it wholly, we shall limit our consideration to the Church of Rome, the largest of the three main divisions into which the Western Church was already broken up at the Reformation.

At the Council of Trent (A.D. 1563) (*Sessio* xxv.) bishops and others in authority were enjoined "to instruct the faithful diligently concerning . . . the invocation of saints: the honour (to be paid) to relics, and the legitimate use of images." This Council's decree upon this subject we have already quoted.[1]

[1] See above, p. 64 sq.

SECOND COMMANDMENT

In this decree, as we have already shown, it is clear that the second Commandment is really ignored. It is true that in the Catechism of the Council of Trent (1566) the Commandment is given, but it is accompanied with comments that explain it away. Images, this Council maintains, are nothing in themselves, yet various acts of worship are to be rendered to them, inasmuch as these acts of worship pass on to their prototypes. This is to state very explicitly what the heathens said implicitly [1] in defence of image worship in their controversies with Origen, Augustine, Arnobius and other outstanding champions of the Christian faith. The images, according to the chief heathen teachers, were nothing in themselves, but the prayers and the other religious offices rendered before them were believed to pass on to the reality behind the images. This doctrine of the Council of Trent is thus purely pagan and may henceforth be dismissed as such from our consideration.

The official action of the Church of Rome then was, as we have shown by the Canons and Catechism of the Council of Trent, to give the second Commandment, but to issue injunctions that directly contravened it or else explained it away.

But long before the Council of Trent the mediæval Church had been unable to escape the conviction that its teaching with regard to image worship was in direct conflict with the second Commandment; and, dissatisfied with the official interpretations of this Commandment, which really explained it away, it had

[1] See above, p. 65 sqq.

THE DECALOGUE

recourse to another and more effective measure. Instead of printing this Commandment and following it up with laboured misrepresentations, the Early Mediæval Church began to omit it wholly. This practice was initiated in England at a Council under Alfred in 887. But the Saxons objected to the omission, and so the second Commandment was added at the close of the Decalogue.[1] But this evil precedent was obviously widely followed in the course of the next three centuries; and, although at first this omission of the second Commandment was illegitimate and without authorisation, it won at last official sanction in England in the Constitutions of Archbishop Peckham, who, as Primate of all England, published the Decalogue without the second Commandment in the decrees of the Council of Lambeth in 1281.[2] In 1287 Quivil, bishop of Exeter, followed the precedent of Peckham, with a few verbal differences. Indeed Peckham's text of the Decalogue was adopted generally by other English archbishops and bishops down to the Reformation.[3]

The omission of the second Commandment by the English Church was no doubt adopted from Continental practice, and especially from that of Rome. In any case from the thirteenth century onwards it prevailed

---

[1] See Spelman, *Concilia orbis Brittanici*, i. 354, 363. London, 1639.

[2] See Wilkins' *Concilia*, ii. 55; London, 1737. The ninth Commandment is here: "Non concupisces domum proximi tu," and the tenth, "Non desiderabis uxorem ejus, non servum, non ancillam," etc.

[3] See Coulton, *Social Life in Britain from the Conquest to the Reformation*, p. 264.

SECOND COMMANDMENT

throughout the entire Western Church down to the Reformation. So strongly had this mutilated form of the Decalogue entrenched itself in Western Christendom, that in 1529 we find even Luther publishing his larger and smaller Catechisms without the second Commandment, and in 1548 Archbishop Cranmer authorising the publication of Justus Jonas'[1] Catechism in Latin and English with the same mutilation. The English version, however, of Jonas' Catechism includes a long excursus on the second Commandment.[2] This excursus gives this Commandment in full in English, but not in Latin. In 1549 the second Commandment was inserted in the Church Catechism, but without the final words, "For I the Lord thy God," etc. The full text of the second Commandment appears for the first time, after the lapse of six or seven centuries, in our Church Catechism of 1552, and since that date there have been no attempts to omit this Commandment in the Anglican Church. Practically from the middle of the sixteenth century all the Reformed Churches throughout Europe have restored the second Commandment to its place in the Decalogue.

It is now incumbent on us to ask what recognition has this Commandment received in the Roman Church since the Council of Trent in 1563 ? We have already seen that it was restored to its place in the Decalogue

[1] Justus Jonas (1493-1555) was a great personal friend of Luther and other German reformers.

[2] That is, according to the reckoning of the Anglican Church. The Lutherans and Romanists make the second Commandment part of the first, as we have already seen. See p. 16 sqq.

72 THE DECALOGUE

in the Catechism of the Council of Trent in 1566. This Council could not do otherwise, so fierce was the light of criticism that beat upon its proceedings. But, though it restored the words of this Commandment, it explained away their meaning. It is not surprising, therefore, that in 1588 in *The reformed Office of the Blessed Virgin*, printed at Salamanca and published by the order of Pope Pius v., it was again omitted.

What Pius v. did has been the general custom in the Roman Church throughout the world ever since. There have, of course, been exceptions. Thus two Catechisms printed in Dublin contain this Commandment: the Douay Catechism, published 1752, and Bishop Hornihold's Catechism,[1] published in 1813. The latter uses the words "Thou shalt not adore nor worship them." Let me remind you that whereas the word "adore" refers to the worship of God or the Trinity alone, the word "worship" was used of images. These words, therefore, "thou shalt not adore nor worship them," taken strictly, forbid the religious worship of images in any form.[2]

But this apparently is the last protest against image worship in Ireland; for though, in 1843, Dr. Doyle in his Catechism seemingly follows in Dr. Hornihold's steps, he is careful not to do so. He gives the second Commandment as follows: " Thou shalt not make

[1] *The Real Principles of Catholics, or a Catechism by way of General Instruction.* Dublin: Richard Coyne.

[2] But Hornihold is careful later in his Catechism to justify implicitly the worship of images. Thus he writes: "Cursed is he who commits idolatry; that prays to images or relics, or *worships them for Gods.*" But even the cultured heathen, as I have shown, would not have objected to these words which I have italicised.

SECOND COMMANDMENT

to thyself either an idol or any figure to adore it." Here he deliberately omits the words "nor worship" which are found in Hornihold's Catechism, and thus the second Commandment is construed by him as admitting image worship. Since 1813, then, so far as my information goes,[1] every Roman Catholic Catechism in Ireland has omitted the second Commandment down to the Maynooth Catechism, published in 1891 with the full authority of Cardinal McCabe, the Archbishops and Bishops of Ireland.

In England the Roman Catholic Catechisms generally omit the second Commandment.[2] "The Catechism of Christian Doctrine" (published by Dolman in 1843) omits. *The Catholic Faith*, a compendium authorised by Pope Pius x. and published in England in 1911, removes this Commandment from the text and relegates it to the notes.[3] On the other hand, a popular penny

---

[1] For most of these facts regarding the Roman method of dealing with the second Commandment in Ireland and elsewhere, I am indebted to the Rev. J. C. Hammond, Superintendent of the Irish Church Missions, Dublin.

[2] *Why does the Church of Rome hide the Second Commandment from the People?* Quoted by Collette in his *Novelties of Romanism*² (London: R.T.S.), p. 95 sq.

[3] This unstraightforward method was already adopted in *The Larger Catechism*, by Fr. Fustet, Rome and New York, 1906. The four Roman Catholic Archbishops of Ireland in their enlarged and revised form of Butler's *Small Catechism*, represent the second Commandment with an "etc." (p. 34, published by Duffy & Co., Dublin). On p. 42 they justify kneeling before images of Christ and the Saints, but say that prayer is not to be offered to them, but, that in honouring the images they do honour to the originals. Relics are to be honoured because the bodies of the Saints had been temples of the Holy Ghost, and at the last day will be glorified for ever in heaven. This clearly implies a resurrection of the physical body.

Catechism, published in recent years without a date and entitled *A Catechism of Christian Devotions*, and approved by the Roman Catholic bishops of England and Wales, contains this Commandment. Here undoubtedly the influence of the Anglican Church on the Roman has brought about this restoration.

In America the same twofold usage prevails. Some Roman Catholic Catechisms contain the Commandment, others omit. It is omitted in a huge work of over seven hundred pages entitled *The Catechism Explained*, and published in 1899 at New York, Cincinnati and Chicago with the imprimatur of the Roman Catholic Archbishop of New York.

As regards the Roman Catholic Church on the Continent and elsewhere, I may close this part of my subject with a quotation from Dr. McCaul, who studied the usage of the Church of Rome on the Continent : " Here there are twenty-nine Catechisms in use in Rome and Italy, France, Belgium, Austria, Bavaria, Silesia, Poland, Ireland, England, Spain and Portugal, in twenty-seven of which the second Commandment is totally omitted : in two mutilated."

From the foregoing examination of this question it follows that at the present day no Christian Church, whether Anglican, Reformed or Eastern, omits the second Commandment save that of Rome, and that, where the influence of the Anglican, Reformed and Eastern Churches is least felt, there it is most frequently or generally omitted. Rome cannot plead in her own defence that the second Commandment is given in about one out of ten or one out of twenty of her Catechisms. What she has to do is to justify, not its omission in nine-tenths or nineteen-twentieths of her Catechisms, but its omission in any. Such justification she cannot find, seeing that the real ground for the omission is her consciousness that it is due to her image worship—an image worship that is, as we have seen, exactly the same in essence as that of the golden calves in Palestine, or as that of the cultivated heathens in the first four centuries of the Christian era, and is assuredly the same as that condemned by the Old Testament prophets as idolatrous from the eighth century B.C. onwards; by the writers of the New Testament, and by the Fathers of the first four centuries.

In my last lecture on this subject I drew your attention to the fact that image worship followed naturally, and indeed inevitably, in the wake of the worship of the saints; inasmuch as devotions offered in the presence of images were believed to pass on to their prototypes, that is, to the saints. In the twenty-second article of the English Church these two evils, image worship and the invocation of saints, are condemned together. With such a large subject as the worship of the saints we cannot deal here, and yet we cannot ignore it altogether, seeing that it has been the fruitful mother of many Christian idolatries. We shall accordingly confine our attention to the most outstanding of these idolatries—that is, to Mariolatry, or the worship of Mary, the mother of our Lord, and show that in the early centuries this worship was wholly unknown, but that from the sixth century onwards the cult of Mary made gigantic strides, till in the twelfth century she was throned in heaven; and in many, if not in most, of Rome's homiletical and devotional books from the twelfth century to the present time she is practically put on an equality with the Three Persons of the Godhead.

The evidence for the above theses I will give under two heads—first, the evidence furnished by mosaics and monuments; and, secondly, the evidence furnished by the Fathers and later works.

(i) First, then, as regards the evidence of ancient monuments, it may be stated categorically that in the Catacombs there is not a trace of any kind of worship of the Virgin.

Mary appears at least a score of times in scenes representing the worship of the Wise Men, but their adoration is always directed to the Child and never to the Mother. She is never graced even with a halo in the Catacombs, and she is represented only in scenes that are directly suggested by the Gospels.

Passing from the Catacombs to the Italian churches we find a most interesting piece of evidence in the mosaics of the chancel arch of the Church of Santa Maria Maggiore, in Rome. These mosaics were given to the Church by Pope Sixtus III. about A.D. 435.[1]

---

[1] This mosaic was altered in the eighteenth century. See Marriott, *Testimony of the Catacombs and of other ancient Monuments*, 1870, pp. 37, 63. Fortunately we have an engraving of the original mosaic by Ciampinus in his *Monumenta Vetera*, i. 200, accompanied

SECOND COMMANDMENT

Here as in the Catacombs we have the adoration of the Wise Men, but the natural and traditional arrangement of the figures, that is, the seating of the Child on the knees of His mother, is abandoned in order to show that the worship is directed to the Child alone. For the Child is placed alone on a throne of state with a halo round His head, while His mother, so far from sharing this throne, is relegated to a subordinate position and is represented without a halo. In fact, in the public monuments of the fifth century there is not a trace of any divine honour paid to the Virgin. In the mosaics in the Church of St. Paul on the Via Ostiensis, which were presented by Pope Leo in 441, and in the mosaics at Ravenna, 451 and 462, Christ is represented in glory with the four-and-twenty Elders, and St. Peter and St. Paul, but the figure of Mary appears in none of them.[1]

In the mosaics of the sixth century the Virgin is represented once, and that only in the scene of the Adoration of the Wise Men.[2] In fact, till nearly the close of the sixth century in the public monuments of the Church there is no trace of any cult of the Virgin. So far as I am aware the earliest representation of the

by an elaborate verbal description. Pope Clement XI. also supplies an exact drawing of this mosaic. Thus we know what the mosaic was in the seventeenth century before it was altered under the direction of Boniface XIV. in the eighteenth century in order to bring it into conformity with Romish doctrine and make it attest a doctrine which directly conflicts with that which in its original form it was designed to teach. See Marriott, *op. cit.* 58–59, 63.

[1] See Marriott, *op. cit.* p. 41 sq.
[2] See Marriott, p. 42.

78   THE DECALOGUE

Virgin with a halo occurs in a Syriac MS of the Gospels, dated 586, in a picture of the Ascension of Christ.[1]

Passing over a couple of centuries we find that by the eighth century the worship of the Virgin has established itself and that the superstition has grown to most extravagant lengths. Early in the ninth century Pope Paschalis introduced mosaics into the Church of St. Cecilia, in the centre of which there is a gigantic figure of the Virgin seated on a gorgeous throne and holding the Infant Christ in her arms. The Pope himself is represented as kneeling in an attitude of adoration and addressing his worship—not to the Divine Child, but to Mary. This same Pope presented mosaics to another church dedicated also to St. Cecilia (A.D. 820). Here, as in the former mosaics, the traditional representations of the worship of Christ are wholly superseded by others which exhibit—apparently for the first time—the Virgin seated on a throne and wearing a royal crown.[2] The Holy Infant is seated on her knees. This superstition reaches its climax in the mosaics of the Church of St. Nicholas in Urbe in Rome, begun by Calixtus II. (1119–1124) and completed by Pope Anastasius IV. (1153–1154). Here Mary is seated on a throne, crowned as the Queen of heaven. The Divine Child is seated on her knees with a halo but without a crown. Archangels flank the throne on either side, and the two Popes kneel at her feet, embracing them in an attitude of adoration.[3] Their worship is directed, not

[1] See Marriott, *op. cit.* p. 44 sq.   [2] See Marriott, *op. cit.* p. 49.
[3] See Marriott, *op. cit.* pp. 54–56, where this mosaic is reproduced.

to the Divine Child, but to Mary. In this crowning monument of mediæval superstition there can be no doubt as to the meaning of the crown on Mary's head. She is thereby represented as the sovereign of heaven and earth, and the Divine Child is wholly secondary in importance. In fact, Dr. Northcote, a Roman Catholic theologian, a former President of St. Mary's College, Oscott, goes so far as to assert in his *Account of the Roman Catacombs* that, if the Virgin mother and her Child appear in the same representation, we may assume that He is represented " simply with a view to showing who she is."[1] This statement is wholly false as regards the early monuments, but from the twelfth century onwards it can be amply justified.

(ii) We shall now turn to the evidence furnished by the Fathers and later works on the growth of Mariolatry, or the worship of Mary.

Of the worship of Mary there is not, as we are aware, a single trace in the New Testament. Nay more, there is not a shadow of an attempt to secure her intervention in order to influence the action of Christ. On the other hand, it would almost seem as if the Evangelists had in view the possibility of such idolatrous worship, and with a view to preventing such an evil had selected special incidents from the life of our Lord which reveal the attitude He adopted towards His mother during His ministry. Thus at Cana of Galilee (John ii. 4, 5) when Mary took the initiative and suggested to our Lord the line of action He should adopt, He requested

[1] See Marriott, p. 9.

her in unmistakable words not to interfere in a province that was peculiarly His own : " Woman, what have I to do with thee ? Mine hour is not yet come." Mary took the words in the right spirit, and retiring into the background advised her friends simply to await and do Christ's bidding. On another occasion when He was teaching and His mother and His brethren sent for Him, seemingly in an unduly peremptory fashion,[1] according to St. Chrysostom and St. Cyril, He appears to have paid no heed to the request, but simply replied : " Who is My mother, and who are My brethren . . . behold, whosoever shall do the will of God, the same is My brother and sister and mother " (Mark iii. 31–35 ; Matt. xii. 46–50). Once more, when at the close of one of His great discourses a woman cried out amid the multitude : " Blessed is the womb that bare Thee," He rejoined : " Yea rather, blessed are they that hear the word of God, and keep it " (Luke xi. 27, 28). Thus so far are the Gospels from sanctioning the idea of Mary's intervention in the work of Christ that they disallow it from the outset and absolutely. And outside the Gospels in the rest of the New Testament this attitude is still more marked. In the Acts (i. 14) she is mentioned directly only once, and then simply as the Mother of Jesus. In the thirteen Pauline Epistles there is only one indirect reference to her in Gal. (iv. 4), where it is said that Christ was " born of a woman, born under the law " ; while in the Epistle to

[1] " St. Chrysostom," Migne, viii. 141 ; " St. Cyril of Alexandria," iv. 1064, 1065.

SECOND COMMANDMENT

the Hebrews, in the seven General Epistles of St. Peter, St. John, St. James and St. Jude, there is not even the remotest allusion to her. The same fact holds true of the Apocalpyse, which goes further and denounces twice any attempt to worship a created being.

Finally, that Mary was not present at the Transfiguration or the Institution of the Lord's Supper, that she was not with the Apostles when they first greeted their Lord on Easter Day or parted with Him on Ascension Day, are facts full of significance. Mary's place was in the background from the beginning of Christ's ministry.

In the first three centuries there are occasional references to Mary as the mother of Jesus, but there is nothing amounting even to a suggestion that there was a cult of Mary. If such a cult existed it would of necessity have appeared in the Church Liturgies and Services of these centuries.[1] But in these liturgies her name is not once mentioned. But just as we have learned that image worship began amongst heretics, so it is with the worship of Mary. In certain apocryphal

---

[1] In fact we might say that in the Church services there was no special mention of Mary till the fifth century. "The leaders of the Church neglected, until the middle of the fifth century at earliest, to insert in the liturgical prayers used in divine service any separate honourable mention of Mary. This omission must be regarded as all the more remarkable, since it had become usual in all the churches, during the fourth century, at each celebration of the Holy Sacrifice, to make special mention of the Patriarchs, Prophets and Apostles, and to celebrate the memory of the Martyrs or to recommend oneself to their prayers" (Lucius, *Anfange*, etc., p. 471 : quoted by Coulton, *Five Centuries of Religion*, p. 138 *n.*). See this last work, pp. 138–154, on "The Mother of God."

works [1] of the second century which are full of the most absurd fictions and pretend to furnish Mary's biography, there is the preparation for such a cult. Thus it is from the apocryphal Gospel of James, which Pope Gelasius condemned along with other heretical works and placed on the Index (A.D. 492–496), that the name of Anna as Mary's mother is derived. Thus even the name of Mary's mother is unknown and unrecorded unless in works of religious fiction, which were fiction in the worst sense, that is, pious frauds, and even rejected as such by the early popes.

When we pass from the first three centuries to the fourth and fifth we find the first real instance of a cult of the Virgin in Thrace, Scythia and Arabia in the fourth century. This cult was strongly denounced by Epiphanius, bishop of Cyprus (c. A.D. 370) [2] (*Hær.* lxxix.). The special honours that were paid to her in Ephesus in the fifth century are described by Sir William Ramsay as a recrudescence of the pagan worship of the Virgin Mother of the heathen world (*Pauline Studies*, p. 126). At Constantinople signs of this cult appear in an oration delivered by Proclus, patriarch of Constantinople, about A.D. 450.[3]

The writings of St. Basil of Cæsarea (*ob.* 379), St.

[1] The *Protoevangelium of James* and the later works: *Liber de Infantia Mariæ et Christi Salvatoris, Evangelium de Nativitate Mariæ.*

[2] *Hær.* lxxix. 7: "Let Mary be honoured, but let worship be paid to the Father, the Son and the Holy Ghost. Let none worship Mary." ἐν τιμῇ ἔστω Μαρία, ὁ δὲ πατήρ, καὶ υἱός, καὶ ἅγιον πνεῦμα προσκυνείσθω, τὴν δὲ Μαρίαν μηδεὶς προσκυνείτω.

[3] προσκυνεῖται καὶ ἡ Μαρία—*Laudatio Deiparæ Virginis*, iv. p. 343.

SECOND COMMANDMENT 83

Chrysostom, St. Cyril of Alexandria,[1] show no trace of the cult of the Virgin, and throughout the twelve folio volumes of Augustine's works there is not a single prayer addressed to the Virgin.[2]

In the mediæval period the cult grew apace. Prayers began to be addressed directly to her. In the Liturgy of St. Mark, one of the most ancient liturgies of the Church, and the Syrian liturgies, prayers addressed to the Virgin were interpolated. I can only notice a few more facts in regard to the growing deification of Mary.

In the twelfth (?) century Peter Damian spoke of her as "deified" (*Sermo de Nativ. Mar.*, P.L. cxliv. p. 740). In the thirteenth century the Franciscans maintained, against the Dominicans, that Mary was conceived without sin, a doctrine that is now declared to be an essential element of the faith of the Roman Church. St. Bonaventura (1221–1274), known as the "Seraphic Doctor," brought out an edition of the Psalms. In this edition he replaced appeals to God by an appeal to Mary. Two examples will sufficiently represent the peculiar labours of this canonised saint of the Middle Ages. The first we take from Ps. xxxi. 1, where, instead of "In Thee, O Lord, have I put my

[1] Petavius (*ob.* 1652) (*Theol. Dogm. de Incarnat.* xiv. 1) denounces the language used by these three Fathers regarding Mary as "shocking" (*infanda*). (Quoted by Marriott, *Testimony of the Catacombs*, etc., p. 197.)

[2] St. Augustine (x. 1133 A, 2101 C) says that Mary was born of the concupiscence of the flesh, and that (*De Sancta Virginitati* 3, vi. 580 B, C) "she was more blessed in apprehending the faith of Christ than in conceiving the flesh of Christ."

84 THE DECALOGUE

trust: let me never be put to confusion: deliver me in my righteousness," Bonaventura rewrites the text thus: "In thee, O Lady, have I put my trust: let me not be confounded for ever: in thy grace take me." The second is the concluding verse of the last psalm, where for "Let everything that hath breath praise the Lord," Bonaventura writes: "Let everything that hath breath praise our Lady." To the Te Deum he applied the same method with like results. Such mental degradation is unintelligible outside the Church of the dark ages, and the Roman Church which is their legitimate successor.

Another Franciscan, Bernardinus de Bustis (*ob.* 1500), outstrips all his predecessors in incredible blasphemies. Thus in his *Mariale* he writes: "Of so great authority in the heavenly palace is that Empress that . . . we may appeal to her for every grievance." Yea more, he declares that "any one may appeal to Mary if he feels aggrieved by the justice of God." Again (Part ix., Sermon ii. p. 605, also quoted from *Anglican Essays*, p. 206, 1923): "Since the Virgin Mary is the Mother of God . . . she is herself superior to God, and God Himself is her subject by reason of the humanity derived from her."

The Council of Trent decreed that worship should be offered to Mary differing in kind to that offered to God, but exceeding that paid to the rest of the saints. But are these kept distinct? Certainly not in Rome's devotional literature, as we have already seen. And what are we to say to this prayer from the Roman

SECOND COMMANDMENT 85

Breviary: "Hail, O Queen, Mother of Mercy! Hail our life, our sweetness, our hope! To thee we fly, the banished sons of Eve."[1]

The Breviary is now almost as full of the praises and powers of Mary as of those of Christ. But to credit Mary with the power of hearing every prayer and of succouring every soul in trouble, is to endow her with essentially divine powers; for " Omniscience alone can hear the cry of every human heart, and Omnipotence alone can deliver everywhere." In fact, Mary dominates the devotional life of the Roman Church. This is conspicuous in the case of *The Glories of Mary*—a book written in 1730 by Liguori, a canonised saint of the Roman Church. This book, which draws freely on earlier devotional and homiletical books and is not always so extravagant as its forerunners, circulates throughout Roman Christendom, and has done so for 170 years. It is pre-eminently a text-book, if not the text-book, of Roman devotion. It has been translated into many languages. The English translation, which has been revised by a former Roman Catholic Bishop of Southwark, is commended to the faithful by the imprimatur of two Cardinals of Westminster—Wiseman and Manning. It thus possesses an authority of a very high order. I will conclude this study by quoting some of the extraordinary and blasphemous statements of Liguori regarding Mary. These are only normal

[1] Antiphon to *Magnificat* in Roman Breviary, reformed by the order of the Council of Trent, published by Pius V. and revised by Clement VIII. and Urban VIII.

specimens of the multitudes that are to be found in its 670 pages.

Liguori states that Mary is "the Queen of heaven" (*Glories of Mary*, translated from the Italian);[1] that "the splendour of the assumption of Mary into heaven . . . (was) more glorious than the ascension of Jesus Christ" (p. 390); that "Christ is a faithful and powerful mediator between God and men, but in Him men fear the majesty of God. A mediator then was needed with the Mediator Himself, and none more fitting could be found than Mary" (pp. 169–170). Hence he calls Mary "the city of refuge" (p. 94), "the hope of all (men)" (p. 83), "the holder of the keys of all the divine mercies" (p. 151). To her power there are no limits; for, as Liguori declares, "Jesus, who is omnipotent, has made Mary omnipotent also" (p. 155). Not content with such an extravagant statement, he quotes with approval the words of an earlier writer: "At the command of Mary all obey, even God"; though he explains these words as meaning that "God grants the prayers of Mary as if they were commands" (p. 155), he accepts the statements of other writers, to the effect: "that for the blessed Virgin . . . God created the whole world," and that "its existence depends on her will" (p. 334); that "Mary is the dispenser of the divine graces: her Son grants nothing but what passes through her hands" (p. 575): that "no one

[1] Published by Burns and Oates. The second edition was issued in 1868. Since then it has apparently been reprinted frequently. The edition I have used has evidently been published lately, but no date is given. I have at times given my own translation of the notes.

SECOND COMMANDMENT

can be saved without the protection of Mary " (p. 575) : that " Mary does not pray, but commands " (p. 570).

It is no wonder that Roman Catholics credit such absurdities and profanities, seeing that their Cardinals and religious leaders not only tolerate, but actually commend to the acceptance of the faithful the following blasphemies to which Liguori gives expression regarding the Incarnation. Thus we read that " Mary's most humble eyes held God in such a way captive that this Blessed Virgin, with a kind of most sweet violence, drew the Word Himself of God the Father into her womb. . . . " Thus it is that we can understand," says the Abbot Franco, " why the Holy Ghost praised the beauty of this His Spouse, so greatly on account of her dove's eyes. . . . For Mary, looking at God with the eyes of a simple and humble dove, enamoured Him to such a degree by her beauty that with the bands of love she made Him a prisoner in her chaste womb. . . . Where on earth could so beautiful a virgin be found, who could allure the King of heaven by her eyes and by a holy violence lead Him captive, bound in the chains of love ? " (p. 328). One more quotation from Liguori regarding the reception of Mary into heaven. " Let him who can," writes Liguori, " comprehend with what love the Most Holy Trinity blessed her. Let him comprehend the welcome given to His Daughter by the Eternal Father, to His Mother by the Son, to His Spouse by the Holy Ghost. The Father crowned her by imparting His power to her ; the Son, His wisdom ; the Holy Ghost, His love. And the three

Divine Persons, placing her throne at the right of that of Jesus, declared her Sovereign of heaven and earth" (pp. 394–395).

On the prurient and blasphemous imaginings of these writers we cannot dwell longer; but, since it has been my duty to apply the teaching of the second Commandment to human life and religion from early Hebrew days down to the present, it would have been sheer dishonesty on my part to have passed over the idolatrous beliefs that came to the birth in the Christian Church in the sixth century, and at last reached their full development and expression in the devotional and homiletical works of the Roman Church —works, be it remarked, which have received for centuries the sanction of Roman Cardinals and Archbishops throughout the entire world. Such idolatrous beliefs have of late been making inroads into the ranks of the Anglican clergy. The outward symbols of this apostasy of the heart from a true and spiritual worship of God are frequently in evidence. Of these the most obvious and indefensible is the representation of the Virgin crowned and seated on a throne.[1]

Multitudes, it is true, are not conscious of all that this and kindred symbols imply, since the accredited authorities of the Church are often silent, and so they go blindly onwards, led by a minority of disloyal clergy in the Anglican Church—a Church which denounces in the strongest terms the worship of images and the invocation of saints.

[1] See above, p. 78 sqq.

THIRD COMMANDMENT

"Thou shalt not take the name of the Lord thy God in vain; for the Lord will not hold him guiltless that taketh His name in vain." [1]—Ex. xx. 7.

THE third Commandment follows naturally on first and second. In the first Commandment the duty is laid down of worshipping God and worshipping Him only. In the second Commandment man is required to worship God in spirit and not through the mediation of images. On these two follows appropriately the command not to dishonour God by invoking His name to attest what is untrue. A false oath is not only a violation of the third Commandment. It is more: it virtually amounts to atheism, and is, therefore, a violation of the first; and it is most prevalent where image worship, that is, the violation of the second Commandment, prevails. An oath is defined by Philo [2] as "an invocation of God to attest the truth of things when they have been called in question": and to this Philo appends the remark: "To invoke God to attest

---

[1] This phrase is taken by Wellhausen, as already by Josephus, (*Ant.* iii. 5. 5), to mean "falsely." Dillmann and Kautzsch interpret it as meaning "sinfully" or "criminally." In my lecture I have confined myself mainly to the former. The latter follows from it.

[2] *De decem Oraculis,* § 17.

the truth of a lie is a most impious deed." To the Commandment not to take God's name in vain is added the warning: "for the Lord will not hold him guiltless that taketh His name in vain." The nature of the penalty is not mentioned here, but we find it in Deut. xix. 15-21, where it is enacted that the same penalty was to be inflicted on the false witness which his testimony, if true, would have brought on the accused: or in the direct and vigorous words of the Deuteronomist: "Then shall ye do unto him as he had thought to have done to his brother" (Deut. xix. 19). Though Deuteronomy is much later than the Book of the Covenant, there can be no doubt that it has preserved this ancient usage of Hebrew law: for we find that the penalty enacted for perjury in the Code of Hammurabi [1] was of a like character.

The name of God according to Hebrew usage stands for all that is known of God, and sums up all that God has made known of His nature, character and will. For the members of a nation to attest their evidence by the use of the Divine name implies that society rests on a Divine foundation. The State is a Divine institution no less than the family and the Church. The powers that be are ordained of God. The object with which the Divine name is invoked in the attestation of an oath and the object likewise of judges in courts of law are one and the same—that is, that the will of God may be

---

[1] For false witness in a capital suit the penalty was death. See Johns, *Code of Laws promulgated by Hammurabi*, 2285-2242 B.C., 1903, § 3.

THIRD COMMANDMENT

done on earth. The witness, on the one hand, is reminded that his evidence should not be perverted by passion or malice, by greed or fear. It is a reminder to the judges, on the other, that it is their task to execute the justice of God impartially in the temporal sphere of human life.

The breach of such an oath—in other words, perjury—is a great crime, and should be visited with the severest penalties. If tolerated, it would destroy human society and shatter the very foundations of the State. Hence, when the accused aggravates the guilt of his wrongdoing by the crime of perjury, he should in every case incur a twofold retribution.

Even towards the close of the Roman Republic, Cicero (*De Off.* iii. 29-30) taught that an oath is a religious obligation, and should be observed as a matter of justice and honour without regard to consequences. "What you solemnly promise . . . to that you must hold fast." No degree of expediency, he teaches, can make honourable that which in itself is dishonourable.

In Philo [1] we find a most pointed and effective exposition of the sin of perjury. He writes thus of the perjurer: "You say to God, if not with your mouth and tongue, at all events in your mind: Bear witness to the truth of my lie, aid me in my wrongdong, help me in my crime. My one hope of preserving a fair reputation amongst men is to conceal the truth. . . . Do Thou, who art God, best of all beings, become a wrongdoer for the sake of another . . . (even) for the sake

[1] *De decem Oraculis*, § 18.

of a man, and that, too, a knave." But the third Commandment may be taken as directed not only against perjury, but also against every wrong, or idle, or irreverent use of God's name, as we may reasonably infer from Lev. xix. 12, which gives a fuller definition of this Commandment in the words : " Ye shall not swear by My name falsely, neither shalt thou profane the name of thy God." Profanity is a flippant and reckless use of the Divine name.

This sin is not so common as it was a hundred years ago. It has now come to be regarded as vulgar, and, since it has incurred social ostracism, it has largely disappeared. Multitudes of men are less afraid of the guilt of irreverence than of " bad form," that is, of violating the conventions of what is called good society. Where profanity is still rife, as it is in certain circles since the war, it is due either to a want of self-control, to a limited vocabulary, or to a lack of education. In the case of the uneducated such profanity does not, as a rule, count for much. In any case it is less reprehensible in them than in those who know better.

But to return to the oath as a confirmation of one's word, we are all aware that in early days objection was taken to its use for such a purpose. Our Lord's words in the Sermon on the Mount are the most significant of all: "Swear not at all . . . but let your communication be Yea, yea: Nay, nay; for whatsoever is more than these cometh of evil" (Matt. v. 34, 39). St. James (v. 12) repeats this injunction. It is found in 2 Enoch xlix. 1-2; very frequently in Philo; in

Justin Martyr (*Apol.* xvi.), St. Chrysostom [1] and other early Fathers. The Essenes [2] avoided swearing, and esteemed it "worse than perjury; for they say that he who cannot be believed without swearing by God is already condemned." What lessons are we to draw from the above injunctions? There are certainly two. The first is that swearing should be avoided as much as possible, since its use may foster the idea that, when the oath is not taken, a man's word is less binding. Thus the introduction of an oath in certain cases may be taken to imply that in other cases where it is omitted there is not the same obligation to adhere to the truth. Accordingly a practice, which was obviously adopted in order to promote truth, may result in doing it essential damage. Even Philo notices this fact when he writes that, when a man resorts to an oath to confirm his word, his good faith becomes suspect.[3] Hence the main lesson is that all communications between man and man should be taken up into the sphere of truth, pure and simple. Men's speech should be, "Yea, yea, and Nay, nay." But this command of Christ does not preclude the judicial use of oaths; for Christ Himself took the judicial oath in its most solemn form, and answered affirmatively when the High Priest adjured Him in the name of the Living God (Matt. xxvi. 63 sq.). Similarly, St. Paul several times calls God to witness to the truth of his assertions (2 Cor. i. 23; Phil. i. 8; Gal. i. 20).

[1] *Hom. IX. in Acta Apost.* [2] Josephus, *De Bello*, ii. 8. 5.
[3] Philo, *op. cit.*, § 17.

But, since the occasions for taking judicial oaths are exceptional in the lives of most men, the tendency in a society that is making moral and spiritual progress must be to set less and less store by such oaths and more and more by the simple unattested word, wherein a man's Yea is yea, and his Nay nay.

We are thus brought to the second and essential lesson of the third Commandment, and this is its requisition that a man should speak the truth for the truth's sake. To this subject—a subject that calls for our most diligent thought and practice in everyday life and yet which is hardly ever made the preacher's theme, I will now ask your attention.

For the sake of clearness we shall consider truth under three heads : truth of word, truth of life and truth of thought.

(i) First, then, as to truth of word. Falsehood in this sense belongs essentially to the primitive and barbarous periods of civilisation. It has prevailed, of course, at all times ; but when it does so in the advanced eras of civilisation, it is a reversion to primitive and barbarous types of life, and therefore carries with it an intensified degree of guilt. For, though lying in the most primitive stages of culture was used by the weak in self-defence and by the strong to reinforce their strength, and that as a rule without any consciousness of guilt: in the later stages of civilisation even the weak cannot resort to it without some sense of shame and self-reproach.

Now, according to common usage, there are various

THIRD COMMANDMENT

kinds of lies. First of all there are the so-called white lies of social life. To this mixture of truth and falsehood we might apply Bacon's words, that it is "like alloy in coin of gold and silver, which may make the metal work the better, but it embaseth it." These are generally a mixture of truth and falsehood, and are told in the name of courtesy in order to avoid hurting the feelings of others. And yet the lies which are told in the name of courtesy not only bring true courtesy into discredit, but are also, as a rule, wholly needless. For what is true courtesy but the manifestation of the respect and consideration we owe to our neighbour, of the truth that is always his due, and of the trust and honour that so often are his due, however unequal we may be to discharge these obligations. There are many people whose outward courtesy varies directly in the measure of their insincerity. Let me take two very minor examples of such insincerity. The first is the use of the phrase "not at home," when, as a matter of fact, the statement is not literally true. Of course it is urged in defence of this practice that it is a mere convention and accepted as such on all hands. But this is questionable. Is the maid who delivers this message from her mistress unaffected by it? Is she not encouraged thereby to go further in the direction of conventional lying? This question was debated in Ancient Rome over two thousand years ago. Thus Cicero (*De Orat.* ii. 68) tells that Publius Scipio Nasica, who belonged to the greatest family in Ancient Rome, was deeply offended with his friend Ennius the poet for greeting him with these words through his maid. The story is worth repeating. This great noble called at Ennius' house and asked to see Ennius. When the maidservant said "not at home," Scipio went away much offended, as he was convinced that Ennius was at home. A few days later Ennius called on Scipio and asked to see him. Thereupon Scipio himself from within called out that he was not at home. When Ennius rejoined, "Surely I recognise your voice?" Scipio replied: "You are an impudent fellow. When I called on you I accepted your maid's word that you were not at home, but you refuse to accept my own word." Scipio Nasica made this call on Ennius nearly 200 B.C.

The second example of such insincerity, and insincerity of a deeper type, is what we may call the society smile. A true smile is spontaneous, and for the most part it is an unconscious manifestation of real feeling. The emotions being aroused, react on the features of the face and throw them into a tumultuous movement. Accordingly the smile so produced only gradually subsides, and that with the subsidence of the emotions that called it into being. On the other hand, the society smile has nothing whatever to do with the emotions. It is false, root and branch. It is merely a flexure of the muscles of the face, called into action by the will, and by the will alone. As such, it disappears the moment the will ceases to act. You can test these facts for yourselves. If you meet a person you regard with suspicion and hostility and yet greet him with a smile, you will find that the moment you have passed him your smile has vanished. But if you meet a trusty and dear friend, your smile has unconsciously greeted him from afar, and long after you have passed him your face is still displaying the tokens of the friendship you feel. The features naturally take time to recover their composure, as they reflect the feelings within. Now, if you turn your attention from yourselves and observe the smiles of some of your acquaintances, you will arrive at some astonishing revelations as to the profound gulf that lies behind the smile of one acquaintance and that of another.

Flattery and certain kinds of exaggeration border closely on falsehood. Flattery generally springs from a corrupt motive, and, as such, naturally expresses itself in falsehood. The person who flatters another can hardly fail to magnify his good points, to extenuate his failings and to show him a deference he does not feel.

But though flattery generally embodies the element of falsehood, certain kinds of exaggeration may be quite free from it. A lively imagination and strong feelings naturally lead to exaggeration. In such a case the exaggeration is generally unconscious and free from deceit. Its whole aim is to win the sympathy of the hearer or reader. Such exaggeration is far from unusual in the orator or in the enthusiastic child. But, when the exaggeration is deliberate and used with a view to self-interest, then it is a breach of the law of truth.

Passing from debatable forms of falsehood to those which are unquestionably such, we must first of all distinguish between the lie uttered in self-defence, which is the refuge of the weak and the craven-hearted, and the lie of covetousness, malice or hatred. The latter is, of course, incomparably the worst. But since its viciousness is universally admitted, we may confine our attention to the former. If to shield ourselves in matters of slight moment we yield to some compromise with truth, we have already crossed the danger limit. Such compromises tend to grow on the soul that has recourse to them. And the more they are used, the more deeply their victim becomes ensnared in the meshes of falsehood. The first step in this direction may seem quite harmless and prudent: the excuse is all but wholly true. But the first excuse soon entails a second, which involves some real sacrifice of truth, and then a third, that is all but wholly false.

Since in every life there are temptations to palter with truth, there is room for heroism in the most unheroic surroundings. When our pride or vanity, our hypocrisies, our mistaken conceptions of honour, or the shame of actual wrong-doing, combine in tempting us to compromise or falsehood, there is need of the heroic spirit, if we are to stand fast by truth. For the scales are often very heavily weighted against the truth-teller. Nevertheless, we must not on that account hesitate, when the call for action comes : we must not pause to balance the advantages or disadvantages attendant on truth and its opposite, but decide forthwith on the highest grounds, and take in our own persons the consequences as they come, be they what they may.

THIRD COMMANDMENT

Again, attuning our thoughts to a higher level, we must not postpone our adhesion to truth till we are assured that we are making a profitable venture, but we must step forward and take its side when there is neither appearance nor promise of any such return. Only when we do so is Truth justified of her children. For the divine reward of such loyalty to truth manifests itself eventually in character and not in self-satisfaction apart from character. The lover of truth has no selfish end in view. If truth is cultivated with any such end, it ceases to be truth. Only when truth is told for its own sake, does a man enter into the heritage that belongs to its children from eternity.

(ii) Still harder than truth of word is *truth of life*. Truth and trust form the foundations of society, when society is worthy of the name. Hence we must be on our guard, on the one hand, against the studious concealment of our real opinions and principles, and, on the other, against the deliberate expression in our lives of what is false. If by our silence we are creating false impressions, we have already outstepped the limits of truth. If through cowardice we fail to avow our sentiments on the right occasions, we become also the slaves of our fears: we lose our self-respect and foster the growth of poltroonery and baseness in our characters. On the other hand, by avowing our convictions and translating them into concrete deeds we strengthen both ourselves and our convictions.

And no less definitely should we shun pretence or simulation, that is, the deliberate expression of what is false, whether by word or deed, in order that we may win a reputation for being what we are not, or for possessing powers, knowledge, or wisdom to which we have no claim. We are to be ourselves, not the caricature of others. We are to develop ourselves on the lines that God has laid down for us. For these our heredity and environment are the raw material out of which by the good guidance of God's Spirit we are to fashion the true personality that God has willed us to acquire.

A breach of trust is also a breach of truth, that is, truth of life. We undertake a certain duty, but it makes irksome claims on our time, on our courage, on our energies. Hence we often let it go by default. And so shirking the tasks that are definitely ours, we hand them over to subordinates to mismanage or pervert them to their own purposes. Yet all the time we may be getting the credit of doing our duty. In such case, though we have told no direct lie, we have lived one. Or again: we accept a definite wage for a definite day's work, but in obedience to the dishonest rules or customs of our profession, our guild, our trade, we either scamp our work or deliberately loiter over it, and yet accept payment in full. The burglar and housebreaker are noble characters compared with such ignoble rogues; for it is at the hazard of their liberty and possibly of their lives that they rob their neighbours. But the ca-canny rogue in all classes risks neither and yet pockets the swag.

Hence, if we would be true in life, we must hold fast to our courage with both hands: we must sit loose to the world and its demands upon us. For we cannot accept its terms, nor can we have recourse to its underground and secret policies, its hidden dishonesties, its finessing and chicaneries, alike in business, in society, in Church and State. For, if a man submits to their unjust claims, he must lose touch with truth, with his own soul, and with God.

Candour, open-mindedness, honesty, singleness of motive, transparency of character, are part and parcel of the truth of life. God's cause is best served by a fearless perseverance in an honest and right course in scorn of consequence. Sooner or later we may be assured that cause will prevail. If, then, it is our chief aim to serve this cause, we shall more and more discover

"That we can wait and not be tired by waiting,
   Or being lied about, not deal in lies,
Or being hated not give way to hating,
   And yet not look too good or talk too wise.

That we can bear to hear the truth we've spoken
   Twisted by knaves to make a trap for fools,
And watch the things we gave out lives to broken,
   And stoop and build them up with worn-out tools." [1]

(iii) From truth of life we pass to the hardest of all —truth of thought. How rarely is it to be found! Vast numbers that are seeking to be true in word and true in life never attempt to attain truth of thought. How is this to be explained?

[1] I have ventured to change the second personal pronouns into the first, and also "if" in two lines into "that," as the reader will recognise.

THE DECALOGUE

It is intelligible that the desire for such truth cannot take root and flourish healthily in hearts that are given up to conceit or vanity, or are the victims of ignorance, whether unconscious, self-incurred or self-chosen. Nor can truth of thought live and thrive in the hearts of men whose main principle in life is expediency and safety. For the desires for truth and safety must sooner or later come into collision. It is then that the so-called safe men, who are so often leaders in Church and State, must, so far as their influence extends, prove to be the ruin of both; for these safe men are seldom to be found amongst the small and noble fellowship of those whose sole aim is truth in and for itself.

Again, truth of thought is beyond the reach of those who submit to the jurisdiction of a so-called infallible authority; for such an authority prohibits the very quest of truth, and the tendency of such a prohibition is to transform the unlearned and feeble-minded into bigots and fanatics, and men of robust understanding into cynics and sceptics. When men blindly acquiesce in any religious system, their aim is safety and not truth. Seeking to save their life they take the surest way of losing it. Blind acquiescence in any religious system has a pernicious influence on the mind. It will make men ready to give false reasons for desired conclusions, false evidence for established beliefs, false sanctions for current traditions.

"Ultramontanism," according to Lord Acton,[1] the most learned historian that the Roman Church has ever

[1] *Letters*, ed. Figgis and Laurence, 1917, p. 43.

THIRD COMMANDMENT

produced in this country, "not only promotes, it inculcates distinct mendacity and deceitfulness. In certain cases it is made a duty to lie. But those," he continues, "who teach this doctrine do not become habitual liars in other things." This saving clause we cannot accept. If an infallible authority makes it "the duty" of its votaries "to lie in certain cases" it cannot prevent this vice from making inroads into every province of the moral life. Even Newman after nineteen years' experience within the Roman Communion was obliged to confess the mendacious character of the Church to which he had passed over. When asked to join in founding an Historical Review based on Roman principles he refused, and the ground he gave was just this, that "unless one doctored one's facts one would be thought a bad Catholic."[1]

A discipline in mendacity[2] naturally unfits men

[1] *The Month*, January 1903, p. 3.

[2] Mendacity must more and more become one of the chief assets of an infallible Church. It could not be otherwise. Being infallible, it cannot disown its errors and false judgments in the past. If it is urged that its claims cannot be reconciled with historical fact, it simply brushes aside such objections as irrelevant and restates its superhuman claims to obedience. And it must be conceded that the persistent repetition of a lie has its effect on weak souls who long to find some authority ready to relieve them of their responsibilities, and so they become worshippers of the Roman lie. Manning[1] writes: "To appeal from the living voice of the Church to any tribunal whatsoever, human history included, is an act of private judgment and a treason . . . (it) is also a heresy, because that voice is infallible." Thus infallibility must perforce protect the mendacity of its mouthpieces and at the same time anathematise those who dare to question its lies.

[1] *Daily Telegraph*, October 8, 1875.

for coming to a right judgment. Seeking not truth but safety, they suborn their judgment and disqualify it for the determination of truth; in fact, they make such sinners of their mental faculties as ultimately to credit their own lies. Accordingly, when the adherents of such a system have their eyes opened to the falsity of any part of it, they too readily jettison the whole and with it their belief in truth itself. Disasters of this nature are frequent in the Roman Church: seldom in the Anglican hitherto. Furthermore, submission to an external authority makes a man incompetent to recognise any truth beyond the horizon of his own limited beliefs, and only such practical truths within this sphere as he can verify in his own spiritual experience. Unquestioning submission necessarily biases and finally atrophies the judicial faculty in man. Hence in addition to other evils it begets in man the vice of superstition generally, and especially the superstition that the thought, gestures, customs and dress of any particular age should be the unquestionable rule for all ages. Accordingly in the present day we have a reversion to the darker ages, a resuscitation of their half-pagan beliefs, a materialising of religion and, still more, a delight in contemplating the physical anguish and agonies of Christ as portrayed on realistic and repulsive crucifixes. This delight in the contemplation of physical torture and death shows its affinity with and its provenance from the savage religions of the East. Ruskin [1] denounces " the thirst

[1] *Lectures on Art,* pp. 53 sqq., 57.

for horror" and "the strange love of death" that has marked Christian worship in connection with the Crucifixion. He emphasises strongly the truth that "the Master is not dead," that He "is not now fainting under His cross, but is requiring us to take up ours." Westcott from the standpoint of theology opposed the crucifix as a symbol of death. It is a false symbol; for Christ is the Lord of life. In confirmation of this truth we cannot too often insist on the fact that the crucifix was unknown in the first five centuries of the Christian Church.[1] But with the advent of the darker ages these conceptions and practices successfully established themselves within its borders. For such ages they had no doubt a force and significance that were in keeping with the violence and religious darkness of the time.

But their reproduction in the present day is a spiritual anachronism. At best it is but a revived antiquarianism. No doubt its votaries think to possess themselves of the spirit of that twilight age of religion by imitating its customs and repeating its symbols. In these respects they do imitate the past, and imitate it successfully, but they do not inherit its truth and inspiration, unless their mental development is essentially that of the mediæval period.

The fruits of unquestioned submission to a so-called infallible authority are to be seen in Spain, Portugal, and, not to speak of other countries, most strikingly of all in the southern provinces of Ireland. Designed by God to disperse the superstition and ignorance, the

[1] See above, pp. 42-47.

falsehood and dishonesty, the hatreds and injustices that prevail in these countries, to be, according to the words of our Lord, as lights set on the hills to enlighten all within their range, the Roman Churches in many countries have, nevertheless, through their corruption lost in the main the illuminating power of truth and righteousness and love, and are at the best serving only as night-lights in the darkness of dying civilisations, the guilt of whose destruction lies at their door. Such a religious system debases the character of its victims and robs them, as we have already shown, of the sense of truth, of the power of judgment and of the knowledge on which such judgment should be founded, and hence of the right of being enrolled as citizens in Christ's Kingdom of the divinely true and free. By their voluntary submission to a power which is the antithesis of this Kingdom, its votaries disfranchise themselves and proclaim their unfitness for the citizenship of Christ's Kingdom. And yet all men are potentially citizens of this Kingdom; for our Lord has promised to His disciples, "Ye shall know the truth, and the truth shall make you free."

Again, when once men vote themselves out of the kingdom of truth and freedom, they proceed to exult in their servitude and glory in their shame. Unconscious of their degradation, they become the most ardent proselytisers, and stop at no measures which may constrain their neighbours to embrace the same yoke of bondage. They manifest the most unblushing intolerance. This their temper of mind is not unnatural, seeing that, having never striven to find truth for themselves, they are wholly unconscious how hard it is to attain unto truth. The attainment of the truth in their eyes is synonymous with subscribing to or learning by rote the creed that they confess, which they have received by tradition or else adopted as a measure of safety.

Of course, it is objected that the field of truth is too vast for any man to explore. This is quite true. No man is able, nor is any man required, to examine the entire province of truth. He takes for granted the main body of Christian tradition, but he accepts it with an open mind. It is and must always be subject to the test of examination by the disciplined judgment, by the trained intelligence. He is not required to be the unreasoning bondslave of any external authority, but the free servant and son of the ever-growing and self-authenticating truth of God. Christ's promise receives its never-ending verification in the rational and spiritual experience of His disciples: " Ye shall know the truth, and the truth shall make you free." In the Roman Church there is no room for the exercise of the judgment in any form, in the Anglican the individual enjoys this liberty. This exercise of the private judgment, it is true, is always subject to correction, for the emphasis in the case of the truth-seeker comes more and more to be laid on the word "judgment" and less and less on the term "private." His aim is, through the guidance of God's Holy Spirit, to have a right judgment in all things.

108 THE DECALOGUE

Again it is objected that perfect impartiality is indispensable, if we are to arrive at real truth, but that the attainment of a perfectly open and unbiased state of mind is beyond the reach of human attainment. This also is quite true; but, if this argument is of any weight, it would prove too much. It would prove to demonstration that we are not to attempt to attain any virtue or any grace, inasmuch as it is beyond our power to attain them in their perfect purity and completeness.

Furthermore, impartiality in coming to a decision does not necessarily imply an absence of all inclination for either side, but it imperatively demands that the inclinations should not so intervene as to pervert the evidence and bias the judgment. In matters of moral and spiritual truth the inclinations should not be neutral or indifferent, and yet the judgment must not be based on such inclinations, though it should take account of them. The verdict must be given in accordnace with the evidence only. Truth becomes a consuming passion to see things as they are. Hence, if we would be children of the truth, we must give no countenance to wrong opinions, however beneficial they may seem in their immediate effects, nor connive at delusions, however salutary their apparent results may be on the faithful. For faith—even apart from truth—may work miracles of healing; but miracles [1] in themselves are

[1] Thomas Aquinas defines a miracle as an effect beyond the order of the whole of created nature. But no man is competent to say that any event is of this nature, since no man knows thoroughly nor can know even a fragmentary part of the universe.

no evidence of truth. When a material miracle of this or any other kind occurs—that is, when a thing occurs that is at once abnormal and unintelligible to the spectator—it is no proof of anything beyond the fact of its own occurrence. When the Pharisees asked our Lord for a sign in proof of His Divine claims, He refused their request. Miracles in themselves, as the Pharisees knew well, were no evidence of truth; for they themselves attributed Christ's miracles to Beelzebub.

Faith, apart from truth, is founded on a lie and must ultimately perish. To such cheats and chicaneries men do not have recourse, save only when they love their party more than their Church, their Church more than truth, and themselves more than all things else beside.

FOURTH COMMANDMENT

FIRST LECTURE

"Remember the Sabbath day, to keep it holy. Six days shalt thou labour, and do all thy work: but the seventh day is a Sabbath unto the Lord thy God: in it thou shalt not do any work, thou, nor thy son, nor thy daughter, thy manservant, nor thy maidservant, nor thy cattle, nor thy stranger that is within thy gates [: for in six days the Lord made heaven and earth, the sea, and all that in them is, and rested the seventh day: wherefore the Lord blessed the Sabbath day, and hallowed it]."—Ex. xx. 8–11.

THIS Commandment is given differently in Deut. v. 12–14: "Observe the Sabbath day to keep it holy, as the Lord thy God commanded thee. 13. Six days shalt thou labour, and do all thy work: 14. But the seventh day is a Sabbath unto the Lord thy God: in it thou shalt not do any work, thou, nor thy son, nor thy daughter, nor thy manservant, nor thy maidservant, nor thine ox, nor thine ass, nor any of thy cattle, nor thy stranger that is within thy gates; that thy manservant and thy maidservant may rest as well as thou."

The subject with which I have to deal in this and the next two lectures is one full of difficulty, but most of the difficulties may be resolved by a careful study of our authorities. In this study I shall, of course, accept the main results arrived at by the best modern critics of the Old Testament. Such a study leads to the recognition that two entirely distinct conceptions of the Sabbath are presented to the reader in the Old Testament, and that these two distinct conceptions are embodied in the two different versions of the fourth Commandment, which you will find respectively in Ex. xx. and Deut. v. The later conception is that set forth in the twentieth chapter of Exodus. The older is that which is given in the fifth chapter of Deuteronomy. The radical difference between these two conceptions of the Sabbath is due to the different reasons which are adduced for the observance of the Sabbath by these two versions of the fourth Commandment. The remarkable results that follow from these differences have never, so far as I am aware, been duly recognised. Let us now set forth over against each other the different reasons given for the observance of the Sabbath and see what follows.

The reason given in Deut. v. 14 for the observance of the Sabbath is admittedly the older one. Therein man is bidden to " observe the Sabbath day to keep it holy . . . in order that thy manservant and thy maidservant may rest as well as thou." So far as these words go, it is clear that the Sabbath was made for man and not man for the Sabbath—the great principle that was first enunciated by our Lord in connection with the Sabbath. The Sabbath was thus instituted purely for the good of man. Besides rest, the duty of worship was associated with the Sabbath

THE DECALOGUE

so conceived as we learn from the eighth century prophets (Isa. i. 13; Hos. ii. 11). Now we may ask: Is the reason given for the observance of the Sabbath by the author of Deuteronomy, who wrote in the seventh century B.C., due to this author, or did it appear in the current form of the Decalogue, which the author of Deuteronomy as well as the author of Exodus used? Though the like thought is found elsewhere in Deuteronomy,[1] there can be no doubt as to the fact that it is not due to the author of Deuteronomy; for it is found in what scholars call the "Book of the Covenant,"[2] which was in circulation in the ninth century B.C., if not earlier. In this Book of the Covenant, in Ex. xxiii. 12, that is, outside the Decalogue, we find the following words: "Six days thou shalt do thy work, and on the seventh day thou shalt rest, in order that thine ox and thine ass may have rest, and the son of thine handmaid, and the stranger, may be refreshed." This is exactly the reason given for the observance of the Sabbath in Deut. v., though in slightly different phraseology. The oldest conception, therefore, of the Sabbath was that of a day of rest from all toil, but also a day which was originally in some way associated with the worship of God, and which in later times came more and more to be so associated.

This conception of the Sabbath held the field down to 500 B.C. and possibly later, when the Priests' Code and subsequently the Book of Exodus, compiled of

[1] Cf. xii. 12, 18, xiv. 26b, xvi. 11.
[2] *i.e.* Ex. xx. 22–xxiii. 33.

FOURTH COMMANDMENT

documents originally distinct and in many cases very ancient, were given to the Jewish world. The Decalogue, as it appears in Exodus, has undergone drastic revision, in the course of which the meaning of the fourth Commandment has been absolutely changed. For the reason adduced for the observance of the Sabbath is no longer the humanitarian one given in Deut. and in Ex. xxiii. 12, but a purely theological one. The Sabbath is to be kept holy, and the reason given is: "For in six days the Lord made heaven and earth, the sea, and all that in them is, and rested [1] the seventh day: wherefore the Lord blessed the Sabbath day and hallowed it" (Ex. xx. 11).[2] Now Old Testament scholars have concluded on adequate evidence that this clause relating to God's resting on the Sabbath day was interpolated in the fourth Commandment by the same hand, or rather by a scribe of the same school, that wrote Gen. i.–ii. 3, which closes with these words: "And on the seventh day God finished His works which He had made; and He rested on the seventh day from all

[1] The Hebrew verb is here נוח = "to rest after labour." In Gen. ii. 2, 3, the word used in the same connection is שבת, which can mean simply "to desist," and which Driver adopts here, though the Oxford Hebrew Lexicon translates it by "to desist from labour, rest." The three Targums give the same meaning and render it by נח. In Ex. xx. 11, however, the writer used נוח (*i.e.* וינח), and so also the Targums. See note on the strong anthropomorphism in Ex. xxxi. 17 on p. 115 n.

[2] It has been frequently observed that, if the author of Deuteronomy had found Ex. xx. 11 in the Decalogue when he wrote, he would not have omitted it, as we may judge from his practice elsewhere. Ex. xx. 11 was, it is justly inferred, introduced in Ex. xx. subsequently to the date of Deuteronomy upon the basis of Gen. ii. 2 and Ex. xxxi. 17. (See Driver, *Literature of O.T.*[7], p. 35.)

114   THE DECALOGUE

His work that He had made. And God blessed the
seventh day, and hallowed it : because that on it He
had rested from all His work which God had created
and made." These two passages, which put forward the
new ground for observing the Sabbath, belong to what is
called by Old Testament critics the " Priests' Code."
The Priests' Code[1] was written after the Exile (about 500
B.C.) on the basis of earlier authorities of various dates.
It is a great misfortune that the framers of our
Prayer Book did not adopt the earlier form of the
fourth Commandment that is given in Deuteronomy.
It was a still greater misfortune that the Jews rejected
this older conception of the Sabbath in order to enforce
the later that appears in Exodus. For the idea of God
that is emphasised in this later conception of the

[1] On the date of the Priests' Code (about 500 B.C.), see Driver,
Literature of the O.T., p. 135 sqq. : on the extent to which it has been
utilised and preserved in the Pentateuch and Joshua, see p. 159.
The fragments of P, preserved in Exodus, are approximately i.
1–5, 13–14 ; ii. 23b–25 ; vi. 2–vii. 13, 19–20a, 21b–22 ; viii. 5–7,
15b–19 ; ix. 8–12 ; xi. 9–10 ; xii. 1–20, 28, 37a, 40–41, 43–51 ; xiii.
1–2, 20 ; xiv. 1–4, 8–9 ; 15–18, 21a, 21c–23, 26–27a, 28a, 29 ; xvi. 1–
3, 6–24, 31–36 ; xvii. 1a ; xix. 1–2a ; xxiv. 15–18a ; xxv. 1–
xxxi. 18a ; xxxiv. 29–35 ; xxxv.-xl. (from Driver's *Introduction to
the Literature of the O.T.*, p. 159. There are three successive stages
of Hebrew legislation. These are represented by JE (*i.e.* the
Jahvistic and Elohistic elements), Deuteronomy and P (*i.e.* the
Priests' Code). Driver, *op. cit.* 142 sq., writes in regard to P : " The
completed Priests' Code is the work of the age subsequent to Ezekiel.
. . . The Priests' Code embodies some elements with which the
earlier literature is in harmony . . . : it embodies other elements with
which the same literature is in conflict. . . . In its main stock the
legislation of P was not (as the critical view of it is sometimes
represented by its opponents as teaching) manufactured by the
priests during the Exile : it is based on *pre-existing Temple usage*,
and exhibits the form which that finally assumed."

Sabbath is far from being a lofty one. It implies that God was fatigued with the work of the six days of creation and was, therefore, in some measure obliged to rest. Indeed this statement is made bluntly in Ex. xxxi. 16, 17, which also belongs to the Priests' Code, and reads thus: "Wherefore the children of Israel shall keep the Sabbath. . . . It is a sign between Me and the children of Israel for ever; for in six days the Lord made heaven and earth, and on the seventh day He rested and was refreshed." Here the very same word " refreshed " is used of God as was used in the early Book of the Covenant with regard to man only. This passage (Ex. xxiii. 12) I have already quoted, but it is worth quoting again: " On the seventh day thou shalt rest: that thine ox and thine ass may have rest, and that the son of thine handmaid, and the stranger, may be refreshed." This Hebrew word meaning " refreshed "[1] occurs once more in the Old Testament, namely, in 2 Sam. xvi. 14, which recounts the flight of King David and his men before Absalom. The text here runs: "And the king, and all that were with him, came weary, and were refreshed there." It is a word that describes man's recovery from fatigue and exhaustion. And yet this word is applied to God in the Priests' Code. From this theological figment of the

[1] The Hebrew word is וַיִּנָּפַשׁ, which occurs only three times in the Old Testament, i.e. here and in Ex. xxiii. 12 and 2 Sam. xvi. 14. In the two latter passages it is used of man. There can be no doubt, therefore, as to its implying that God needed rest after His labours in the passage in Ex. xxxi. 17. The Targums follow the Hebrews literally, וְנָח שָׁבַת.

Priests' Code—that God was wearied by His six days' work of creation and needed rest and refreshment—sprang the preposterous laws of the Sabbath that are to be found in the Talmud as well as in earlier works. The lofty teaching of the prophets on the omnipotence of God in creation ought to have guarded these Priestly writers from such a degrading conception of the Godhead. Thus about 540 B.C. the second Isaiah (xl. 28) writes : " Hast thou not known ? hast thou not heard, the everlasting God, the Lord, the Creator of the ends of the earth, fainteth not, neither is weary ? " In keeping with the teaching of the prophets, and in direct opposition to the view that the Sabbath originated, not in human but in Divine infirmity, our Lord declared in unmistakable terms : " The Sabbath was made for man." The Sabbath, as observed originally by the Jews, was adapted exclusively to a being needing physical and mental rest, and that at definite intervals. Physical strength ebbs, the will flags, thought grows weary, the nerves become hypersensitive, and so rest in many ways becomes indispensable to our humanity, and still more needful for the renewal of man's spiritual life in God. But the Jews of the sixth and fifth centuries were not content with this conception of the Sabbath. Ignoring the infinite interval between the Divine and the human capacities, they conceived God as in actual need of rest after the work of the six days' creation, and so they shrank not from applying to the Creator a law originating in and adapted to purely human infirmity.

FOURTH COMMANDMENT

Having now distinguished the two different conceptions of the Sabbath in the Old Testament, we shall trace some of the main developments of the Sabbath in Hebrew and Jewish history.

First of all the word Sabbath carries with it the idea of rest and cessation from toil. In itself this idea is purely negative. But it must have meant more than this. It cannot have been destitute of all religious meaning. Its consecration among the Hebrews must have had in view some intelligible form of religious worship. This was an idea quite familiar to the ancient world. But the Hebrew Sabbath combined the idea of rest from ordinary work for purposes of worship with a second element, and the second was the division of time into weeks.

As regards the first—the suspension of daily toil in connection with a religious festival—we know that this was a common practice amongst ancient peoples. It prevails also in the present day amongst many of the lower races.[1] Abstinence from work has always been recognised, amongst other rites, as a way of expressing man's reverence for the Deity. The Greek historian Strabo, writing before the Christian era, declares : " The Greeks and barbarians have this in common, that they accompany their sacred rites by a festal remission of labour " (x. 3. 9). At the outset, therefore, the Sabbath had a humanitarian character. Men secured a rest from the often oppressive toil of ordinary life.

[1] With the exception of those living in Australian, Melanesian and American areas. See *ERE* x. 885 sqq.

118 THE DECALOGUE

So much for the first element in the Sabbath—the suspension of ordinary work with a view to worship.

The second element is the division of time into weeks. This division of time into weeks arose most probably in connection with the quarters of the moon, which may be divided roughly into four sections of seven days each. The fact that in the older books of the Old Testament [1] the new moons and Sabbaths are generally mentioned together, supports this hypothesis.[2] The week most probably originated in Babylon in connection with astrology, but came in due course to be used as a civil division of time. This weekly division of time passed thence to Western Asia, Egypt and Eastern Europe.

The question next arises, Was this day of rest, called the Sabbath by the Hebrews, connected by the Babylonians with the seventh day of the week? The facts are shortly as follows.

The seventh, fourteenth, twenty-first and twenty-eighth days of each month were observed in Babylon as holy days of rest by certain classes [3] of the community. The seventh day was not called Sabattum, but *û-ḫul-gallum*, which they translated by "evil day." The word Sabattum,[4] which may be the same as the Hebrew

[1] At first each month began with a fresh week, but, as there was thus a residue of two or three days each month, this unsatisfactory arrangement was abandoned and the weeks were reckoned in an unbroken series from the beginning to the close of the year.

[2] Is. i. 13; Amos viii. 5; 2 Kings iv. 23; Hos. ii. 11.

[3] See Pinches in *ERE* x. 890.

[4] The Semitic Babylonians rendered this word by *ûm-nûḫ-libbi*, "day of rest of the heart."

FOURTH COMMANDMENT

Sabbath, was current in Babylon and was used in connection with a festival of the moon's "resting" on the fifteenth day of the month, but was not applied to the seventh day of the week. Moreover, the interval of seven days between each festival was not rigidly observed. In one case it was eight days, and in another six. So far, then, as we know at present, the institution of the Sabbath as a weekly festival on the seventh day of every week was due to the Hebrews.[1]

In the eighth century the new moons and the Sabbaths alike summoned men to the Sanctuary (Isa. i. 13), and on both alike ordinary work in the field or in commerce was forbidden (Amos viii. 5). It is noteworthy that in every case before the Exile where the new moons and Sabbaths are mentioned together, the new moons are mentioned first.[2] The impression is thus given that before the Exile the new moons were regarded as the more important festivals. With the Exile the order is reversed, and the Sabbaths take precedence of the new moons.[3] In the Pentateuch, which was put together after the Exile, the new moons and the Sabbaths are never mentioned together at all. The new moons at this stage have quite fallen into the background, save in the ritual of the temple : for the Deuteronomic

[1] If, on the other hand, the Hebrew borrowed the Sabbath from Babylonia, they put an end to its connection with the moon, and reckoned every seventh day as a Sabbath, wholly irrespective of the days of the moon.

[2] See also Hos. ii. 11 ; 2 Kings iv. 23; Ezek. xlv. 17 (latest occurrence of this order). Hosea does not set a high religious value on these festivals.

[3] Ezek. xlvi. 3 ; 1 Chron. xxiii. 31 ; 2 Chron. ii. 4, xxxi. 3.

reform in the seventh century had suppressed the local sanctuaries outside Jerusalem, and with their suppression the importance of the new moons waned steadily, and the Sabbath came to be the peculiar and universal festival of Judaism, observed everywhere, at home or in exile, even though wholly divorced from ritual. At this period the duty of religious observance with abstention from labour was defined and accentuated in the post-exilic prophets (Jer. xvii. 19-27).[1]

We have above remarked that the consecration of the Sabbath must have had in view some intelligible forms of religious worship in addition to its being a day of rest. Of the forms that accompanied its observance from the time of its institution by Moses down to the time of David and Solomon we have not the slightest knowledge. Nor do we know anything of the nature of these rites even in the days of David and Solomon save from the Books of Chronicles, which are a very late source.[2] On the other hand, there is evidence of its general observance[3] in the ninth century, and especially in the eighth.[4] The Sabbath in these early centuries first of all required cessation from field labour[5] and trading,[6] and the fulfilment of certain religious rites at the temple and the various northern Sanctuaries and high places.

With the suppression of the northern Sanctuaries and

[1] Not written by Jeremiah. See p. 124 n.
[2] 1 Chron. xxiii. 31 ; 2 Chron. ii. 4.   [3] 2 Kings iv. 23.
[4] Isa. i. 13 ; Hos. ii. 11 ; Amos viii. 5.
[5] Ex. xxiii. 12, xxxiv. 21.   [6] Amos viii. 5.

FOURTH COMMANDMENT

high places, the Sabbath may for most Israelites have lost its association with public—though not with private —worship, and become mainly a festival made for man, such as it appears in the Decalogue in Deut. v. 14. But even when dissociated for the most part from public worship, it could not have failed to exercise a spiritual and ethical influence. It was a standing witness also that, though sore travail was the inevitable lot of man in this world, yet man was not made to spend all his days in feverish, or monotonous, or unremitting toil, to be for ever the thrall of his own physical needs, but rather that he was made for spiritual and moral growth, for freedom, and peace, and joy.

But in the course of the sixth and fifth centuries the conception of the Sabbath underwent, as we have already observed, a radical change. It came forward with unique and transcendent claims on man's obedience. In the Priests' Code, which came into being in these centuries, the older conception of the Sabbath was essentially transformed. The cause of this transformation was the introduction into Judaism of the dogma that God had created the heaven and the earth exactly in six days, and that God needed rest and refreshment on the Sabbath, and that for this reason man was to observe the Sabbath day. This belief is set forth in the Priests' Code, particularly in the account of the Creation in Gen. i.-ii. 3, Ex. xxxi. 17, and in the interpolation made in the fourth Commandment in the twentieth chapter of Exodus. Regarded from this standpoint the Sabbath was an observance, obviously

THE DECALOGUE

not made for man, but one that had originated in the needs of the Godhead. If the Sabbath was observed originally to meet a necessity of God Himself, then all beings created in His image would naturally be subject in some measure to the same necessity, and therefore all men would be under an everlasting obligation to keep the Sabbath. But since this revelation was made to Israel alone, Israel alone amongst mankind was originally subject to this obligation. This revelation to Israel therefore constituted a peculiar bond and everlasting sign between God and Israel.[1] So conceived, the Sabbath was in no case made for man, whereas in a very essential sense it would hold true that man was made for the Sabbath.[2]

---

[1] Ex. xxxi. 13, 17 ; Ezek. xx. 12, 20.

[2] That this new conception of the Sabbath is due to a combination of the older idea of the Sabbath and a day of rest necessary to man, and of the later idea of God's creation of the world in six days and His need of rest and refreshment on the seventh, has, I hope, been made clear. It is noteworthy that Mr. Abrahams in his *Studies in Pharisaism and the Gospels* (p. 129), unwittingly supports the view above advocated. He maintains that in the "higher sense . . . man was made for the Sabbath," and in support of this doctrine quotes the Rabbis. His first quotation from Shabb. 119b, which is based on Gen. ii. 1-3, implies beyond question the derivation of the Rabbinic conception of the Sabbath from its connection with God's rest after the creation in six days. The sense of the quotation is given thus by Mr. Abrahams. "The observance of the Sabbath constitutes a man the partner (rather 'as it were a partner') of God in the creation of the world." Now since Mr. Abrahams accepts the outstanding results of O.T. criticism, he must therewith accept the conclusions that follow from them. Accordingly he must admit that that supernatural conception of the Sabbath derived from the account of God's creation of the world in six days and His rest on the seventh, was unknown to Judaism until the sixth century or thereabouts. No educated man

FOURTH COMMANDMENT

Certain results naturally followed on the adoption of this new and transcendent view of the Sabbath. It was no longer a Sabbath ordained purely for man's physical and spiritual well-being, but a Sabbath which, observed in heaven itself by God,[1] Israel was now privileged, nay more, was obliged to observe. The withholding of the manna on the Sabbath day was construed by the Rabbis to be a proof of God's observance of it. Naturally any breach of the Sabbath so conceived became henceforth a capital offence, and the penalty of death appears *now for the first time in connection with a breach of the Sabbath*. This new conception of the Sabbath is found, as I have already said, for the first time in the Priests' Code.[2]

The natural results of such an extravagant conception of the Sabbath are easy to trace. In the Old Testament they are only beginning to assert themselves. The Commandment, as originally conceived, rightly required cessation from field labours,[3] from buying and selling,[4] from travelling,[5] unless for some religious purpose.[6]

now accepts the literal account of the Creation in six days. This supernatural conception of the Sabbath is without any basis in actuality.

[1] Jub. ii. 18. See also ii. 19-21, 31; Mek. 104a, b (quoted in *Jewish Ency.* x. 589).

[2] Ex. xxxi. 14b, 15, xxxv. 2; Num. xv. 32-36.

[3] Ex. xxxiv. 21 (E).

[4] Amos viii. 5. Cf. for later enforcement of this law, Neh. x. 31, xiii. 16, 17.

[5] Ex. xvi. 29 (J).

[6] 2 Kings iv. 23. According to this passage men might go great distances on the Sabbath if the aim of the journey was a religious one. The later Rabbinic law current in our Lord's time is in conflict with this earlier usage.

THE DECALOGUE

But even this exception was disallowed later. When we come down to the fifth century we find that the carrying of burdens is prohibited;[1] but this was quite legitimate, for the burdens here referred to were of considerable size and were connected for the most part with trading and commerce. So far the observances required on the Sabbath are reasonable and not in conflict with the spontaneous and natural expression of a people's worship.

But the Priests' Code, which represents the latest form of the religious usages of the Temple and of the devout classes of the people, attests further developments.

According to this new conception of the Sabbath, it became a breach of the Sabbath to light a fire (Ex. xxxv. 3), to bake bread or boil meat (xvi. 23); and to gather sticks for such purposes (Num. xv. 32) was an offence punishable by death.

Here we have the beginning of the process which ultimately made the Sabbath a burden to all save a small body of men. The bulk of the Jews, or at all events of mankind, could only regard the later Sabbath laws as a burden which, to use St. Peter's words, "neither we nor our fathers could bear" (Acts xv. 10). And

[1] Neh. xiii. 15, 19. The passage in Jer. xvii. 19–27, which lays such emphasis on the keeping of the Sabbath, is rejected by Kuenen and more recently by Stade, Cornill and Giesebrecht and Cheyne as the work of a contemporary of Nehemiah. Driver admits that "the importance attached on it to the Sabbath or the appreciation expressed in xvii. 26 for sacrifice, are not in the usual spirit of Jeremiah (LOT^7, p. 258), and yet he argues for its authenticity on the ground of its style.

FOURTH COMMANDMENT 125

yet it is a question whether without the drastic discipline enforced by later Judaism the Jewish faith could have escaped annihilation in the centuries that followed.

Of the endless laws on Sabbath observance laid down after the close of the Canon of the Old Testament we can only mention a few.[1] One of the most striking was the enactment that a man might not fight even in self-defence on the Sabbath. Of this law the generals of Antiochus Epiphanes took advantage early in the second century B.C. and put to the sword on the Sabbath[2] one thousand unresisting Jews who were engaged in worship. But the Maccabean leaders succeeded in modifying this law, and henceforth defensive warfare was declared to be admissible,[3] but with limitations.[4]

We have now come down to New Testament times,

[1] See Jub. ii. 17–32, i. 6–13, where the growing strictness enforced on the Sabbath day is manifest.

[2] 1 Macc. ii. 34–38; Jos. *Ant.* xii. 6. 2.

[3] 1 Macc. ix. 34–43; 2 Macc. viii. 25–28.

[4] Jos. *B.J.* ii. 19. 2. The destruction of siege works raised on the Sabbath was not allowed. Here again the adversaries of the Jews availed themselves of this restriction, and Pompey was able to complete his earthworks against Jerusalem and capture the city (Jos. *Ant.* xiv. 4. 2). Other enemies of the Jews took the same base advantage of the loyalty of the Jews to the most extreme requirements of the Sabbath law: as Ptolemy the son of Lagus (Jos. *Ant.* xii. 1), and Appollonius, a general of Antiochus Epiphanes (2 Macc. v. 24 sqq.). Cf. the attempt of Nicanor (2 Macc. xv. 1 sqq.). But on one occasion the Jews broke this Sabbatical law and attacked the Romans (Jos. *B.J.* ii. 19. 2), and on another occasion treacherously in breach of a sworn covenant (Jos. *B.J.* ii. 17. 10). Owing to the strictness of the Sabbath laws the Romans were forced to release the Jews from the duty of military service (*Jos. Ant.* xiv. 10. 11–19). Offensive wars were not to be begun during the three days preceding the Sabbath, but, if begun earlier, they could be prosecuted even on the Sabbath (Shabb. 19*a*; Yad. ii. 23–25.

126   THE DECALOGUE

and are in a position to sum up the positive and spiritual gains achieved for religion by the institution of the Jewish Sabbath. The Sabbath was recognised as a day of rest from ordinary work, but still more as a holy day set apart for the building up of the spiritual element in man,[1] for private prayer, meditation, and for public worship in the Synagogue[2] or the Temple. Even the hours preceding the Sabbath were accounted holy. On the eve of the Sabbath or the Day of Preparation[3] no business might be undertaken that might encroach on the Sabbath. And yet the Sabbath was not to be a fast but a feast day, as we learn from the Book of Judith (viii. 6). In the second Isaiah it is called a delight.[4] With a view to its celebration as a feast day three meals of the best food available were to be prepared for it but not on it.[5]

But though the Sabbath had these spiritual and social privileges associated with it, it began steadily to deteriorate exactly in these respects through the labours of the scribes and Pharisees. And yet we cannot wholly blame the scribes and Pharisees; for the laws they laid down followed logically from the wrong conception of the Sabbath which they had inherited from their forefathers, and which they found stated cate-

---

[1] Philo in Eus. *Præp. Evang.* viii. 7 (Gifford's ed. i. 359); Jos. *Ant.* xvi. 2. 4.

[2] Mark i. 21, 23; Luke iv. 31, 33, vi. 6, xiii. 10; Acts xiii. 14 sq. 43.

[3] ערב שבה or the παρασκευή. Cf. Mark xv. 42; Matt. xxvii. 62; Luke xxiii. 54; Jos. *Ant.* xvi. 6. 2.

[4] lviii. 13, ענג.   [5] Peah. viii. 7; Shabb. xvi. 2.

FOURTH COMMANDMENT 127

gorically in the sections of the Pentateuch which are derived from the Priests' Code. Accordingly we must not censure Jewish scholars, if in the Mishnah and the Talmud the rightful claims of the Sabbath are overlaid by a mass of regulations of the most trying and vexatious description (Shabb. xxiv. 3). These scholars were simply the victims of a false conception of the Sabbath, as many teachers of the Christian Church were in the past and are in the present day the victims of certain false conceptions of the Christian Faith.

In the Mishnah and Talmud the development of legalistic minutiæ comes to a head. The Mishnah (Shabb. vii. 2) defines 39 classes of forbidden work. But since all work is forbidden alike in heaven and on earth, the province of forbidden work requires still closer definition. Hence each of these 39 classes of forbidden works is subdivided into 39 sub-classes, which are casuistically developed from the former. The number of these sub-classes thus comes to 1531 ($=39 \times 39$).[1] I will mention a few of the 39 chief classes (Shabb. vii. 2) of forbidden works: namely— (1) sowing, (2) ploughing, (3) reaping, (5) threshing, (6) winnowing, (10) kneading dough, (11) baking, (13) washing, (16) spinning, (18) making two cords, (19) weaving two threads, (20) separating two threads, (21) making a knot, (22) untying a knot, (26) killing, (32) writing two letters, (33) blotting out for the purpose of writing two letters, (34) putting out a fire, (37) lighting a fire, (39) carrying burdens.

[1] J. T. Shabb. vii. 2. See *Jewish Ency*. x. 596.

THE DECALOGUE

Let us apply these rules and their corollaries to the actions of our Lord and His disciples. When the disciples as they passed through the cornfields on the Sabbath plucked the ears of corn and rubbed them in their hands, they were guilty of a double offence against the Sabbath—*i.e.* of "reaping" and "threshing." When our Lord (John ix. 6 sqq.) made clay and applied it to the eyes of the blind man, a double breach of the Sabbath was thereby incurred. First He kneaded the clay. Now kneading was work, and therefore forbidden (Shabb. xxiv. 3). In the next place, since the application of saliva to the eyes was supposed to have a curative action it was, therefore, forbidden (Shabb. 108*b*). When the man, that had been a cripple for thirty-eight years, took up his bed at the bidding of Christ (John v. 10), he was, of course, breaking the law, for he was carrying a burden. Since, as we have already observed, healing was a work, it was therefore forbidden. Hence these casuists said : You may on the Sabbath put a plaster on a wound, if the object is to prevent the wound getting worse, but not with a view to secure its getting better or well. It is specially recorded in the Gospels that on certain occasions the sick were brought to Christ at the close of the Sabbath *after sunset*. The reason was that it was unlawful to heal on the Sabbath day, unless it was a case of life and death.

Amongst other trivialities and absurdities laid down in the Talmud we might adduce the following. Yet we must remember that these are not trivialities or absurdities from the standpoint of the later conception of the Sabbath. Thus bones might not be set on the Sabbath—not even the dislocated limb of a child— nor any medical or surgical operation be performed, nor emetics given (Shabb. xxii. 5), unless life was imperilled. A man might go about with wadding in his ear, if he had inserted it before the Sabbath; but, if it fell out, he might not replace it. He might not wear false teeth; for, if they fell out and he lifted and carried them, this would be a breach of the Sabbath. Women were forbidden to look in a mirror lest they might discover white hairs and attempt to pull them out—an act that on the Sabbath would be a grievous sin. Neither might they comb nor plait their hair (Shabb. x. 6). Women might wear false hair at home but not in the streets. It was unlawful to kill a flea on the Sabbath (Shabb. 107*b*), for that was taking life; or to eat an egg laid on that day, unless it was laid by a hen that was kept for fattening and not for laying (Beza, 2*b*). A scribe might not carry his pen for some hours before the Sabbath began, nor a tailor his needle (Shabb. i. 2). To scatter two seeds on the earth was to sow, and hence forbidden. To pluck a blade of grass was forbidden likewise. It was unlawful to wear any garment which one might put off and carry in the hand, for this would be a burden.

The best part of the Sabbath was to be devoted to the study of the law. The Psalms, Job, Daniel and the remaining books of the Hagiographa were not to be

130   THE DECALOGUE

read except in the evening, as they were held to be of inferior worth.[1]

But certain higher considerations superseded these rules, and thrust aside the Sabbath.[2] Actual danger to life justified a breach of the Sabbath law (Yoma, viii. 6).[3] The duty of observing the Sabbath was not to be put forward as a reason for permitting a man to die on the Sabbath,[4] since the law was given that men might live thereby. Such breaches of the Sabbath were justified by an appeal to Lev. xviii. 5, where it is said that if a man do God's judgments he shall live.

The bulk of the Rabbinic law [5] regarding the Sabbath is really based on the later and unjustifiable conception of the Sabbath which was introduced in the Priests' Code, and which represented this day as the day on which God was apparently obliged to rest after the six literal days of creation. Since on this theory the Sabbath owes its origin to an actual need of the Godhead, and

[1] For a nearly complete analysis of the law of the Sabbath, see Edersheim, *Life and Times of Jesus the Messiah*, ii. 777–787.

[2] רוחין השבת.

[3] כל ספק נפשות דוחה את השבת. But the Rabbis were very lax in applying this Canon about mortal diseases, or else they reckoned amongst them many we could not regard as such. See Edersheim, *Life and Times of Jesus the Messiah*[4], ii. 59, 60.

[4] Aboda Zara, 27b.

[5] The laws were modified from time to time. In the second century B.C. several severe laws were in force that were abrogated or mitigated later. See my edition of *Jubilees*, p. lxv sqq.; Abrahams, *Studies in Pharisaism*, p. 131 sqq. On the other hand, it is clear that the law which our Lord appealed to in Matt. xii. 11, 12, which justified a man in lifting his sheep out of a pit on the Sabbath, was later made more rigorous, as we learn from the Talmud, and all that a man was permitted to do was to furnish the sheep with food or supply it with the means of making its own way out (Shabb. 128b).

had been observed by God immediately after the Creation, and according to many Jewish writings ever since the Creation, the obligation of its observance by man followed inevitably. So conceived and interpreted the Sabbath was in no sense made for man, but man was in a large degree made for the Sabbath.[1]

Having now studied the earlier and later conceptions of the Sabbath as they appear in the Old Testament, we are in a position to study the attitude which our Lord adopted to these two conceptions, and to appreciate the transcendent insight wherewith, without any knowledge of modern criticism, He arraigned the inherent falseness of the conception [2] taught in His day, which was really a later conception, and yet recognised the element of truth underlying the Sabbath, which was observed in the earliest ages.

But this question must be adjourned to our next lecture.

[1] Classical writers refer to the Sabbath rather as a fast or day of sheer idleness; cf. Tac. *Hist.* v. 4; Suet. *Aug.* 76; Juv. xiv. 96, 105 sqq.; Mart. iv. 4. 7; Persius, v. 179–184; Seneca, *Epist.* ix. 47; Plutarch, *De Superstit.* 8 *ad fin.*

[2] To the non-Jew as well as to a large section of ancient Judaism the yoke of the Sabbath as conceived by the Rabbis appears an intolerable burden. And yet to a considerable body of Jews, both ancient and modern, the Rabbinic Sabbath has made an extraordinary appeal. As a modern Jew writes : " The Sabbath is celebrated by the very people who observe it in hundreds of hymns, which would fill volumes, as a day of rest and joy, of pleasure and delight . . . to which such tender names were applied as 'the Queen Sabbath,' ' the Bride Sabbath,' or ' the holy, dearly and beloved Sabbath.' "— Schechter, *Some Aspects of Rabbinic Theology*, 153 sqq., 1909.

FOURTH COMMANDMENT

SECOND LECTURE

"The Sabbath was made for man, and not man for the Sabbath."—MARK ii. 27.

"Let no man therefore judge you . . . in respect of a feast day, or a new moon, or a Sabbath day: which are a shadow of the things to come; but the body is Christ's."—COL. ii. 16, 17.

"One man esteemeth one day above another: another esteemeth every day alike. Let each man be fully assured in his own mind."—ROM. xiv. 5.

IN my lecture last Term I showed that there were two distinct conceptions of the Sabbath in the Old Testament. The older is attested in the fourth Commandment as it is given in Deut. v. 12–14 and parallel passages, where the ground for its observance is purely humanitarian—the physical and spiritual well-being of man. Its origin is due to human infirmity. The Sabbath, so conceived, was made for man. This conception held its ground down to the sixth century B.C. In that century, or somewhat later, the doctrine of the creation of the world in six literal days was introduced into Judaism by the authors of the Priests' Code, and introduced in combination with the older conception of the seventh day as a Sabbath of rest for man. The object of these writers was obviously to establish the observance of the Sabbath on a cosmic and everlasting basis. This attempt succeeded in Judaism. When these two ideas were fused together as they are in Gen. i.-ii. 3, the conception of the Sabbath was wholly transformed. According to this view, the Sabbath originated not in human needs, but in Divine. If, then, the Sabbath originated in God's need of " rest and refreshment," to use the actual Biblical terms from the Priests' Code,[1] and if man was made in God's image, then the necessity of observing the Sabbath devolved inevitably on man, and man was undoubtedly in some measure made for the Sabbath. From this new conception of the Sabbath all the extravagant ideas of the Rabbis followed logically and inevitably.

Now in the face of this later conception of the Sabbath, which had wholly superseded the earlier, our Lord declares : " The Sabbath was made for man, and not man for the Sabbath."[2] Previously to our Lord's

[1] Cf. Ex. xxxi. 17 (שבת וינפש). The last of these words is used in an earlier document of man's rest and refreshment at the close of the week of moil and toil, Ex. xxiii. 12. The Hebrew word supposes recovery from weariness and possibly from discouragement in 2 Sam. xvi. 14 (see above, p. xxxix, 112-116, 121-125).

[2] Rabbi Greenstone of Philadelphia, writing in the *Jewish Encyc.* x. 597, states that this saying of our Lord's is " a free translation of the Mekilta's comment on Ex. xxxi. 13,"—" the Sabbath is given over unto you, you are not delivered over unto the Sabbath." That this statement is untrustworthy, is easy to prove. In Yoma, 85a, a saying akin to that of our Lord is attributed to R. Jonathan ben Joseph, who lived early in the second century A.D., or to R. Simon ben Menasya, who lived at its close. The saying is : " It (the Sabbath) is given over to you, but you are not given over to it " (היא מסורה בידכם ולא אתם מסורים בידה). (See also Mekilta on Ex. xxxi. 13.) This principle is said to be derived from Ex. xxxi. 14 : " Ye shall keep the Sabbath ; for it is holy unto you." But no sane exegesis

declaration of this principle, a sharp controversy had arisen between Him and the Pharisees. The latter charged our Lord with breaking the Sabbath. The controversy was occasioned by the action of Christ's disciples, who as they passed through the cornfields on the Sabbath plucked the ears of corn and rubbed them in their hands (Mark ii. 23 sqq.). The Pharisees attacked our Lord, saying : " Why do Thy disciples on the Sabbath day that which is not lawful ? " Our Lord rejoined that David, when an hungered, ate of the shewbread, and also they that were with him, which it was not lawful for them to eat : and that the priests in the Temple necessarily broke the Sabbath law without incurring guilt [1] (Matt. xii. 4, 5). On another Sabbath the controversy was renewed in connection with the healing of a man with a withered hand. The Pharisees,

can derive such a principle from such a context. There is no connection in thought between them. There are passages in the earlier sections of the Old Testament which are not at variance with this principle, as our Lord showed in His controversy with the Pharisees, but the spirit of the Priests' Code is against it. Still more against it is the prevailing spirit of the Talmud on this question. In short, such a principle is not at home in the Priests' Code nor in the Talmud. On the other hand, since it is essentially at one with the spirit of the New Testament from its beginning to its close, and further, since it was uttered by Christ nearly a hundred or two hundred years before some Rabbi gave utterance to a weaker reproduction of it, the natural inference is that the Rabbis in question were acquainted with the Lord's words, and utilised them in order to mitigate the rigour of the Sabbath law, just as Mr. Abrahams (*Studies in Pharisaism and the Gospels*, p. 129 sq.) adopts it with the same end in view.

[1] A priest might do things in the Temple on the Sabbath which he could not do outside it (Shabb. 74a). Thus if he hurt his hand he might bind it with rushes when in the Temple, but not without it.

we read, "Watched Him whether He would heal him on the Sabbath day, that they might accuse Him" (Mark iii. 2). Whilst the man with the withered hand stood before them, Christ appealed to the reason and conscience of the Pharisees: "What man shall there be of you that shall have one sheep, and if this fall into a pit on the Sabbath day, will he not lay hold on it and lift it out?[1] How much then is a man of more value than a sheep?" (Matt. xii. 11, 12). And still further urging the claims of righteousness upon them He added, "Is it lawful on the Sabbath day to do good or to do harm, to save a life or to kill?" (Mark iii. 4). But they held their peace; and when Christ healed the man, they straightway went forth and took counsel against Him to destroy Him (iii. 6).

It was in connection with the first controversy with the Pharisees that our Lord laid down the fundamental principle: "The Sabbath was made for man, and not man for the Sabbath." Accordingly, whereas the Pharisees taught that help should not be given on the Sabbath unless life was endangered, our Lord uncompromisingly rejected this principle, and throughout His ministry made it clear, both by word and deed, that *acts of mercy, whether urgent or not, were not to be foregone because of the Sabbath.* Thus our Lord appears

[1] It is remarkable that this question as to the lawfulness of lifting an animal out of a pit on the Sabbath is discussed in the Talmud (Shabb. 117b, *ad med.*), and that it was decided that it was unlawful, though it could be supplied with food and furnished with means whereby it could make its own way out (Shabb. 128b). What led to this increased rigor of the law?

to have left it largely to a man's own conscience to decide what he should do or leave undone in the way of work on the Sabbath, exactly as St. Paul did later. This conclusion is confirmed by a remarkable incident in the life of Christ, which, it is true, is recorded only in one of the earliest Greek MSS (*i.e.* D) at the close of Luke vi. 4. The exact words are : " On the same day, seeing a man working on the Sabbath, He said unto him : ' If, O man, thou knowest what thou art doing, blessed art thou. But if thou dost not know, thou art accursed, and a transgressor of the law.' " These words are regarded by Dean Alford and Dr. Plummer [1] as authentic, and by certain other scholars as a fragment of a true tradition.[2] Their meaning is equivalent to St. Paul's words in his Epistle to the Romans (xiv. 5) regarding the Sabbath and other festival days : " One man esteemeth one day above another : another esteemeth every day alike. Let each man be fully assured in his own mind." In other words, he that works on the Sabbath on the ground of conscientious conviction in order to satisfy the claims of love, of duty, or of necessity, such an one is blessed in his work ;

---

[1] Dr. Plummer thinks that "both Paul and James possibly derived from this source the phrase παραβάτης νόμου (" transgressor of the law "). The former uses it twice in Rom. ii. 25, 27, and the latter in Jas. ii. 11. The former uses ἄνθρωπε, " O man," in Rom. ii. 1, 3.

[2] Montefiore thinks that this saying is "too subtle and Pauline" to be authentic. Does this scholar not recognise that this saying is only an individual application of the general principle laid down by our Lord : " The Sabbath was made for man " ? Can Christ not apply His own principles to life in the concrete ?

but he that has no such conscientious conviction is accursed, and a transgressor of the law.

The principle laid down by our Lord is that all ritual and positive ordinances are made for the sake of the worshipper, and not the worshipper for the sake of the ordinances. In the Pauline Epistles this general principle is given in its fullest comprehensiveness, and its object is thus defined : the law, which in addition to higher things contains all ritual and positive ordinances, is only a schoolmaster to bring us to Christ. Thus this idea was not imported into the religion of Christ by St. Paul ; it was already an integral principle of the teaching of Christ.

Passing from the Gospels to the Pauline Epistles we find there, as we have just observed, the same attitude adopted towards the Sabbath by the great Apostle of the Gentiles. In his Epistle to the Colossians (ii. 16, 17) he writes : " Let no man therefore judge you in meat, or in drink, or in respect of a feast day, or a new moon, or a Sabbath day : which are a shadow of the things to come ; but the body is Christ's." In his earlier Epistle to the Galatians (iv. 10, 11) he had already rebuked their superstitious observance of days : " Ye observe days, and months, and seasons, and years. I am afraid of you, lest by any means I have bestowed labour upon you in vain." And again in Rom. xiv. 5, 6 : " One man esteemeth one day above another : another esteemeth every day alike. Let each man be fully assured in his own mind. He that regardeth the day, regardeth it unto the Lord ; [and he that regardeth not

138   THE DECALOGUE

the day, to the Lord he doth not regard it :][1] and he that
eateth, eateth unto the Lord, for he giveth God thanks;
and he that eateth not, unto the Lord he eateth not,
and giveth God thanks." So far as regards the eating
of certain meats or abstinence from them, the observance of certain days or their non-observance, St. Paul
treats such things as in themselves indifferent for the
man who has grasped the principle of Christian liberty.
But, on the other hand, the Apostle requires each man to
be fully assured in his own mind that in such observance of
days or non-observance he is doing right. This principle
applies alike to Jewish or Christian ordinances. As an
Oxford scholar writes: "The Christian who has grasped
the freedom of the Gospel recognises the indifference in
themselves of such ordinances; but he voluntarily submits
to the rules of the Church out of respect for its authority,
and he recognises the value of an external discipline."[2]

The Jewish Sabbath was well known throughout the
Roman world at the beginning of the Christian era.[3]
It was observed universally by the Jews. It was
observed also by Jewish Christians for some generations, and by the Ebionites always.[4]

---

[1] The words in brackets are omitted by the chief authorities.
But they are not improbably original, and may have been *deliberately* omitted, as Alford suggests, when the observance of Sunday was
regarded as binding, and not have been *accidentally* omitted through
homoioteleuton.

[2] Sanday and Headlam, *Romans*, p. 387.

[3] Josephus (c. *Apion*, ii. 40) declares that the Jewish Sabbath
was known to all nations. References to the Sabbath are frequent
in classical authors: Tibullus, i. 3. 18; Ovid, *Ars Amatoria*, i. 415;
Martial, iv. 4. 7. See also note on p. 131, n. 1.

[4] Eus. *H.E.* iii. 27.

FOURTH COMMANDMENT

But Gentile Christians, following the teaching of St. Paul and the spiritual teaching of Christ, rejected the Sabbath wholly as a part of the old law. They repudiated all connection between the Lord's Day and the Sabbath. Thus Ignatius[1] in the early years of the second century exhorts his readers no longer to observe Sabbaths, but to fashion their lives by the Lord's Day. Early in the fourth century, to pass over other testimonies, Athanasius writes thus : " We keep no Sabbaths : we keep the Lord's Day as a memorial of the beginning of the new creation." [2]

The Lord's Day [3] is the oldest specific title which the

---

[1] *Ad Magn.* 9: μηκέτι σαββατίζοντες ἀλλὰ κατὰ κυριακὴν ζῶντες. Tertullian (*Adv. Jud.* iv.) teaches that the Jewish Sabbath was unknown before the time of Moses, and that its observance was never designed to be eternal, but only temporary. But a nobler meaning—that of abstaining from evil—was attached to σάββατον and σαββατίζειν by the early Christians. Thus Justin Martyr, *Dial. c. Tryph.* xii., writes : " The new law of Christ wills that you should keep Sabbath continually (σαββατίζειν ὑμᾶς ὁ καινὸς νόμος διὰ παντὸς ἐθέλει (but ye who are idle for one day think that ye are pious, seeing that ye discern not why it was prescribed for your observance. . . . But in these things the Lord your God hath no pleasure. If there be any perjurer or thief among you, let him cease to be so . . . then hath he kept the delightful and true Sabbath of God (σεσαβάτικε τὰ τρυφερὰ καὶ ἀληθινὰ σάββατα τοῦ θεοῦ). So also in Clem. Alex. *Strom.* iii. 15. 99 (p. 337), iv. 3. 8 (p. 566).

[2] *De sabb. et circum.* 4. The Sabbath still, however, continued to be recognised in the East during the early centuries. The *Apostolic Constitutions* (vii. 23. 36) recognise both Sabbath and Sunday, while the Council of Laodicea (A.D. 363), though condemning a Judaising observance of the Sabbath, accepted it as a festival and day of worship.

[3] The probable origin of this phrase is as follows. In Egypt the 25th of each month was called "the King's day" in the reign of Ptolemy Euergetes, because this monarch had succeeded his father on that day of the month. This prepares us for the next

first day of the week bears in the New Testament. It occurs only in Rev. i. 10 : " I was in the Spirit on the Lord's day." But the name was speedily adopted by the entire Church. In the Epistle of Barnabas (xv. 8, 9) it is called "the eighth day." [1]

Passing from the name to the duties of Sunday, as we shall for convenience designate the Lord's Day, we are struck at once by certain outstanding facts which mark it off from the Jewish Sabbath. In not a single passage in the New Testament is the observance of Sunday commanded, whereas the observance of the Sabbath is constantly enjoined throughout the Old Testament. But that Sunday had a special significance, we infer from three passages outside the Gospels. St. Paul impresses on his converts in Corinth the duty of putting aside money every Sunday for Church purposes (1 Cor. xvi. 2). Shortly afterwards he preached at Troas at a service, which is described as of regular occurrence on the first day of the week (Acts xx. 7). We may, therefore, reasonably infer that the

development. In Asia Minor and Egypt the first day of the month was called Σεβαστή, or " Emperor's Day," according to Lightfoot (*Apost. Fathers*, I. ii. 714), Mommsen and Usener. But Buresch and Deissmann (*Bible Studies*, 218 sq.) go further and contend that Σεβαστή was *a day of the week*. Since they are probably right in this contention, the conclusion follows naturally that the Christians named the first day of the week " Lord's Day," in opposition to and in defiance of the heathen name " Emperor's Day." With the reign of Domitian the Church adopted an attitude of antagonism to the great world-power of Rome.

[1] In this same passage the author states that "the eighth day " was observed because that on it Christ rose from the dead. This Epistle may belong to the last third of the first century or the first of the second.

observance of Sunday as the *only* day of common or public worship, began in the Pauline Churches. About thirty years later the Seer in the Apocalypse writes of his being in the Spirit on the Lord's Day (Rev. i. 10). Here the idea of private devotion on the Sunday is mentioned for the first time, though no doubt it must have been long a common practice in the Christian Church.

In the next place, it is not even implied in any passage throughout the New Testament that Christians were to observe Sunday as a day of cessation from ordinary labour in the same way as the Sabbath was observed by the Jews. This latter fact is only what we might expect; for rest from manual or other toil was not, as a rule, possible till the Christian Church became so strong that it could require exemption from labour for the sake of worship. For the first two or more generations the members of the Church were mainly slaves or persons of humble rank, who were not masters of their own time and convenience. Accordingly the early Christians had to worship when their several secular avocations allowed, and so only simple services were possible early in the morning before the day's work began, or late at night after it was over, if Christians were to meet at all for united worship. When Eucharistical services were celebrated early in the morning, they were celebrated at that early hour owing to the exigencies of the time, and not on the ground of any supposed spiritual principle.

Now beyond such simple services—early in the morning or late at night—the Church had not advanced at the beginning of the second century,[1] as we learn from the letter of a great Roman official, Pliny the younger, who was appointed by the Emperor as Governor of Bithynia, and Prætor with consular powers (A.D. 103-105). This letter is addressed to the Emperor Trajan (*Ep. ad Trajan.* 96), and gives an account of Pliny's methods of dealing with the Christians who were charged with disloyal and immoral practices. To be a Christian at this date, in this province as in others, was a capital offence.[2] According to this letter the question Pliny put to the accused was, "Are you Christians?" If they confessed that they were, Pliny condemned them to be executed. Secret societies were absolutely prohibited as dangerous to the State, and the Early Christian Church was regarded as such a society. Yet Pliny confesses that he could not discover any evil in the conduct of the Christians beyond that of an inflexible obstinacy in adhering to their professions. Pliny derived all his information from Christian apostates, and yet records that all these apostates maintained that the sum and substance of their fault was that they were accustomed to meet before dawn on a fixed day (*stato die*), which was obviously Sunday,[3] to sing hymns to Christ as God, and

---

[1] Tertullian, writing at the beginning of the third century, impresses on his readers the duty of common worship, and as he wrote during a time of persecution, he said : " If you cannot assemble by day, you have the night " (*De fuga in persecutione*, 14).

[2] See Ramsay, *The Church in the Roman Empire*, p. 223.

[3] Cf. Justin Martyr, *Apol.* i. 67 : τῇ τοῦ ἡλίου λεγομένῃ ἡμέρᾳ πάντων . . . ἐπὶ τὸ αὐτὸ συνέλυσις γίνεται.

FOURTH COMMANDMENT

to bind themselves by a solemn oath (*sacramento*) [1] to abstain from theft, robbery and adultery, to keep their plighted word, and not to withhold a deposit when reclaimed. After this service they separated and met again for a common meal.[2] What this common meal was, which was taken after sunset, whether a love feast or a love feast conjoined with the Eucharist, is a subject of controversy.

Fifty years later the Christians had increased in numbers as well as in social position and influence, and were able to arrange for fuller services and probably at more convenient hours. Writing about A.D. 150, Justin Martyr gives the earliest Christian account outside the New Testament of such a service. Christians, he tells us (*Apol.* i. 67; see also 65), met on Sunday, both in town and country, for common worship. Such services began with lessons from the Gospels and Prophets. Next a sermon was delivered by the president of the assembly, and this was followed by a series of prayers, in which all the congregation joined standing. At the close of the prayers bread and wine and water were

[1] Lightfoot (*Epp. of S. Ignatius*, vol. i. p. 52 *n.*) thinks it *possible* that Pliny's witnesses were not referring to either sacrament, but prefers to believe that Pliny had confused the two sacraments together, the words *se sacramento obstringere* referring to the baptismal pledge and the phrase *stato die* to the Eucharist. But there is no evidence of any kind from which it could be inferred that *sacramentum* had acquired among Christians in Bithynia any special Christian meaning, in case they spoke Latin. In case they spoke Greek, then the word is Pliny's own, and employed in the ordinary classical sense.

[2] "Quibus peractis morem sibi discedendi fuisse rursusque coeundi ad capiendum cibum." See Lightfoot's *Epp. of S. Ignatius*, i. 52 *n*.

brought to the president. The president thereupon offered prayers and thanksgivings, and the deacons distributed both elements to the members of the congregation and conveyed them to those that were not present. To this service of A.D. 150 our own service of Morning Prayer followed by a sermon and the Eucharist bears a close resemblance. *The Teaching of the Twelve Apostles*, xiv. 1, which dates from the same century, ordains that there should be a celebration of the Eucharist every Lord's Day.

Within the next twenty years Melito of Sardis wrote a treatise on the Lord's Day,[1] and still later Tertullian inveighed against the deacons and priests and bishops who forsook their flocks in the time of persecution, leaving them shepherdless [2] and so unable to meet in common worship.[3]

I have shown sufficiently that Sunday was first and essentially conceived, not as a day of rest from physical toil, but as a day when Christians should meet together for common worship, the chief features of which in the second century were the reading of lessons from the Gospels and Prophets, the preaching of a sermon, and the celebration of the Eucharist.

The next question we have to consider is how and when the conception of Sunday as a day of rest from manual and other ordinary labours arose. So far as I am aware, the first direct reference to this conception of Sunday is found in Tertullian, about A.D. 200, who writes that on that day " we ought to avoid every posture betokening

[1] Eus. *H.E.* iv. 26.   [2] *De fuga in persecutione*, 11.   [3] *Op. cit.* 14.

FOURTH COMMANDMENT 145

anxiety . . . even putting aside the claims of our business,[1] lest we should expose ourselves to temptation." But this conception of the Sunday only slowly gained ground, owing, no doubt, to the difficulty which Christians experienced in the first three centuries of getting release from their secular duties on Sundays, unless where they were themselves more numerous or influential than their heathen neighbours. Notwithstanding, there was a steady movement in the West towards regarding the Sunday as a day of rest from physical labour, and therefore in this respect as the heir of the Sabbath. This movement originated with the Church at large and not with its leaders. It was furthered by two new departures in the ecclesiastical and political worlds.

In the ecclesiastical world, attendance at public worship came more and more to be made compulsory, whereas in earlier generations it had naturally been spontaneous. A Spanish Council at Illiberis in 305 went so far as to decree that the man who absented himself from divine service for three Sundays in succession should be excommunicated. Such a decree would have been impossible had not the belief, that the observance of Sunday was necessary, already become prevalent in the second century.

In the political world, Constantine issued in the year 321 a decree that Sunday should be kept as a public holiday, but that field labour should be pursued as usual

[1] *De Orat.* 23: "Differentes etiam negotia." Cf. *De Idolatria*, 14 *ad fin.*

146 THE DECALOGUE

when necessary for the ingathering of the crops. Some sixty years later (*i.e.* 386) Theodosius the Great put down all games in the theatre and in the circus, and forbade all legislation and litigation on Sunday.

A succession of Church Councils took similar measures, which grew in severity with each century till the Council of Macon in 585, which proscribed every kind of business on Sunday.[1] Even Pope Gregory the Great, about 600, was obliged to protest against the extension of these prohibitions to the use of a bath on Sunday.

Now these new departures in Church and State as regards the observance of Sunday were beneficial to a certain extent. But both authorities were moving on a dangerous incline. Their measures were proceeding inevitably to the identification of Sunday with the Jewish Sabbath, and consequently to the prohibition of all work on Sundays and the infliction of severe penalties for any breaches of this prohibition. Notwithstanding, it was not till the close of the eighth century that Sunday was actually called the Sabbath.[2] Thenceforward Sunday was identified by Councils and Synods with the Jewish Sabbath till the time of the Reformation, and on this ground all save necessary work, both in town and country, all markets, fairs, legal business,

---

[1] See a list of such Councils in Bright's *Early Church History*, p. 334 *n*.

[2] *i.e.* by Alcuin in his *Hom.* 18 *post Pentec.*: "Cujus observationem mos Christianus ad diem dominicam competentius transtulit." Under the guidance of Alcuin, Charlemagne issued in 789 a decree prohibiting all labour as a breach of the fourth Commandment. In the Eastern Empire, field labour was not forbidden till A.D. 900 by Leo.

FOURTH COMMANDMENT 147

and hunting, were strictly prohibited. Amongst outstanding authorities who maintained this identity of the Sunday and the Sabbath were Bernard of Clairvaux [1] and Thomas Aquinas.[2] But these great Churchmen and their successors not only identified Sunday with the Sabbath. They went further. They brought all holy days under the rule of Sabbatical observance— that is, under the fourth Commandment. This gross misinterpretation of the scope of the fourth Commandment and its misapplication to Sunday and Saints' Days led to most disastrous results in the Church at large before the Reformation and in the Roman Catholic Church since the Reformation. Saints' Days were first put on an equality with Sunday—a measure that was in due course followed by another development. For Saints' Days grew so numerous in the growing centuries, that they elbowed Sunday into the background, and so it came about that, whereas Saints' Days were observed as holy days, and all labour was prohibited on such days, labour on Sunday was not proscribed with the same strictness.

On the other hand, though all kinds of work were prohibited, little or no restriction was put on the people's amusements on Sunday from the tenth century

[1] Bernard brought not only Sunday, but holy days generally, under the fourth Commandment. "Spirituale obsequium Deo præbetur in observantia sanctarum solemnitatum, unde tertium (quartum) præceptum contexitur." From Heylin, *Hist. of the Sabbath*, ii. 5. 457.

[2] Thomas Aquinas (*Summa*, ii. ; qu. ciii. Art. 3) states definitely : "Sabbatum . . . mutatur in diem dominicum . . . similiter aliis solemnitatibus veteris legis novæ solemnitates succedunt."

148 THE DECALOGUE

till the Reformation. The liberty accorded in this direction naturally degenerated into licence as the decrees of the sixteenth-century Councils, alike of the Roman and Reformed Churches, clearly attest, not to speak of the Puritan reaction which such excesses brought about. The Roman Church sought to put an end, or at all events a check, to this licence that had practically grown inveterate in the preceding centuries, and introduced decrees against dicing and conjuring, dancing and theatrical performances, wanton songs, public feasts and fairs.

The Reformed Churches had to face a more difficult problem. Though they accepted the statements regarding the Jewish Sabbath in Genesis and Exodus as historical, they could not accept them as furnishing valid grounds for observing Sunday, nor could they identify Sunday with the Sabbath. Luther, Calvin [1] and other Continental Reformers maintained that the fourth Commandment was abrogated by the New Testament, and that from the ideal Christian standpoint there was no distinction between one day and another.[2] The Augsburg Confession (A.D. 1530), which

[1] There is a tradition that when Knox called on Calvin on a Sunday in Geneva, he found him playing a game of bowls. I cannot recover the reference.

[2] Calvin (*Institutes*, ii. 8. 33) teaches that the Lord's Day was instituted with a view to " decency, order and peace in the Church." In ii. 8. 34 he writes : " I do not cling so to the number seven as to bring the Church under bondage to it, nor do I condemn Churches for holding their meetings on other solemn days." Calvin in the same section brands the teachers as false prophets who allege " that nothing was abrogated but what was ceremonial in this commandment . . . while the moral part remains, *i.e.* the observance of

represents the views of the Reformed Churches on the Continent, states this shortly as follows: "They that think that the Church instituted the Lord's Day as a day necessary to be observed in place of the Sabbath do greatly err. The Scripture . . . has abrogated the Sabbath. And yet because it was necessary to appoint a certain day, that the public might know when they ought to come together, the Church appears for that purpose to have appointed the Lord's Day."

This statement is in certain respects sound, but it failed in a large measure to appeal to men who had hitherto been trained by the Church to accept just what they were told and not to use their own judgment as to the validity of the beliefs or duties enjoined. In the Reformed Churches, therefore, Sunday lost much of its authority, and its observance claimed less attention especially on the Continent. In Roman Catholic countries the case was still worse.

In England, however, the observance was stricter under Henry VIII. and Elizabeth, though at its best it left much to be desired. James I., by his publication of the *Book of Sports* (A.D. 1618),[1] and Charles I. by his

one day in seven. But this is nothing else than to insult the Jews by changing the day, and yet mentally attributing to it the same sanctity; thus retaining the same typical distinction of days as had place among the Jews." Hooker (*Eccles. Pol.* v. 70. 9) comes under Calvin's criticism when he writes: "We are bound to account the sanctification of one day in seven a duty which God's immutable law doth exact for ever."

[1] The evil effects of this publication were somewhat mitigated by the *Sunday Observance Act*, 1625, which settled the amusements that were legal on Sunday, and forbade men to go outside their own parishes in search of amusement.

republication of this work in 1633, brought the disorders connected with the observance of Sunday to a head. In this work the King gave his sanction and that of the Church, so far as he could secure it, to the furtherance after morning service on Sundays of games and sports—such as leaping, vaulting, fencing, archery, Whitsun Ales, morris and other dances. The Court set an example by giving balls, masquerades, and plays on Sunday evenings. The clergy were required to read this book in Church, and in case of refusal threatened with severe punishment. Such clergy as refused to conform with its demands were to be driven into exile. By the order of Parliament this book was burnt by the common hangman ten years after its republication by Charles I.

This policy of James I., Charles I. and their advisers was not without some justification. It was initiated to counteract a movement which had begun towards the close of Elizabeth's reign with the publication of *The True Doctrine of the Sabbath*, by Dr. Nicholas Bownd of Norfolk, in 1595. In this book Dr. Bownd maintained that to Sunday attached the full and unrestricted claims and authority of the Sabbath, and he urged accordingly that its observance should be enforced by the State. This book appeared opportunely for the object its author had in view; for it gave vigorous expression to the reaction that had set in against the desecration of Sunday as a day of worship in his own and earlier days. Bownd's book had an immense circulation and a no less immense influence. It led to

FOURTH COMMANDMENT 151

a controversy which was pursued with great vehemence for one hundred years, in the course of which its views were adopted by the Westminster Confession and by the Longer and Shorter Catechisms, and enforced by several Acts of Parliament. On the Restoration these Acts were annulled, but the good effects of the Puritan conception of Sunday have never been wholly lost to England, though the Puritan conception itself was wrong.

FOURTH COMMANDMENT

THIRD LECTURE

" The Sabbath was made for man, and not man for the Sabbath."—MARK ii. 27.

" One man esteemeth one day above another: another esteemeth every day alike. Let each man be fully assured in his own mind."—ROM. xiv. 5.

IN my last lecture I showed how our Lord and St. Paul—the two greatest and most convincing Modernists in all history—rejected the Jewish doctrine of the Sabbath, and how the early Church followed their example and replaced the Sabbath Day by the Lord's Day. Next we traced the salient features in the history of Sunday, its identification by the entire Church with the Sabbath from the seventh century to the Reformation, when its original character was in the main restored; and then with a brief account of the Puritan reaction and the identification of Sunday with the Sabbath we came to a close.

We cannot pursue further the history of Sunday [1] in

[1] See Hessey, *Sunday, its Origin and History* (1861); Glazebrook's art. on " Sunday " in Hastings' *Encyc. of R. and E*. xii. 107-111; Lecky's *History of the Eighteenth Century* (1896), ii. 17, 84, 87, 532, 534, v. 162-163; *Democracy and Liberty* (1896), vii. 81-89; Abbey, *Life in the English Church* (1885), 316-321; Lea's *Studies in Church History* (1869), 469.

FOURTH COMMANDMENT

England and elsewhere. We must content ourselves with the statement that the English Church rejected the Puritan conception of Sunday by refusing to identify Sunday with the Sabbath. But whilst it has refused to identify Sunday with the Sabbath, it has, according to some of its most distinguished theologians,[1] retained what is called the moral element of the Sabbath, that is, the sanctification of one day in seven. How far the Church of England is justified in these two decisions may best be seen by setting the characteristic and essential elements of the Sabbath and of Sunday side by side. These can be arranged under six heads.

1. First the observance of the Sabbath is enforced in both versions of the Decalogue and throughout the entire Old Testament. On the other hand, there is not a single specific command to observe Sunday in the New Testament.

2. The Sabbath can only be legitimately observed on the seventh day. On the other hand, Christians treat the seventh as a common day, and keep the first.

3. The Sabbath lasts from sunset to sunset : Sunday from midnight to midnight.

4. The Sabbath, according to the Decalogue in Exodus and the Priests' Code, was instituted to commemorate God's need of rest after the six days of creation. Sunday, to commemorate Christ's first manifestation of

[1] Cf. Hooker, *Eccles. Pol.* v. 70. 9, who speaks of "the moral law requiring therefore a seventh part throughout the age of the whole world to be that way employed," and again: "We are bound to account the sanctification of one day in seven a duty which God's immutable law doth exact for ever."

Himself to His disciples as the Lord of life after His crucifixion.

5. The Sabbath law as stated in the Decalogue required physical rest and nothing more. Herein, of course, the claims of the Sabbath were not fully stated. Worship in some form, public or private or both together, was associated with Sabbath observance from the beginning. Before the Exile, public worship could only have been occasionally observed on the Sabbath, but when Synagogues were established throughout Palestine in the centuries that followed the Exile, such worship became an almost indispensable element of Sabbath observance. Private worship, though not mentioned in the Decalogue, may be presumed to have existed in some form from the beginning in connection with the Sabbath. The devout Hebrew, we may reasonably assume, spent part of the day in prayer and in teaching his household what God had done for and required from Israel. But throughout the Old Testament the emphasis is laid first and mainly on abstention from ordinary work: worship is often mentioned in connection with it, but it is treated as secondary in its claims and importance.

Now let us turn to the first two centuries of the Christian Church, including New Testament times. What do we find during this period in relation to Sunday? We find just this, that Sunday is first and always conceived as a day when Christians assembled for common worship, and that for a long time in secret. Not once in these two centuries, so far as I am aware, is

Sunday spoken of as a day of physical rest. Physical rest could not be obtained owing to the overwhelming heathen environment of the Church. Thus to put this contrast in a few words: the chief element of the Sabbath was rest from the ordinary labours of life: the chief element of Sunday was worship. In due course physical rest was won also for Sunday.

6. The penalty for breaking the Sabbath, as it was conceived after the Exile, was death; for the violation of Sunday no penalty was imposed for many centuries after the Christian Era.

Thus—to sum up shortly the essential differences between Sabbath and Sunday—the Sabbath is positively enjoined in the Old Testament, but in the New Testament there is no such injunction as to Sunday: the Sabbath is kept on the seventh day of the week, Sunday on the first: the Sabbath is kept from sunset to sunset, Sunday from midnight to midnight: the Sabbath is kept for one reason, Sunday for an entirely different one: the Sabbath lays the emphasis on rest from ordinary work, Sunday lays the emphasis on worship. The penalty for the violation of the Sabbath according to the later conception of it was death: there was no such penalty connected with Sunday.

Christians who are Sabbatarians are, therefore, brought face to face with insuperable difficulties. Thus though the seventh day is prescribed in the Old Testament, they observe not that day but another: though specific reasons are adduced in the Old Testament for its observance, they discard these and observe it for quite different reasons : and, though definite rules are laid down for the manner of its observance, they observe the Sabbath in a manner essentially different.

And yet, if we were called to decide between the precisianism and severity of the Puritans in respect of the fourth Commandment, and the utter indifference and worldliness, the riot and licence that prevail in many foreign countries, and, alas ! in a growing measure in our own, even the most secularly minded amongst us could hardly fail to decide for a modified version of the former.

But we cannot go back to this Jewish festival. Christianity has abrogated the Sabbath. It has altered the day of the week, the hours when it begins and closes, and likewise the grounds for, and the manner of, its observance. Hence nothing remains of the fourth Commandment save the proportion of one day in seven. But, if all the rest of the fourth Commandment is rejected as temporary and relative, on what principle can we declare that this element is unalterable and absolute, and that the observance of the Christian festival of Sunday derives its sanction by an immutable and absolute law from the Sabbath ? No valid reason for such a view can be adduced. We cannot analyse the fourth Commandment into its original elements and maintain that all these elements are merely ceremonial and indifferent save one that is moral and unchangeable, unless we adduce some valid ground for this conclusion. But no such ground is discoverable ; for there is no spiritual significance in itself in the proportion of one day's rest in seven, though this proportion of rest to work is sound and therefore expedient, if judged from the physiological and intellectual needs of man. On this question St. Paul's words give no uncertain sound. He classes Sabbaths and new moons together as Jewish ordinances belonging to the past. "Let no man therefore judge you . . . in respect of a feast day, or a new moon, or a Sabbath day" (Col. ii. 16).

But this objection is not to Jewish sacred days only, but to the principle of attaching intrinsic sacredness to any day. Hence he rebukes his Galatian converts for their superstitious observances of particular days as foreign to the true spirit of Christianity: "Ye observe," he writes, "days, and months, and times, and years. I am afraid lest I have bestowed upon you labour in vain." And again in Rom. xiv. 5, "One man esteemeth one day above another: another esteemeth every day alike. Let every man be fully convinced in his own mind." "Every day" in this passage embraces first days as well as sevenths, Sundays as well as Sabbaths. St. Paul clearly had no idea of establishing a new calendar of holy days in the place of the old, or of transferring the traditional sanctities of the old Sabbath to the new Sunday.

And this principle which St. Paul taught so definitely was, as we have already shown, only a more elaborate and detailed statement of the principle already laid down by Christ: "The Sabbath was made for man, and not man for the Sabbath." And, furthermore, this principle, which was so applied by our Lord to the Sabbath and by St. Paul to all times and seasons, applies not only to times and seasons, but to all human interests. It is only a specific application of the universal principle, which holds true as regards the relations of one nation or individual to another, of one place to another, of one building to another, of so-called clean to unclean meats, and of certain so-called sacred callings to other so-called secular callings. This principle is based on the great claim made by Christ that all things are God's. Such a principle comes into inevitable conflict with the ideas of material sacredness or holiness, which men connect with certain peoples, places, buildings, times and vocations. But holiness according to the New Testament is not as in the Old Testament frequently, and in heathen religions all but universally, a material but a spiritual thing, and can belong essentially only to spiritual beings: and only to these so long as they are striving to live by a Divine standard. Holiness cannot attach *essentially, but only indirectly*, to a place, or a time, or a calling, and to these only so far as they are associated with a spiritual being.

On this principle no intrinsic holiness attaches to one nation or individual more than to another, except in so far as they realise the ends for which they were created: and from such holiness none are excluded; for in Christ Jesus " there can be neither Jew nor Greek, there can be neither bond nor free : there can be neither male nor female " (Gal. iii. 28 ; cf. Col. iii. 11). No place, or house, or food or calling is intrinsically more sacred than any other. No intrinsic holiness attaches to any place. Thus our Lord declares: "The time cometh and now is, when neither in this mountain nor in Jerusalem shall they worship the Father" (John iv. 21). No house is intrinsically holier than any other. No human consecration can localise God in space. "The Most High," as St. Stephen declares, "dwelleth not in houses made with hands." We consecrate one house—not that all other houses may be treated as secular, but that all alike may be hallowed. As regards meats (Acts x. 10–13), St. Peter was taught the same lesson when, in the vision of the many kinds of living things, he refused to eat what the law condemned as unclean. This lesson—that meats are not in themselves clean or unclean and so cannot defile a man, but that a man can only be defiled by himself (Mark vii. 14–21)—had already been taught by our Lord to His disciples, but they had failed to apprehend it. As regards vocations, no vocation is in itself to be regarded as sacred and other legitimate vocations as secular. The best instruction of heaven is committed to the daily round and common tasks and callings of ordinary life: for in the meanest calling that God has made necessary for man there is room for the divinest instruction of heaven. All right occupations are in the purpose of God alike sacred, and do not differ from each other in kind but only in degree of sacredness, according as one is more adapted than another to be a channel of divine light, and truth and grace.

To return, however, to our immediate subject, there appears to be no valid ground for maintaining that

Sunday is based upon, and borrows its sacredness from, the Sabbath, nor yet for the claim that the setting apart of the first day in each week followed in accordance with a divine and immutable law such as the Jews believed to exist in regard to the Sabbath.

On what grounds, then, did the Early Church set apart one day in seven for Christian observance ? It was not, as we have already seen, on the ground of man's need of physical rest; for the Christian Church could not secure rest from physical labour for many generations after the institution of Sunday. Moreover, if Sunday was instituted solely to meet man's physical needs, such an institution would have placed man on no higher level than that of the ox or the ass.

Nor was Sunday primarily instituted on the ground that the observance of one day in seven was, in virtue of a divine and unchangeable law, necessary to meet man's moral and spiritual needs ; for there is no essential relation discoverable between the observance of one day in seven and such moral and spiritual needs. Such moral and spiritual needs cannot be wholly relegated to one day of the week. As spiritual needs, they should find satisfaction, not on one day, but on every day of the week, alike in our thoughts, in our desires and our actions.

None of the above facts, therefore, explain how the first day of the week came to be accepted spontaneously and unofficially by the Infant Church. But there still remains one fact which in itself appears to afford an adequate explanation, and this is that Christ manifested

Himself to the Apostles for the first time after His crucifixion only on the first day of that first week.

That Christ manifested Himself on the first day of the week after His crucifixion to His Apostles, is the most transcendent fact alike in the events of those weeks and in the history of the Church. This great fact, the manifestation of Christ to His disciples, brought into being two other great historic facts. The first and greatest of these is the transformation of a body of timorous, disorganised and ignorant peasants into a fearless and united band of Christian men, bound together by a new faith and inspired by a new hope. The first Sunday was thus the birthday of the Christian Church.

The second fact is the unofficial institution of Sunday as a *weekly* commemoration of Christ's first manifestation to His disciples, and the consequent supersession of the Sabbath by the Sunday as the chief day of worship in the week. Christ manifested Himself on the first day of the first week after His crucifixion. To have commemorated the Resurrection of their Lord once a year or even once a month, would have wholly failed to express the thought and joy of the Infant Church, or to meet its spiritual needs. Nothing less than a weekly commemoration could suffice, and such a festival the Primitive Church instituted spontaneously, and not under the pressure of an immutable law of Jewish origin. The weekly observance of the Sabbath no doubt suggested the weekly observance of the Lord's Day; but it went no further, though behind it lay the strength of the associations and traditions of well-nigh thirteen hundred years. A supreme significance thus attached itself to the first day of the week; but not only to the first day of the first week, but also to the first day of every week, as a commemoration of the first appearance of Christ to His disciples after His crucifixion, and therein as a commemoration of His triumph over death, and of the like triumph of all that are one with Him.

Thus while Judaism from the Exile onwards associated the seventh day with the rest which it supposed that God stood in need of at the close of the six days' physical creation, the Primitive Church from the outset associated the first day of the week with the manifestation of the unwearied, tireless and triumphant Son of God, the Lord of life, the Founder and the Finisher of the new and spiritual creation. Thus, to repeat what we have already said, every recurring Lord's Day is the memorial at once of Christ's first manifestation of Himself to His disciples and of the birthday of the Christian Church.

Let us now try to realise how Sunday was observed in the earliest generations of the Christian Church. During the first generation most Christians were Jews. The Jewish Christians naturally observed not only the Sunday but also the Sabbath, and generally joined in the Synagogue and Temple Worship. But when once Christianity had established itself amongst the Gentiles, the Sunday wholly displaced the Sabbath and came to be the one and sole day set apart for worship— for worship, indeed, but not for physical rest; for the

FOURTH COMMANDMENT

environment of the Infant Church did not admit of Sunday being a day of rest either amongst the Jews who rested only on the Sabbath, or amongst the Gentiles who had no definite Sabbath of any kind. In the earliest generations, therefore, the Christians could observe Sunday, not as a day of rest, but only as a day of worship; and even this worship was restricted for more than a century to the early hours of the morning and to late hours after sunset. Nay more: no individual body of Christians could safely reckon on such restricted opportunities of worship, unless it had registered itself as a burial club. The members of such clubs were allowed by the imperial authorities to meet once a month. The formation of any associations other than burial clubs was strictly prohibited by the Roman emperors. Thus during the latter half of the first century the Christian Churches were tolerated simply as burial societies, but early in the second century they were deprived even of these limited rights and were proscribed as unlawful societies (*Collegia illicita*). Judaism had succeeded in gaining from the Empire its recognition as a lawful society, but Christianity failed in this respect till the time of Constantine, though it was growing by leaps and bounds during all this period.

However, despite all the difficulties that confronted the Church from Judaism on the one side and the Roman State on the other, Christianity spread so rapidly that Pliny in his letter to the Emperor (*Ep. ad Trajan.* 96), in A.D. 104, writes as follows: " this hurtful superstition has penetrated all ranks and ages ": " not

only the cities but the villages are infected by it " . . .
" the temples are almost deserted."

Thus throughout these perilous times the Church maintained at a great cost the practice of common worship. The Christians of that age had learnt a fact of supreme importance for all ages. They found that it is not enough for the individual soul to be brought into living fellowship with Christ : they discovered that for the sustenance and growth of the new life the joint and habitual communion of Christians in common worship is to a certain extent as necessary as the habitual communion of the individual soul with God. Divine gifts and graces are to be won in such common worship in a measure in which they could not be won by the solitary soul apart from it. Even though strength and endurance, truth and purity, wisdom and joy, can be acquired by the faithful individual soul, yet these virtues and graces can be won in still greater depth and fullness, where two or more, meeting together in the Master's name, realise for themselves the truth of His never-failing promise, that He, their Life and Lord, the Source and Sustainer alike of their present good and future well-being, is present with them as they pray.

I have now shown at sufficient length how Sunday arose, not as a substitute for the Sabbath, but as a fresh creation of Christianity, how it originated unofficially as a memorial of Christ's first manifestation of Himself to His disciples, and how its weekly observance was based on this great fundamental fact.

I have shown, further, how it was conceived originally

FOURTH COMMANDMENT 165

as a day of worship and observed as such, and that only after the lapse of three hundred years was its recognition as a day of rest secured. I have shown also that with the latter characteristic as a day of rest the Christian Church during two periods of its history came to identify Sunday with the Jewish Sabbath, and that—the later and wrong conception of the Jewish Sabbath condemned by Christ. To this gross error entire Christendom committed itself from the seventh century down to the Reformation. With the Reformation this error was recognised and denounced by the Reformers, who maintained that the Sabbath, as enforced by the fourth Commandment, was abrogated, and that Sunday was a purely Christian festival. The Roman Church still clung to the fourth Commandment, but emptied it of most of its significance by maintaining that the fourth Commandment applied to every one of its innumerable Saints' Days.

Once again the Sabbatarian view was advanced by an English clergyman and adopted by the Puritan Party in England, in Holland and in America. Thence arose a controversy which was maintained for over a hundred years with such energy and keenness that the echoes of the strife have not yet wholly died out.

We have recognised that the Christian Sunday has two characteristics, it is a day of worship and a day of rest. Let us consider Sunday in the latter aspect first. As a day of rest, it is a social institution. As a social institution, Sunday lays us under the obligation of keeping it as free as possible from ordinary work. Wholly apart from religion, there are abundant reasons for making a break once a week in the world's endless strain and toil; for putting a check on the feverish and often insane devotion of man to things material. Now the proportion of one day's rest in seven has been justified by the experience of the last three thousand years. Physical health fails without such a relief. The first French Republic rejected the one day in seven and ordained a rest of one day in ten. But the experiment was a complete failure, and the Republic had soon to abandon this foolish revolt against the well-justified experience of the past. Again, in the Great War, Sunday labour was tried and the wages doubled for Sunday work. This experiment was also a failure and had to be abandoned. The men who worked seven days, though stimulated to do their utmost by feelings of patriotism and the prospect of increased rewards, produced less than they had done previously in a week of six days. In the coming generations there is not much danger of the neglect of one day of rest in seven unless some immoral Communism or Bolshevism gets into power. The Trade Unions, not to speak of the employers of labour, will see to the observance of rest from ordinary work. The motive of humanity, so far as it relates to man's physical well-being, operates all but universally amongst secularists as well as among Christians.

But though Trade Unions and the public generally recognise the absolute need of one day's rest in seven, so far as they are themselves concerned, they are often thoughtless and indeed quite callous as to the same claims on the part of no inconsiderable bodies of workmen in our midst. How much unnecessary travelling is indulged in on Sunday, and how many public amusements which entail severe labour on a large minority of the people! There must, of course, be certain travelling facilities on Sunday, but for the sake of the community the public should avail themselves of these only when necessary. The problem is a difficult one. The highest benefit of the many has to be reconciled with the least possible hurt to the serving few.

So far as Sunday is claimed as a day of rest and of cessation from ordinary work, the claim is good; but if the claim begins and ends there, Sunday is stripped of every religious and even of every human characteristic and degraded into a thing that meets the needs of the ox and the ass just as fitly and as fully as it meets the needs of their human masters. Here surely it is the duty of the State to intervene in the higher interest of its subjects. The State is not a purely secular institution. It takes account not only of the physical wellbeing of its citizens, but also of their mental and moral welfare, and it has been the exception in the history of mankind when a State has considered religion as lying outside the sphere of its protection and encouragement.

Let us consider Sunday from these three standpoints—that is, in respect of man's physical, his mental and moral, and his spiritual needs.

First of all, the State has to consider man as a being possessed of physical energies. Now for such a being

168   THE DECALOGUE

Sunday as a day of rest is of untold value. Sunday rest does not, of course, inhibit the right use of healthy recreations. And innocent recreations,[1] whether public or private, should be permissible on Sunday, but under clear and definite limitations. Care must be taken that indulgence in such physical recreations should not circumscribe or destroy man's possibilities of moral and spiritual progress. No man, it is true, can be compelled to take the path of such progress, but that path should at least be kept open for all that can and will avail themselves of it. That multitudes do not avail themselves of the opportunities of mental and spiritual discipline is an incontrovertible fact. And yet physical recreations, even of the highest character, can never serve as their substitutes. The men who give themselves no pause amid the fret and fever of the six days of the week cannot maintain that to spend the Sunday in absolute idleness, or in playing football, cricket, tennis or golf, or in the mere delirious quest of pleasure, can restore the flagging powers of a troubled and atrophied soul, or enable a man to realise the spiritual ends for which he was created.

Hence such recreations should not trench upon the hours usually assigned to public worship: no more should they be dependent on the organised labour of others, as in the case of theatrical performances, league football matches and the like. We should not, save at

[1] Recreation means one thing for one man, another for another. The brain worker will naturally resort to some form of physical exercise ; the manual worker will seek rest of body, and will also have recourse to intellectual and social pursuits.

the dictates of necessity, take our pleasure on the day of rest at the price of another's toil. If men seek recreation they should provide the means at their own and not at another's cost. The games that are played for their own sake are immeasurably superior, alike physically and morally, to those that are provided as a spectacle by paid professionals. Sundays, therefore, even when regarded from the lowest standpoint as a day of physical rest and recreation, should be secured against such Sunday games and amusements as are merely industries run on business lines, and naturally run for a profit. Such commercialised amusements tend both to degrade the players and to transform the bulk of the spectators into betters and gamblers.

Where the County and Municipal authorities provide facilities for Sunday games in the parks and open spaces of towns and villages, it is incumbent upon them to resist to the uttermost any attempt to introduce professional games and competitions in the train of such amateur games as they may think it wise to allow.

Though it must be admitted that Sunday games are attended with definite difficulties, no good reason can be adduced against the opening of museums and picture galleries for certain hours of the Sunday. These are not run for profit, and for such as can enjoy them they discipline and enlarge the intellect and imagination in ways and means infinitely beyond the finest games.

But these, too, have their limitations. For even when to the splendours of art and the wonders of science there are added the ministry of music and the healing influences of nature, all these combined are wholly unable to restore to the human spirit its lost balance ; to

> " minister to a mind diseased,
> Pluck from the memory a rooted sorrow,
> Raze out the written troubles of the brain,"
> Or " Cleanse the stuff'd bosom of that perilous stuff
> Which weighs upon the heart."

They may humanise a man, but they do not necessarily lead him to Christianity, or any true form of the spiritual life. There is no necessary bond between æsthetics and religion. The most splendid periods of the arts in Ancient Greece, and eighteen hundred years later in Italy, were notable for the moral and spiritual degradation of both these countries.

As man cannot live by bread alone, no more can he live by the ministries of art, or science or nature. The soul can be spiritually sustained only through communion with God as the body is physically sustained by bread. This communion should be maintained at all times, and the perfect man is he who realises this communion in its fullness. For the perfect man no Sunday, no special season of devotion, is needed; for these are but temporary ordinances for imperfect beings. But where is the perfect man to be found ? We all fall short of our duty from day to day : we all fall short of the divine standard in the tasks of our various callings. Hence the need of special days is indubitable, and the days and hours must be fixed and recur at regular intervals ; for we know well that that which may be done at any time is sure not to be done at all.

FOURTH COMMANDMENT

The men who deliberately or thoughtlessly neglect private as well as public worship are slowly starving their souls, and with this Nemesis, that the more they do so, the more convinced they become of the needlessness and uselessness of all such fixed seasons for worship, and at last also of worship itself. For the unspiritual man to regulate or dispense with the hours of his worship in accordance with his actual desires, is as wise as for the dipsomaniac and the glutton to prescribe their own diet.

On the other hand, there are spiritually-minded men who may refuse to observe our fixed festivals. When they do so on the ground of conscientious conviction they are, as St. Paul declares, as acceptable to God as those who observe them. But such men, the Apostle says, should be thoroughly convinced in their own minds. In the heavenly Jerusalem, we are told, there will be no temple. Nor will there be one time or season more sacred than another in the perfected Commonwealth of God. But for the vast majority of men, and to this majority we, my brethren, all belong, such seasons are necessary. So long, indeed, as we bear about us the weakness of our humanity, we shall need regular hours and seasons of retirement, when the soul must quit the tumult of life and in personal communion with God recruit its exhausted energies of faith and hope and love, alike in private and in the common prayers and services of the Church. But these will be but recurring feast days in the eternal festival, and, as we grow in likeness to our heavenly Master, the Divine sustenance of the soul will more and more be found—not in fixed services, which are only means to an end, but in the daily doing unto God of the daily tasks our God has set us. And, if these duties are fulfilled from their divinest motives, they will feed us wth the bread of life from heaven, even as the Master Himself declared, "My meat is to do the will of Him that sent Me," and we shall keep everlasting festival, ever reaping richer rewards of reverence and faith and love from every task rightly done, and from every obligation gladly acknowledged and dutifully fulfilled in the vocations to which our God has called us.

FIFTH COMMANDMENT

"Honour thy father and thy mother: that thy days may be long upon the land which the Lord thy God giveth thee."—Ex. xx. 12.

THE first four Commandments are concerned with the duties we owe to God. The next six relate to the duties we owe our neighbour, and the first of these naturally deals with the honour children owe to their parents. This Commandment is set first in our duties to our neighbour, in order to show that the well-being of the family is the foundation on which the well-being of every other human association depends, whether that association is the church, the school, the college, the guild, the trades union, the corporation, the nation or the league of nations: one and all depend on the family life for their well-being. Destroy the family and sooner or later you destroy all these.

And not only is the importance of this Commandment emphasised by the foremost position it occupies, but also by the form in which it is conveyed. All the other nine are negative. They declare, you are not to commit this offence, you are not to do that. Even the fourth is as negative as the rest in this respect: it required the Hebrew to do nothing at all on the Sabbath day.

Such negative Commandments are necessary restraints and curbs imposed on the licence of human nature, limits set to the action of the human will in various directions, and to the breach of some of these Commandments severe penalties are attached.

But to the fifth Commandment there is no penalty appended: moreover, it is not a negative but a positive command. It is couched in words dignified and tender —" Honour thy father and thy mother "—words to which the heart naturally responds, and to this command is added the gracious promise—" that thy days may be long upon the land which the Lord thy God giveth thee."

It is maintained by most scholars that this promise is made, not to the individual, but to the nation. As regards the nation, it is, of course, an indisputable fact that where the family life is maintained in honour and uprightness, and successive generations are linked together by such spiritual bonds as the love and respect of children for their parents, the nation has therein the best guarantee for its well-being and permanence. For God sets no limit to the life of any nation on earth. Every nation is capable of enduring as long as the world endureth. But if a nation is to enjoy this relative immortality on earth, it must be able to look back to its past with reverence and look forward to its future with hope. If, on the other hand, a nation thinks of the best in its past only with contempt, it can contemplate the future only with despair. For it has thereby shown itself to be unable to interpret and develop the noblest elements of the past; and, when this is so, its days are numbered. Having ceased to grow it has begun to die. It is perishing through its own vices—it is dying through moral suicide.

But St. Paul in his Epistle to the Ephesians slightly recasts the form of this Commandment so that it carries with it the promise of long life to the individual. " Honour thy father and thy mother : that it may be well with thee, and that thou mayest live long on the earth." And the general experience of mankind has vindicated the justice of this interpretation. Reverence in childhood is generally followed by a virtuous manhood, and such a manhood is generally closed by an honourable old age; whereas disobedience to parents not infrequently ends in a life of discredit or dishonour, and, finally, in a premature grave. Seeing, then, the importance of this duty, let us consider for a moment the facts on which it is based. There are two words which describe the two greatest forces that influence the life of the child. These are heredity and environment. Heredity embraces everything that we derive from our parents, whether it be of a moral, intellectual or physical nature. Our physical strength, our stature, our various faculties, our soundness of brain, our predispositions to good or evil— in fact, everything that constitutes the beginnings of our weakness or of our strength, we derive in an overwhelming degree from our parents. In the next place, the child owes to its parents its earliest environment. Now the child's environment is of far greater importance than its heredity for the making of character. During our helpless years we are wholly dependent on our parents: they provide us with food and clothing; they furnish us with their own outlook on life—whether material or spiritual: upon them we are dependent for all our teaching and discipline, in things practical and intellectual, in things moral and spiritual.

The powers, therefore, committed to parents are stupendous, and the relation between child and parent is a thing absolutely unique in human experience. It is certainly fashioned on a divine original. The authority of the parent transcends that of any prince or autocrat. Kings and emperors have claimed throughout all ages of the past to rule by divine right, and for thousands of years this claim has been admitted, but in the present day the right of monarchs has been so transformed that it has now come to be the same in kind wth every other rightly appointed and subordinate authority within the nation. There is no real difference in kind, but only one of degree, between the authority of the monarch and that of the various representatives of the national life, save that the monarch is the supreme representative of power within the nation. All these authorities, if found inadequate or unsatisfactory, can be removed and replaced.

But the authority of the parent over the child is essentially different in character. The parents' authority is unalterable and irreplaceable. Parents are in an essential sense "*Kings by divine right.*" Into their hands have been committed the lives not only of citizens of this world, but of beings who will outlive this world, and within whose reach God has placed the power and blessedness of an endlessly progressive life. To no beings in this world has God delegated such tremendous powers for the weal or woe of mankind as a whole, and to the mothers more than to the fathers.

Hence while the Commandment "Honour thy father and thy mother" is addressed first and chiefly to children, it cannot but arouse parents to the seriousness of the charge committed to them. The life of the child is derived from God through the life of the parents. The child lives and grows in the atmosphere created by the parents, and its moral nature begins to take shape in this atmosphere as soon as it awakes to self-consciousness. The capacities for love and truth and reverence and every other virtue and grace are latent in the child, only waiting to be developed in a congenial atmosphere. It is this atmosphere that the parents must create. Without such an atmosphere these virtues may never be quickened into life. Hence the home is infinitely more important than the Church, the school, the university, the trade, the profession, the municipal or national life. The greatest achievement open to parents is to be worthy of their children's reverence and trust and love. So far as they realise this ideal they are working not merely for time, but for eternity.

Parental goodness, of course, if it is to evoke such virtues in the child, must be genuine and real. The destiny of the child is to a great degree determined by what the parents are, not by what they pretend to be. There is nothing so bad as make-believe in this relation. Unreality is sure to be detected sooner or later. Precept can never take the place of example. Where the example fails the precept will be ignored, and disobedience and contempt for the parent take the place of obedience and honour. There is no eye that sees so quickly through pretence as the eye of the child, though the child generally keeps its own counsel.

Parentage, then, is God's earliest medium for the revelation of Himself. The parent becomes the type of God Himself to the child. St. Paul in Eph. iii. 15 teaches this truth in the words that God is the Father from whom every family in heaven and earth is named, that is, the Father from whom all fatherhood derives its name and should derive its character.

On this divine relation between the parent and the child is based the command, " Honour thy father and thy mother."

It is difficult to define exactly the character and extent of the duties comprised under the word " honour." And yet the child has little difficulty in recognising what it owes to its parents in the way of duty and affection. The honour due to parents includes at least three elements : respect, obedience, love.

In the earliest years of childhood these are due in unlimited measure. The young child has no right to dispute the commands of his parents. On the parents and not on the child rests the responsibility of the rightness or wrongness of the commands issued. The child has simply to do as he is bid. This is the only case in all human life in which the will of one person is rightly controlled by that of another throughout every detail of conduct. During this immature period the parent stands to the child as the interpreter of God's will. The obedience of the child, therefore, should be prompt and unquestioning; it should not be the offspring of fear, nor should it be won through bribery nor hope of reward. But as the years multiply the child passes out of this state of pupilage, and the authority of the parent is superseded and its place taken by that of God Himself. When the youth comes to be assured that his parents require of him tasks and actions that are inconsistent with his duty to God, it is his duty to resist his parents—firmly, but with all due respect.

Returning now to the elementary duties of respect, obedience and love, it is obvious that no right-minded child can withhold such duties as he rightfully owes to his parents. For if children have any natural superiors on earth it is their father and mother who gave them birth, who cherished them during their years of helplessness, reared them at a cost they cannot possibly appreciate till they enter upon riper years, bore with all their waywardness and weaknesses, and dealt tenderly even with their most flagrant faults. Can any service repay the numberless obligations that men owe their parents? Even if we rendered them love and service to old age, the arrears of obligation cannot be wiped out: the debt can never be discharged, we must die, however advanced in years, debtors to our parents.

THE DECALOGUE

On the children that withhold the obedience and love due to their parents there rests a curse as old as the most ancient civilisation. In the dawn of human history we find an echo of this in the primeval curse on Ham, which reflects the attitude of those days against shameless and unnatural children. This malison is re-echoed in every period and every nation. In the law of the Hebrews it ran as follows : " Cursed be he that setteth light by his father or mother " (Deut. xxvii. 16); " He that honoureth not father and mother, let him die the death," while the wise men of later time declared :

> " The eye that mocketh at his father,
> And refuseth to obey his mother,
> The ravens of the valley shall pick it out,
> And the young eagles shall eat it."
>
> PROV. xxx. 17.

It is a righteous indignation at white heat that gives birth to these imprecations on disobedient children. Next to the curse of God, a parent's curse is the most grievous woe that can fall on the head of any child of man.

Disobedience to parents has generally been the forerunner of a nation's overthrow. In many instances it has been the cause. Now at no time in the history of our own nation has disobedience been so rife and so dangerous to the nation's weal. This has largely been due to the carelessness of the parents themselves. They have not recognised their moral obligations to their children. Having provided them with shelter, food and raiment, they have regarded themselves as having done all that was required at their hands. But man does not live by bread alone, and the parents that withhold from their children the moral and spiritual teaching and example, that are more than food and raiment, must answer for this grievous dereliction in duty alike here and hereafter.

But the present widespread disobedience to parents, while traceable in large degree to the parents, is to be attributed in no small measure to another cause, and that, it is to be hoped, a temporary one, namely, the war and its after-effects. Owing to the necessary absence of millions of fathers from their families on the various fronts of war, and the extraordinary rise in wages at home, young unskilled boys and girls came to earn more than the skilled artisans of pre-war days. Having thus risen at a bound to financial independence of their parents, they cast off parental control, and claimed complete independence and the management of their own immature lives. Such a course has led to moral disaster and shipwreck in thousands of families. Now that the fathers have returned from the war, it is to be hoped that they will address themselves to restore order in their families, and that in due time the Commandment, "Honour thy father and thy mother," will be better observed. The power of the parents will be reinforced by a new Education Bill,[1] which will

[1] But very much—nearly everything—depends on the *nature* of the education. It should prepare the pupils for the tasks that await them.

prolong the period of school life, and thereby adjourn the day when boys and girls can earn their own living and become independent of their parents before they are in the least fit to control themselves. Besides receiving a better education intellectually and morally, they will be longer subject to parental control and discipline. And when in due time they become independent of their parents' support, they will enter on the tasks of life with brighter prospects both for themselves and the nation.

But there are some practical questions which must be considered before we close.

Some young people say that their parents are not wise, and that therefore they cannot respect them : that their lives are selfish, mean, capricious, or even stained by vices of the grosser kind, and therefore they cannot honour them : that they possess no attractive qualities, and therefore they cannot love them.

But the answer to all such disclaimers of the duty to parents is shortly this. The faults of parents—even the gravest faults—cannot absolve children from their duty or in any circumstances justify their disrespect, any more than the faults of children can absolve parents from their children's claims upon them.

The obligation of children to honour their parents is not cancelled by shortcomings on their part, though it may alter the form such duty should assume. We are not released from a debt because our creditor has become a drunkard or a profligate. We owe the debt all the same and must discharge it. No more are children released from the obligation of this Commandment whatever their parents' character may be. This duty is often hard to fulfil, but the line prescribed by duty is generally not the line of least resistance—at all events at the outset. Our love and respect are due first and mainly to our parents, not because they possess certain personal merits, but simply because they are our parents, just as our parents loved us first, and mainly not because of our personal merits, but because we were their children. If our religion has opened our eyes to the failings and sins of our parents, the same religion should also make us more patient with them. There is hardly any parent in whom there are not good elements; but, even where all these are apparently wanting, the duty still remains, and should we withhold from them the honour we owe them, the time will in due course come when they will be taken from us, and the remembrance of our unfilial conduct will remain an ineffaceable regret, however deeply we repent, however bitter be the tears we shed. On the other hand, we can carry with us no happier memories to our latest years than those of the respect and love we rendered freely to our parents from the days of childhood onwards. The fulfilment of this duty in certain extreme cases involves, it is true, immeasurable hardships: yet all the same the duty remains, and calls for fulfilment in some form. Often the best that a dutiful child can do for a discreditable or vicious parent is to be patient with him, to conceal from others as far as possible his shame, and to cherish the charity, the love that hopeth all things; for nothing is so base as for a child to taunt a parent with his shortcomings, to disclose his infirmities, or expose his baseness.

In conclusion, if we owe such far-reaching duties to earthly parents, compassed as they are with manifold infirmities, how much more do we owe obedience, reverence, love to our Father in heaven.

There is hardly to be found on earth such patient and disinterested love as that of parents for their children ; for this love enters into their children's joys, shares their sorrows, and clings fast to them even in the depths of sin and despair. But the love of God for His children infinitely transcends that of the best of earthly parents. For even when we have outworn a father's love and exhausted a mother's devotion, we can still turn to Him whose compassions fail not, who will receive us even when human love has been forfeited, human sympathy lost, and father and mother and all others have turned away and forsaken us. A mother may forget her sucking child, yet will I not forget thee.

SIXTH COMMANDMENT

FIRST LECTURE

"Thou shalt do no murder."—Ex. xx. 13.

AS the fifth Commandment upholds the reverence due to rightly constituted authority in the family and the State, the sixth, eighth and ninth Commandments enforce the rights which every man possesses to the protection of his life, his property, and his good name, while the seventh guards the sanctity of the home.

Every community, however primitive, which was resolved to maintain some form of order within it, was obliged to legislate on such questions. That the Decalogue is very primitive and elementary is clear from the fact that it is content to prohibit crimes against life, property and the like without enforcing positive duties save in the fifth Commandment: and that it takes no account of other offences destructive to any well-constituted society, such as breach of contract, arson and others.

But though the Decalogue is defective and inadequate, considered merely as a criminal code, it would be in the highest degree inequitable to interpret it purely from this standpoint. It is not merely a legal document, but also a religious one. It is therefore to be interpreted from the standpoint of the religious development of primitive Israel. Even when we have done it full justice in this respect, we shall see what a vast advance is made in the New Testament on the teaching of the Old. For though, according to the Mosaic law, a man may be held blameless on the ground that he has committed no open breach of the law, according to the teaching of Christ the same man might in reality have broken all the Commandments.

Let us turn now to our immediate subject, " Thou shalt do no murder." Already in ancient Israel murder and manslaughter were carefully distinguished. " To take life " was not in itself to be guilty of murder. If a man killed another through accident or in self-defence when attacked, he was not guilty of murder. Personal feeling, such as hatred, revenge or covetousness had to be behind the act to constitute murder. In primitive times when a man took the life of another, whether with malice aforethought or through accident, it was the duty of the nearest relative in any and every case to avenge the victim. At this period there were no such organs of justice as regular tribunals, judges, police, executioners. The duty of punishing the slayer of blood devolved by universal consent on the next of kin. This was the unwritten, if not the written, law as regards the avenger of blood. It may be objected that this method of enforcing justice was highly unsatisfactory, was heathen and not religious. This is quite true, but before we show how Hebrew legislation modified this existing and primitive form of justice, it may be well to observe that, notwithstanding the teaching of Christianity for two thousand years, the present relations of one nation to another are just as elementary and heathen as were the relations of individuals to one another over three thousand years ago. When one nation is outraged by another, it has to become its own avenger. This is simply the primitive law of the avenger of blood writ large. The nation does now what the individual avenger of blood did in times primeval. But the Great War has shown that we must advance from this primitive and heathen conception to a loftier and Christian one. And just as this ancient heathen method of individual retribution was superseded in due time by a national judiciary and executive, and the task of the avenging of blood was taken out of the hand of the nearest kinsman and administered by the State, so it is now the duty, especially of the Christian nations, to establish an international judiciary which will decide between nation and nation, and an international executive which will follow up, if necessary, its awards by force.

Returning to the duty of the avenger of blood, it was obvious to the ancient lawgiver that, if this law were carried out immediately in every case, men were sure to suffer death who were really guiltless of murder. To obviate such a miscarriage of justice, ancient Hebrew law ordained that certain sanctuaries should be recognised, to which the slayer of blood might flee until his case was tried by the elders of the city where the offence had been committed. If these returned a verdict of murder, the murderer was delivered up to the kinsman of the murdered man as the natural executioner of the sentence. On the other hand, if he were declared to be guilty only of justifiable or accidental homicide, he was allowed to live in one of the cities of refuge, and protected by it from the avenger of blood.

By thus carefully distinguishing the homicide from the murderer, ancient Hebrew law disengaged the idea of justice from the custom of the vendetta and the wild impulses of revenge. Thus while every care possible in that primeval period was taken to secure the life of the former, every care also was taken to secure the death of the latter. For it was strictly enacted that no composition or fine should be taken for the life of the murderer; for, even if the murderer fled to the altar of God and laid hold on the very horns thereof, he was to be torn therefrom and put to death (Ex. xxi. 14).

In this respect the law of the Ancient Hebrews is far in advance of the Canonical law of mediæval Christendom. Confining our attention to England, we observe that till the Norman Conquest no distinction was made between clerical and lay criminals. But this evil principle, established by a Canon of the Church of Rome, was introduced by the early Norman kings into England. According to this Canon any lay judge who presumed to judge and condemn a criminous monk or priest was to be excommunicated. But the mediæval

Church went further. Abusing its authority to the utmost, it offered sanctuary, that is, protection, to the murderer and the homicide, and to criminals of every description, lay and clerical, save those guilty of treason or sacrilege, and, what is more, it succeeded in delivering such criminals from the rightful penalties of the law of the land. It was mainly on this question that the dispute between Henry II. and Thomas à Becket arose. Unhappily, the great Abbey of Westminster was a notorious offender in this respect from the twelfth to the end of the sixteenth century. According to More (*Hist. of Richard III.*, p. 47, A.D. 1557) these sanctuaries were asylums for every kind of miscreant. "What a rabble of thieves, murderers, and malicious heinous traitors, and that in two places specially, in one at the elbow of the City (Westminster Abbey), the other in the very bowels (S. Martin le Grand)." Thus an infamous community grew up all round the Abbey through the iniquitous claims of the mediæval Church. One of the approaches to this sanctuary of infamous characters was appropriately named "Thieving Lane." And the designation "Broad Sanctuary," belonging to the stately buildings outside Dean's Yard, is derived from the same period. It was not till the reign of James I. that this gross abuse was put down.

In contrast to this evil influence of mediæval Church law the ancient Hebrew Lawgiver enacted, as we have already observed, that the guilt of the murderer, whether a priest or layman, was not to be wiped out by any fine, however great, but that he was to be put to death, even if he sought sanctuary at God's altar.

There are other principles which modern law-makers could with advantage carry more fully into effect which are to be found in the Mosaic legislation. One of these is the principle that a man should be held responsible for the consequences of his criminal neglect, where this neglect affected the lives of his neighbours.

I will take one concrete application of this principle from ancient Hebrew law and another from the Assyrian Code of Ḥammurabi, which was laid down at least seven hundred years before the birth of Moses and is now generally admitted to have influenced Hebrew legislation. This provision in Hebrew law is that which deals with a vicious bull (Ex. xxi. 29–31). Here the law enacted that, if a vicious bull was left carelessly at large by its owner and killed a man, its owner was to be put to death or to pay a heavy fine.

In the Code of Ḥammurabi only a fine is imposed, but in other cases where criminal neglect issued in fatal consequences the death penalty was inflicted on the guilty person. Thus Ḥammurabi (about 2100 B.C.) decreed that, in case a newly built house fell and destroyed human life, its builder was to be put to death. Some years ago, not many hundred yards from the Abbey, a large house was built on jerry-building lines. Before it was fully completed it fell and three workmen were done to death by its fall. When the case was brought into Court, whether the prosecution was weak or the jury too lenient, the culprit escaped. Four

SIXTH COMMANDMENT

thousand years ago in Babylon he would have been promptly put to death.[1]

That life is more sacred than property is acknowledged in principle but not always in practice. The most notorious breach of this principle, in which property and vested interests have been protected at the cost of life, is to be found in the liquor traffic. The abuse of alcohol is destroying, it is said, over one hundred thousand of our people every year, and the State is drawing a large revenue from this abuse. There is not a family in the land that has not to mourn the dishonoured end of some of its members or immediate relations by the abuse of alcohol. You will observe that I speak of the *abuse* of alcohol, for alcohol has its right uses. But the present system of the sale of alcohol in this kingdom is both an outrage from the standpoint of civilization, and, if considered in its actual working and results, it is in no slight degree a violation of the command, " Thou shalt do no murder." For though this system can be administered honourably and uprightly, as in many cases it indubitably is, yet it would require for its right administration a body of men who would be as wise as philosophers and as disinterested as saints. The sale of what is nothing short of an actual poison to a large body of our fellow-countrymen is left completely in the hands of a commonplace body of men, who are

---

[1] The words of the Code are : " If a builder has built a house for a man and has not made strong his work, and the house he built has fallen, and he has caused the death of the owner of the house, that builder shall be put to death." § 229. *Code of Laws promulgated by Hammurabi*, transl. by Johns, 1903.

materially interested in selling as much alcohol as they can to all comers, however unfit they are to have it. The more vigorously the innkeepers, brewers and distillers push their sales, the larger their gains. What matter is it that their gain is made at the cost of their brother's life ? Are they not authorised by the State ? Hence the State is to blame, and the appeal of the reformer must be to the people at large, to the State, to its ministers, and not to the Trade or the vast body of shareholders in this traffic, whose consciences are either hopelessly biased or wholly hypnotised by their greed of gain. These remarks may seem to point to prohibition, but prohibition does not seem to be the best measure to meet this evil. It is not the legislation that befits a free and self-respecting nation that has attained, or is on the way to attain, its moral majority. It befits rather a nation that is still in the condition of moral minors. For self-control and self-discipline it substitutes external coercion in the case of a stimulant in itself legitimate. On the other hand, the State should not by its bad legislation make the task of self-control and self-discipline too hard for its weaker citizens, of whom there are always a vast number. Hence the best remedy will be found rather in State Purchase, in the reduction of public-houses by 80 per cent., in the limitation of the hours of sale to less than half, alike in inns, hotels and clubs, and in the making every public-house a place of public entertainment, the manager of which should draw all his profits from the sale of food, but none at all from the sale of alcohol.

Other breaches of the Commandment, habitually overlooked in the past by the vast majority of the nation, are to-day being recognised more and more fully. Wherever there are fever-breeding districts and ill-ventilated and insanitary houses, wherever there are congested populations, excessive hours of toil, and work done under hurtful conditions, wherever there is under-feeding of the coming and actual mothers of our nation and their offspring, there are breaches of this Commandment, though it may be difficult in each case to discover the main offender and to define equitably the degree of guilt incurred. However, there should be no difficulty generally in bringing to justice the main offenders, and in due time it should be possible to reach all or most of them. For such offenders, whether individuals, companies or corporations, are morally and legally responsible for their criminal conduct, whether such conduct be the outcome of deliberate greed or criminal neglect, however thoughtlessly incurred.

This principle should be applied drastically in these democratic days to every citizen, whether he be a craftsman or employer, a manual labourer or a brain worker. Every citizen should be proud of his work, of the labour of his brain and hands. He should also be held responsible for the quality of his work, for the goods he disposes of, for any evil consequences that may follow from his contribution to the commonwealth. A modest but good beginning in this direction has been made in the case of plumbers. These craftsmen have often in the past borne a bad name, and not undeservedly, but their reputation is changing for the better through the establishment of the Society of Registered Plumbers. Each member of this Guild has his initials or name stamped on his work. It is needless to say that such work is good, and gives satisfaction alike to the craftsman and his employer.

I have now dealt with the nature and scope of this Commandment in Old Testament times, and also shown how applicable it is to the conditions of modern life. So far I have treated it as a Commandment affecting only our outward actions : the New Testament reinterpretation of this Commandment in the Sermon on the Mount, as affecting our inner life, must be reserved for the next lecture.

But there is one more point which calls for consideration. On what ground is the command given, " Thou shalt do no murder " ? Every ancient and modern State, it is true, issued such a command or its equivalent, but the ground on which they ordained this command differs often wholly from that on which the Old Testament ordained it. When the State forbids the crime of murder it generally does so on the ground that the life of the citizen belongs to it, and that accordingly human life cannot be taken unless with its approval or by its own direct action. The physical life of man is thus claimed by the State. And on this ground modern States forbid both murder and suicide, seeing that thereby the State is illegitimately robbed of its property in the lives of its citizens. Whether modern States will advance a more honourable ground for their action in this matter, it is not our duty here to inquire.

But this secular view finds no echo in the Old Testament. The Commandment, "Thou shalt do no murder," is based on the inherent dignity of man. "Whoso sheddeth man's blood, by man shall his blood be shed: for in the image of God made He man." Human nature, even in its earliest stages, is in some degree a reflection of the Divine. Where this inherent dignity of man fails to be recognised, life becomes insecure; for such security is based ultimately on reverence for man as made in the image of God. The likeness to God does not consist in the possession of physical life, but in the spiritual personality and capacities behind this life. The Old Testament does not say, "Thou shalt do no murder" because human life is sacred, but because man in himself possesses a dignity and worth transcending all other things. Physical life is only one of the many things that belong to his personality, and is not by any means the chief. Hence the ultimate religious ground, which justifies the sentence of death on the murderer, is not the so-called sacredness of human life, but the fact that man is made in the image of God. And yet this very definite phrase—the sacredness of human life—is continually used in this connection. When, however, we examine this phrase, it is hard to discover what exactly it means. There are many things in the world far more sacred than life. The countless roll of Christian martyrs who have willingly sacrificed their lives from the earliest ages out of loyalty to Christ attests this fact. And all who have been really baptized into Christ's spirit feel that they must forego life rather than abjure a single spiritual truth which in communion with Him they have made their own. Good faith and honour have in all ages and countries been esteemed by the best men as more sacred than life. Rather than forfeit these we must be ready to face death, and see that those we love face it also.

The three millions of Englishmen who volunteered to fight on behalf of England's honour and freedom are an illustration of this truth without a parallel in all human history. Even loyalty to purely scientific truth is a more sacred thing than physical life, as many great scientists have shown. To take the most notable example of such. Over three hundred years ago Bruno Bauer was burned in Rome because he refused to recant his teaching that the world is round and not flat: that there are a plurality of worlds and other like ideas, most of which are accepted by every intelligent man today. Yet the Roman Church burnt him for maintaining such scientific truths. But time has brought its revenges. Just thirty years ago his admiring countrymen raised a statue to Bruno in Rome on the very scene of his martyrdom.

It is not, therefore, man's physical life that is sacred, but the man himself. Physical life has only a relative degree of sacredness. There is a whole hierarchy of good things more sacred than physical life, and to preserve physical life at the cost of any one of these would be to make life itself a curse. For every man is

SIXTH COMMANDMENT

infinitely more sacred than this passing phase of his existence. Life is not an absolute, but only a relative good. It is valuable not for what it is in itself, but for the potentialities of other and better things which it carries with it.

Moreover, the same principle which requires the individual to surrender his life rather than lose that which constitutes its worth and greatness, requires him to approve the same action in the nation at large when it is confronted by the same alternative. Neither the national nor the individual life is worth preserving if, for the sake of merely living on, it sacrifices the ends that alone make life worth living.

Neither capital punishment nor war can be wholly dispensed with till murderous assaults on the individual and on the nation come to an end.

That nations are justified in resisting foreign aggression needs no vindication. Nay more, even an individual province within the Empire, such as Ulster, would have been justified in resorting to civil war if this country tried by force to deprive it of its full citizenship in the Empire itself, and to subject it to the yoke of other provinces—larger in numbers indeed than itself, but lower in achievement and character, and alien in race, alien in religion, and alien in ideals.

It is necessary to emphasise these truths ; for in the present day there are very many individuals whose minds have undergone a moral perversion. Some of these are opposed both to capital punishment and to war as a whole. Others admit the necessity of capital punishment but deny the necessity of war. In all these individuals there is a lack either on the moral side or on the intellectual, and often on both. The majority of them regard physical discomfort as worse than vice, and physical pain as worse than sin.

They are not more clear-sighted than others : they are simply more stupid. In some of them a perverted or dishonest moral sense has reacted on the intellect and destroyed the judgment : in others, a weak and one-sided judgment has destroyed the moral sense. In either case they have made their conscience the very sanctuary of their delusions, so that they are generally ready to condone any outrage, any infamy, private or national, for the sake of what they call peace. They are moral perverts and degenerates : they have lost the capacity for righteous indignation.

SIXTH COMMANDMENT

SECOND LECTURE

"Ye have heard that it hath been said to them of old time, Thou shalt not kill; and whosoever shall kill shall be in danger of the judgment. But I say unto you, That every one who is angry with his brother shall be in danger of the judgment: and whosoever shall say to his brother, Raca, shall be in danger of the council: and whosoever shall say, Thou fool, shall be in danger of the hell of fire.—MATT. v. 21, 22.

IN my last lecture I dealt with the Old Testament Commandment, "Thou shalt do no murder," not only with the literal breaches of this Commandment, but also with other manifold violations of it in ancient and modern times. Though only an outward Commandment, it was shown that even the most recent legislation of to-day has failed to bring the penalties of this Commandment to bear on those who through criminal carelessness in many trades and many forms of business are literally guilty of their brothers' blood.

The general principle deduced was that every man should be held answerable for the evil consequences that followed naturally and directly from his criminal carelessness.

This morning we shall deal with our Lord's reinterpretation of this Commandment in the Sermon on the Mount. The inadequacy of the law, " Thou shalt do no murder," as a moral commandment, had long been felt before it was transformed in the teaching of our Lord. It was an external law and could deal only with external acts and not with the motive or purpose of the heart. Our Lord therefore finds the guilt—not in the outward act, but in the heart of the offender. Many a man might be in spirit a murderer, and yet be perfectly blameless in the eye of the law. There could be murder without the outward act. It is the motive that determines the character of the action. And since the motives to murder may be various — envy, malice, hatred, contempt—these constitute the very spirit of murder.

This is the direction taken by our Lord's reinterpretation of the Old Testament Commandment. Now I want you to follow the words carefully; for though the difficulty of explaining our Lord's words has been recognised from the earliest times, no satisfactory explanation of them have been given till the present generation. It is only of recent years that the source of this difficulty has been discovered in a dislocation of the text and in the probable loss of three words. Let us again follow the words as we find them in the text.

" Ye have heard that it was said to them of old time, Thou shalt not kill; and whosoever shall kill shall be in danger of the judgment. But I say unto you, That every one who is angry with his brother shall be in danger of the judgment: and whosoever shall say to his brother, Raca, shall be in danger of the council;

SIXTH COMMANDMENT

and whosoever shall say, Thou fool, shall be in danger of the hell of fire."

As the words stand, our Lord enumerates three sins which carry with them the guilt of murder. The first is that of him who is angry with his brother; the second that of him who says to his brother, Raca; and the third that of him who says *môre*,[1] that is " Thou fool." Now in these three we should expect a progressive advance in wickedness. But there is no such advance. The man who calls his brother Raca, is just as guilty as he who calls him " thou fool "; for Raca and the word translated " fool " [i.e. *môros*] are synonyms, both meaning " fool," the first being a genuine Aramaic word, the second being originally a Greek word ($\mu\omega\rho\delta\varsigma$) subsequently naturalised in Aramaic. No real difference of meaning can be established between them. And yet there must be a great difference between them, since the penalties attached to them differ enormously. This is the first and in itself an insurmountable difficulty. But this is not all. A still greater difficulty meets us when we study the three penalties imposed respectively on these three sins. The first offender is the man who is angry with his brother: for this sin he is to be in danger of the judgment. Now, since no civil court can take cognisance of merely angry or malicious feelings, the judgment here must be God's judgment, not man's. The next two offenders are, as we have already seen, guilty of exactly the same offence; that is, each calls his brother " Raca " or " fool." But

[1] $\mu\omega\rho\acute{\epsilon}$, vocative of $\mu\omega\rho\delta\varsigma$.

their respective dooms are wholly incommensurable. The man who says to his brother "Raca" is to be convicted before the local council or Sanhedrin, and to be subjected to a purely human punishment; but the man who addresses him with another word of exactly the same meaning is to be cast into hell fire! Whether, therefore, we regard the sins or their respective penalties, this passage is quite impossible as it stands.

Happily the solution of the difficulty has been discovered.[1] The confusion and incoherency of the two verses are due to a slight derangement of the text. Ver. 22 consists of three sentences. By some unhappy accident the first two sentences got transposed. If, then, we restore the second sentence of ver. 22 to its original position before the first sentence, the whole passage becomes, in the main, clear, and the text falls naturally into three parts. The first part gives the original Commandment: "Ye have heard that it was said to them of old time, Thou shalt not kill." The second gives the traditional expansion of the sixth Commandment by the Jewish Elders. This expansion or comment is: 21. "Whosoever shall kill shall be in danger of the judgment (*i.e.* of being brought before an earthly tribunal): 22. "And whosoever shall say to his brother, Raca, shall be in danger of the council" (or Jewish Court of Law). The third part (in 22a) gives our Lord's reinterpretation of the Commandment, "But I say unto you, That every one that is angry with his brother shall be in danger of the

[1] Peters, *JBL*, 1892, 131 sq.; Bacon, *Sermon on the Mount, in loc.*

SIXTH COMMANDMENT 203

judgment " (that is, divine judgment). " And whosoever shall say,[1] Thou fool, shall be in danger of the hell of fire." This phrase is to be taken as expressing the inward scorn from which the words spring. Thus, whereas the Elders dealt only with two *outward* violations of the Commandment, i.e. *actual murder and contemptuous language, and with their punishment before earthly tribunals*, our Lord deals with the *spirit and temper from which the actions spring and their punishment by God Himsel* .

The spiritual violations of the Commandment our Lord defines as two ; the first is anger—" whosoever is angry with his brother " ; and the second is contempt or scorn—" Whosoever shall say, Thou fool." I might add here that it is probable that after the words " shall say " there stood originally the words " in his heart " ; for the phrase " shall say in his heart " means in Hebrew or Aramaic = " shall think." It is the temper from which the words spring with which our Lord is concerned.

Let us now study the first of these ; that is, anger. To begin with, we must recognise that these words do not forbid all anger ; for anger can be of two kinds—righteous and unrighteous. It is only unrighteous anger that our Lord condemns.

[1] Probably after יימר in the Aramaic there stood originally בְּלְבֵיהּ " in his heart." Cf. Ps. x. 3. If this is right, then our Lord first condemns " anger " and next " contemptuous thought." The loss of the above phrase could be perfectly explained through the dislocation of the text and the subsequent assimilation of the phrase in 22c to that in 22b. The absence of the words τῷ ἀδελφῷ αὐτοῦ in 22c is possibly a further proof that the original phrase was יימר בלביה.

The anger denounced is an active passion springing from envy, covetousness, malice, or hatred. So far as a man yields to this wicked passion, he is a murderer before God, though he may have committed no outward wrong and be blameless in the eyes of men. As St. John says: "Whosoever hateth his brother is a murderer; and ye know that no murderer hath eternal life abiding in him."

When this spirit of anger rises within us against a man who has done us some real wrong and that deliberately, our first duty is to get rid of the personal element in our anger, else our anger will speedily assume an evil character. Now there is one sure way of overcoming this evil element, and that is for us to pray for the man who has wronged us, and to speak well of him when we justly can. If we do so, and that not once or twice but persistently, the spirit of embitterment and hatred will be exorcised, and we shall recover quiet of heart and regain the power of appreciating the latent good in the offender despite all his wrong-doing; for the offender no less than the offended is made in God's image, is a child of God. In this way the personal element is got rid of—the irritation, the exasperation, the embitterment. These feelings, unless promptly resisted, coalesce into hatred against the man who has done the wrong, and can hardly fail to injure him. But however this may be, they demoralise the man who has sustained the wrong, if he indulges in them or suffers them to gain the mastery over him. So far as a man nurses such wrath against another, he makes his own spiritual life impossible : for such wrath unbalances the mind, distorts the judgment, disorganises the body and its functions, and becomes the actual source of numberless nervous disorders.

So strongly did the ancient Stoics feel the dangers of anger that they condemned it and other strong emotions wholly as unrighteous passions. But this is only a mean way of shirking our duty, *i.e.* of disciplining the passions. Besides, when the Stoic succeeded in extirpating his passions, he had robbed his nature of some of its strongest powers. Such passions were given to man to be yoked to the car of duty, as the dynamic force that is indispensable to man in life. But there is no such teaching laid down in the New Testament; for there is a righteous anger as well as an unrighteous. The New Testament inculcates no actual suppression of the passions, but their right guidance and their translation into action, when purified from the personal element. "Be ye angry and sin not," writes St. Paul; but he adds, "let not the sun go down upon your wrath." Here "wrath" is a different word from anger and means the feeling of personal exasperation, which often arises on suffering a wrong and which should not be harboured or entertained, else it will develop into hatred; and the sin of hatred is just as absolutely forbidden as the crime of murder.

But when we have succeeded in getting rid of the personal element of irritation, resentment or revenge, we have only achieved the first stage in forgiveness, that is, the attainment of a forgiving spirit. This is a spiritual conquest of ourselves. But this spirit seeks to be completed in bringing the offender into the same spiritual temper, and so is ready to offer the offender full forgiveness, if he truly repents. But the offender may refuse to repent; and to the unrepentant, whether it be an individual or a nation, neither can our forgiveness nor, what is of infinitely greater importance, can God's forgiveness be granted, though it is to be had in either case for the asking, if the man or the nation be truly contrite. Full forgiveness means restoration to communion, and this is only possible when there is true contrition and a real change of heart.

But nowadays, as at all times, there are not a few individuals who think that, if they overlook or condone the personal element in a wrong done to thèm, they have thereby acquitted the offender of his guilt. But this would be to treat a moral offence as though it were nothing more than a personal affront, and to regard a wrong ignored as a wrong forgiven. But, unless the offender repents, the wrong remains just as much a wrong as ever. Moreover, willingness to put up with deliberate injury and preference of peace to conflict for the mere sake of peace are characteristics not of a lofty but of an easy-going, mean and unspiritual nature.

The man who is not capable of righteous anger is no true man. To be angry at times is our first duty. To fail to be angry under certain circumstances is incontrovertible evidence that we are either intellectually undeveloped, or else profoundly immoral or non-moral. If we can quietly stand by and see wrong done without

SIXTH COMMANDMENT

indignation, then assuredly we are either stupid or bad, or perhaps both. A righteous anger is characteristic of every just and noble mind ; for such anger is simply the spontaneous protest of the generous man against the base, of the chaste man against the lewd, of the genuine man against the hypocrite, of the true man against the liar.

But in every case the man who is stirred to anger must take care that it is righteousness and not merely his own personal resentment that has given birth to it. Wherever envy or coveteousness or malice or hatred singly or jointly are behind the anger, then the anger is that which is condemned by our Lord as being essentially of the nature of murder.

Let us now pass on to the second violation of this Commandment as set forth by our Lord in the words, "Whosoever shall say, Thou fool, shall be in danger of the hell of fire." These words of our Lord are terribly severe. Accordingly we must be careful to interpret them aright. And the right interpretation will be found by considering the temper they indicate and not the words in themselves. Thus one man might say to a friend who had been guilty of some very foolish action, What a fool you are, and yet not be guilty in any sense of the sin here condemned.

In the mouth of another man, however, they might express a permanent spirit of scorn and contempt in the speaker. Whether or not this spirit ever finds actual expression in words is a matter of indifference. If these words rightly describe his mental attitude to others, then he is, as our Lord declares, a murderer in spirit, and in danger of the hell of fire.

This temper of scorn or contempt may be considered from two standpoints : first, as a thing hurtful in itself to the brethren ; secondly, as a special source of censoriousness and rash judgments.

First, then, it is a hurtful thing in itself to the brethren. If you despise your neighbour, you are injuring him, so far as in you lies. Your very temper towards him, however you disguise it, cannot be hidden from him : he feels your depreciation in everything he attempts or does ; and should it chance that he looks up to you or admires you in any way, you are paralysing in him the springs of right action, you are stifling his aspirations, you are turning his heart to stone. So far as in you lies, you are killing—not his physical life, which is only a relative good, but — his spiritual life, which is an absolute good.

On the hatefulness of the contemptuous spirit the Poet Laureate writes the following pregnant lines :

> " Since to be loved endures,
> To love is wise :
> Earth hath no good but yours,
> Brave joyful eyes.
>
> Earth hath no sin but thine,
> Dull eye of scorn :
> O'er thee the sun doth pine
> And angels mourn."

Hence instead of this spirit of scorn towards our neighbour we should cherish the opposite spirit—that of

SIXTH COMMANDMENT

reverence—not perhaps for what our neighbour actually is, for that at times is quite impossible, but for what he is capable of becoming as a child of God. And the grounds for cherishing such reverence are hardly ever wanting to the discerning eye. All the ages have testified to the nobility of character of which our race is capable, and no age has witnessed heroism and self-sacrifice on such a gigantic scale as our own. Countless numbers offered their lives a willing sacrifice in the fulfilment of duty, however obscure was the form in which their duty claimed them, facing untold suffering and shame rather than betray their honour, and winning their souls through the patient endurance of ills unspeakable. The measure of goodness in the world, of actual witness to God, is infinitely greater, then, than had been our highest hopes. Moreover, most ordinary men are better than they appear to the ordinary beholder. Their failings, follies, sins, they often cannot hide if they would, but they can and do hide their bitter anguish over them; they tell no one of their forlorn struggles against the sins that beset and overcome them, of their resistance, so often ineffectual, though carried even to the verge of tears and blood. Still more are they silent as to the many calls upon their self-denial, the many services they render in the spirit of pure kindness, and the fortitude maintained uncomplainingly under hard conditions, even when the hope of bettering them is dead.

But apart from the goodness and heroism so common in ordinary life, it is our duty to honour every man, independently of circumstance and place, as a being gifted with infinite possibilities : to reverence even those who no longer reverence themselves, to look beyond what is repulsive and mean in a man's bearing, word or deed, beyond his chastened insolence or calculating servility, beyond his obvious shiftiness and untrustworthiness, to the soul behind them, not indeed to the soul as it is, but as it is capable of becoming, if once awaked to the knowledge of God in Christ.

Hence the one spirit that makes a man incapable of appreciating and duly honouring his fellow-man is the spirit of contempt or scorn—the spirit which our Lord identifies with that of murder.

Lastly, the spirit of contempt is the parent of censoriousness or of the judging spirit. Judge not, that ye be not judged. This spirit of rash criticism, which finds expression in some variation of the words, "Thou fool," sets us in an unfriendly and unreceptive attitude to our fellow-men ; and, while for the most part it blinds us to a brother's merit, it makes us quick to discern his failings, and daily entices the unwary, and even the wisest of us into precipitate and self-trammelling judgments. Thus mere impressions of the moment are often converted into final conclusions, which commit us to a certain definite view of a man, and so close our hearts to any fresh revelation of goodness that further intercourse with him may give. Every action and utterance are wrested into harmony with the preconception so hastily and heedlessly formed, and so we become more and more ignorant of a brother's character, more and more blind to a brother's worth.

SIXTH COMMANDMENT

Such criticism is irreverent and presumptuous in the highest degree. And yet the feebler a man's discernment, the meaner his capacity, the fewer his spiritual graces, the more assurance he has in pronouncing such baseless and unjust judgments. This censorious spirit tends to destroy its victims, for it has the temper of the assassin. But whether it succeeds or fails therein, it steadily and inevitably destroys the souls that harbour it; for unless it is overcome and cast forth, it carries with it such souls as it thralls down into the hell of fire.

Rather in the presence of the inner life, the unknown capacities and the indefinite possibilities within the reach of every child of man, we should cultivate an attitude of reserve and silence, unless it is our clear duty to speak out without reserve and without hesitation. But, whether it is our duty to speak or to be silent, our attitude to a neighbour should be not scornful and censorious, but expectant and optimistic: the reverence of an undefined hope for even the meanest son of man forasmuch as he also is a son of God.

SEVENTH COMMANDMENT

" Thou shalt not commit adultery."—Ex. xx. 14.
" Whosoever looketh on a woman to lust after her hath committed adultery with her already in his heart."—MATT. v. 28.

THE Commandment, "Thou shalt not commit adultery," had a very definite and limited meaning when given originally, and this limited meaning persisted in Judaism down to and long after the advent of Christianity. In the first place, this Commandment condemned only the outward act and not the impure thought, as it does when it is reinterpreted by Christ. In the next place it condemns unfaithfulness in the married woman as adultery, but only in certain cases in the married man. A married man so long as he sinned with unmarried women was not held by the Jews to be guilty of adultery, but only when he sinned with another man's wife. There is no word in Hebrew or Greek to express a man's unfaithfulness to his wife. The explanation of this strange fact is due partly to the practice of polygamy, and partly to the fact that a wife was regarded as a piece of property. A man was not to injure his neighbour's wife on the ground that he was injuring his neighbour's property. The Commandments both before and after the seventh support this view. Thus as the sixth deals primarily with a man's rights as to his life, "Thou shalt not kill," the eighth as to his possessions, the ninth as to his good name, so the seventh insists on his rights of property in his wife. So far then as the seventh Commandment went, it took account not so much of the sin of impurity as of a sin against property. It was limited therefore to the sin of the married woman and her paramour, whether he was married or unmarried. No account, therefore, is taken of fornication in the Old Testament Decalogue. Elsewhere in the Old Testament there are, of course, many condemnations of the sin of fornication, as when Job declares, " I have made a covenant with mine eyes. How then shall I look upon a maid ? " or in the terrible warnings against this sin in Proverbs, which refer to the strange woman as one

> " Whose house is the way to hell,
> Going down to the chambers of death."
> PROV. vii. 27.

But the sin of fornication was never condemned in the Old Testamant in the same strong terms as that of adultery.

The Oriental view of woman that prevails in the Old Testament was not favourable to the new legislation required on this subject. Woman had no lofty place in the social system. From the dawn of Hebrew history the relation of the sexes, though much higher than that which prevailed among the neighbouring nations, was from the Christian standpoint a very low one. Polygamy and concubinage prevailed throughout most of the Old Testament times. A man might have as many wives and concubines as he could support. Another conspicuous token of women's servitude comes to light in the fact that the right of divorce was lodged in the hands of the husband only, and never in those of the wife. Even when our Lord was setting forth the new laws of the kingdom with regard to divorce, the Jewish schools were still debating the extent to which the husband's right of divorce might be exercised. The strict school, that of Shammai, insisted that the husband could not divorce his wife except for sexual immorality (Gittin, ix. 10; Jer. Tal. *Sot.* i. 16*b*). The school of Hillel, however, which represented the accepted view in Judaism, held that the husband need not assign any reason whatever; that any act on her part which displeased him entitled him, without the intervention of any court, to give her a bill of divorce and dismiss her. This loose teaching of the school of Hillel prevailed down to the eleventh century of the Christian era.

Even till the present day the Oriental view of women prevails amongst the Jews, and, since the progress of a race is to be measured by the respect in which its women are rightly held, there is not much prospect of further advance in Judaism in this direction, so long as in their daily worship in the family circle or in the Synagogue, according to their Authorised Prayer Book, the men still say, " Blessed art Thou, O Lord our God, King of the Universe, who hast not made me a woman." On this prayer the women follow with the humble response,

"Blessed art Thou, O Lord our God, King of the Universe, who hast made me according to Thy will."

Let us now turn to the New Testament reinterpretation of this Commandment in the Sermon on the Mount, where after enunciating this Commandment our Lord proceeds to say, "But I say unto you, Whosoever looketh upon a woman to lust after her hath committed adultery with her already in his heart." In another discourse our Lord declares, " Out of the heart of man . . . proceed fornications, thefts, murders, adulteries " (Mark vii. 21, 22). Our Lord here does not limit the sin to the unlawful intercourse of a married woman and her paramour, as did the Jews, but extends it to the sin of the married man, whether his paramour were married or not: nay more, He makes it co-extensive with all impurity between man and woman. The guilt of fornication is thus placed essentially on the same level as that of adultery. But this is not all: our Lord declares that he that has sinned in thought in either respect has committed a breach of this Commandment. We have here a complete revolution of thought as to the purity binding on both sexes.

The sin of impurity holds a strange position. It is more ignored and thrust into the background than any other sin of which man is guilty, and yet there is none against whose inroads the Christian conscience should keep more sleepless watch and ward. Every normal human being is assailed by the temptations of the flesh. This is a warfare from which none can escape; the strife is inevitable, and every man must determine whether he is to be the master of his own body or its slave.

The temptations of the flesh are amongst the most dangerous in youth; for they come when man seems least fitted to meet them. They burst upon the boy at the age of puberty, at an age when the powers of the intellect are only beginning to develop, the moral faculties are only beginning to recognise their tasks, and the character is in the earlier stages of its formation. Thus the fight is difficult and the risks are terrible. Furthermore, the extreme hardness of the struggle to which man is exposed is not fully appreciated till we compare the profound difference between man and the lower animal creation in reference to the desire of sex. In the case of the brutes the age of puberty coincides with the age of mating, and for this mating the lower animals are sufficiently developed in every other respect. But in the case of man this age arrives from four to eight years in advance of his physical development, in advance of his intellectual development, in advance of his moral development—in other words, from four to eight years before man is fit for marriage. If children were married at the age of puberty, physical, mental and moral degeneracy would ensue and bring with it the complete degeneracy or even the brutalisation of the race.

But, if this period is the time of the severest trials that beset and sift men in the struggle of life, it offers them also the greatest opportunity for winning the battle for self-control. If they win this battle, they can win all others. Most young people that lose their purity lose it before the age of eighteen. There are few fallen women on the streets who have fallen after eighteen. Hence the supreme importance of protecting our boys and girls during these perilous years.

Another characteristic of this vice, which accentuates the malignity of its allurements, arises from its appeal to the imagination. Merely to let the mind dwell on it is to be tempted by it. Some sins are indefinitely more than others sins of the imagination. Now the sins of the flesh are essentially of this character. Other sins, such as theft, arson, perjury, murder, make no appeal to the normal healthy mind. You may read countless tales of such crimes in the daily press and not be tempted in the least to become a thief, an incendiary, a perjurer, or a murderer, because in healthy minds the desires leading to such crimes are absent, and the tales of such crimes create only abhorrence. But it is otherwise in regard to sins of the flesh. Every healthy human being is influenced, and rightly influenced, by the attraction of sex. On the chaste regulation of this desire stand the rise and fall not only of individuals and families, of empires and races, but also of the whole Kingdom of God on earth.

Before I turn to the right methods for overcoming the sins of the flesh, there is an important psychological fact that must be noticed. This fact is that whatever stirs a man greatly in any one department of his being reacts on every other. There is a close interconnection of all man's passions and desires; for a man's mind is not built in water-tight compartments. Let one passion or desire be strongly aroused and every other is affected more or less. Now for our immediate convenience we might distinguish certain of the chief springs of action in man into the appetites and sentiments. The appetites are those of food and sex : the sentiments are those of wonder which leads to science, of admiration which leads to art, and of reverence which leads to religion. Now in man the lower springs of action—the appetites—are mysteriously and perilously interwoven with the higher springs of action, the sentiments. The passions, if strongly aroused by art or science, may react on man's lower nature, and this connection of the sensual propensities with the æsthetic delights of art, or the mental curiosity of science, forms the most insidious feature of this species of temptation. And yet attempts have been made in recent times to bring about a moral, nay even a religious, reformation by art exhibitions and the like. And on the part of science it has been urged that the temptations of the flesh will disappear, if the physical differences of the sexes are dealt with openly and in a purely objective manner in the elementary and secondary schools, and the appalling dangers that follow on the abuse of man's sexual powers are clearly set before the opening mind.

But dread of consequences will not keep a human being chaste. At the most it will make him more prudent and wary in the indulgence of his vice, and therefore the more detestable. It is well, indeed, that the penalties for such sins should be made known ; for they are God's laws written in our nature, but no such knowledge will deter the greatly tempted from sin.

That neither art nor philosophy, nor both combined, can avail to save man from these evils, or exercise even a restraining influence on his sensual vices, we can learn from the past. If we turn to the age of Pericles in the fifth century B.C., when Greek philosophy and Greek art and Greek literature attained an elevation never transcended and never equalled in any subsequent age of the world, the Greeks were the most civilised race of their day, and likewise the most degraded in respect of the sins of the flesh. The same moral perversion prevailed in Italy under Pope Alexander VI. and Leo X., though Italian art was then in its zenith, represented by such masters as Andrea del Sarto, Leonardo da Vinci, Michael Angelo, Raphael, Titian, and many others.

But it is not only the excitements of art or the facts of science, used pruriently, that may react hurtfully on man's lower passions, war has always the same effect, and often great religious revivals—this strange result being due to the fact that the feelings or passions stirred to action in one province of man's being react on those in every other. The disastrous influences of the Great War on the morals of the present day are known to all. I am, of course, not referring to the deliberate and organised infamies practised by the Germans and Turks on the women they captured, but only to the epidemic of sensual passion stirred into activity by the excitements and enthusiasms of the War in all countries, and particularly in our own. Now these excitements and enthusiasms are mighty forces for good or evil, according as they are subordinated to good or evil ends. It was well for England, when the stormy enthusiasms of our boys and girls were threatening our country with a moral pestilence, that the forces for goodness and order arose, and took measures to control and guide the fevered temperaments of our young people back into the paths of self-control and of service to God, to King and Country. If the passions aroused by the War had not found this healthful outlet in self-denying toil and drudgery to save both King and country, it would be hard to estimate the depths of infamy to which these passions would have debased the younger generation. The evil already wrought is great, as tens of thousands have found to their cost, but it would have been incalculably greater had not the wise leaders of the nation taken advantage of the passions so aroused and, yoking them to the car of duty, brought into rightful subjection to the service of God and of the State millions of young women and young men whose uncontrolled enthusiasms would otherwise in large measure have wrecked the nation.

Sins of the flesh have been an evil of all ages and all lands. They have destroyed empire after empire. The mighty Empire of Rome perished in the maelstrom of its own vast impurities. Is there no remedy for this evil ? No healing for this tragedy of human frailty and human suffering ?

Assuredly there is, though Art must own " It is not in me," and Science avow that it has heard thereof,

SEVENTH COMMANDMENT

and legislation confess that it is beyond the wit of man to imagine. But though these are helpless in themselves, religion can give to mankind, and not merely to individual men, the mastery of this passion.

But many, perhaps most people, may say: that such a statement is merely the expression of a foolish optimism, the vain hope of a fond heart. The best reply to such doubters and pessimists is to be found in the study of the past, and to ask history what it has to say on kindred questions.

During the half-dozen centuries immediately preceding the Christian Era, the ancient world, especially of Greece and Rome, was profoundly defiled with the unnatural vices mentioned by St. Paul in the first chapter of his Epistle to the Romans. References to the prevalence of these vices are found through centuries of Greek and Roman literature. The best men of those centuries, and amongst them Plato[1] (*Laws*, viii. 841),

[1] Plato entertains some hope that men may through three principles be compelled not to transgress. These are: " the principle of piety, the love of honour and the desire of beauty, not in the body but in the soul. These are, perhaps, romantic aspirations; but they are the noblest of aspirations, if they could be realised in any state, and, God willing, in the matter of love we may be able to enforce one of two things—either that no one shall venture to touch any person of the free-born or noble class except his wedded wife, or sow his unconsecrated and bastard seed among harlots, or in barren and unnatural lusts; or at least we may abolish altogether the connection of men with men " (Jowett's translation). Even Cicero says that it was regarded as a shame for young men not to indulge in unnatural vices ("Opprobrio fuisse adolescentibus, si amatores non haberent," *De republica fragment*. iv. 5. 10 (ed. Noble, p. 1196)). Nearly all the Latin poets and dramatists reveal a moral debasement unknown to modern times save in Russia and other countries affected by Bolshevism.

were just as hopeless of getting rid of these unnatural vices as most men of the present day are of getting rid of natural vices such as prostitution and other breaches of the seventh Commandment. And yet it was just against these unnatural lusts, that had held through unnumbered ages the mastery of the ancient world, that Christianity entered the arena, and in the course of a truceless war for over three hundred years triumphed over them completely, and, thus, what Greek wisdom and Roman legislation had despaired even of attempting, that Christianity undertook and carried into effect. It first transformed the popular view of these vices and made them abhorrent to the Christian conscience, and then secured the recognition of the Christian view in the legislation of the Empire.

Surely the conquest of these age-long evils of the ancient world cannot but inspire us with hope in this fresh crusade, and be the earnest of a new and greater victory. And should one ask, Who are to undertake this crusade? the answer naturally is: First, the nation in its legislative capacity as a whole; next, every family as a moral unit of the nation; and, thirdly, every individual soul.

First, society is an organic whole. If one member suffers, the whole body suffers with it. Either the disease must be cast forth or the body will perish. Public opinion is ripe for fresh legislation on the subject. The first measure in this direction must provide adequate housing for the people—houses, in fact, in which it will be possible to be moral and cultivate a sense of decency.

Most of the fallen men and women in our community have been born in surroundings in which decency and morals could only be maintained by persons of very strong character. This measure, which would have been carried into force by the present Parliament but for the Bricklayers' Trade Union, is the first step necessary in the direction of better morals. It is a deplorable fact that a small body of working men are on purely selfish grounds blocking the measures that are being taken to remove this evil—an evil which affects in an intensified degree the body of working men as a whole. The next measure will deal directly with the vice itself. Here some may object that you cannot make a man moral by Act of Parliament. This is quite true. Notwithstanding, legislation can reduce the extent of this vice as it has done that of gambling and the Liquor Traffic, though, of course, not as effectively.

One hundred years ago a gambling shop could be found in every street. Now through the vigorous application of the law this pernicious and illicit practice can only be pursued in the haunts of secrecy and darkness.

Next, as regards the Liquor Traffic, the Government Report published during the War states that men and women mainly fall into drunkenness—not through any predisposition to intemperance, but—through evil environment such as bad housing, insufficient amenities for refreshment in works and factories, absence of healthy recreation, but especially through the excessive number of public-houses and the evil methods by which these houses are administered—methods destructive not only to the public at large, but in an almost incredible degree to the publicans themselves. Thus the mortality amongst publicans is almost as great as that which prevails in the fever swamps of Africa.

Seeing, therefore, that legislation *following on a moral advance in public opinion* has dealt successfully with the problems of unnatural vice, with gambling, and in part with the Liquor Traffic, we feel confident that with a kindred moral advance of public opinion legislation will cope successfully with impurity and prostitution, will suppress the obscenities in literature and art that contribute to these foul vices, raise the age of consent from sixteen to eighteen as it was previously raised from thirteen to sixteen, and visit with the heaviest penalties every one connected with their maintenance.

Herein it is to be hoped that all classes will use to the full their powers to impose restraints on all for the good of all.

It is a grievous defect in modern sentiment and legislation that the sin of the man is regarded in this connection as a minor offence compared with that of the woman. But, since Christianity clearly teaches that the obligation of purity is equally binding on the man as on the woman, the forces that work for social purity must not relax their efforts till the public conscience is awakened and makes compulsory on man the same degree of purity that it requires in woman.

In this matter Christianity will win as in the past. It has already made great advances on the morals of the eighteenth century, as every one who has studied the literature of that century is well aware. Legislation on this subject has, in recent years, been attended with encouraging success. If the nation will take this subject in hand as one of instant and unequivocal obligation, it will achieve most of its ends in the course of a few generations.

But the success of the nation in achieving this end will be conditioned by the character and action of the units that compose it—that is, of the families. The purity of the next generation depends on the purity and wisdom of the parents in this generation. The measure of responsibility, therefore, that lies upon parents, and above all on the mothers, can hardly be exaggerated. This responsibility owns no limit of time. It is a question whether eternity itself can exhaust the results that flow from it.

Ye, therefore, that are parents, guard the sacred trusts which God Himself has committed to you, and for which you will one day be called individually to give account. The longer your children are preserved from contamination, the more the powers of their soul are strengthened, the more easily they will overcome the temptations that will later befall them. Most of the fallen girls on the street, as I have already remarked, have fallen before eighteen, large numbers before sixteen or even fourteen. The same is true of boys. Hence the need of encompassing them during their years of weakness and innocence with the shield of your protection—nay more, of surrounding them as with a wall of fire. You must not, indeed, keep them in ignorance of these subjects, but you must counsel them wisely, or secure them trusty counsel from others. May you, therefore, be faithful in bringing up for God those young souls, whose worth outweighs not empires, but worlds.

But if the unit in the nation is the family, the unit in the family and the Christian Church is the individual. To individuals, therefore, the Church addresses its most direct and urgent appeal. Keep yourselves rigorously and strictly pure, and require the same tone in the society you frequent. Refuse to harbour impure thought, for such thought, if dallied with even for a moment, becomes a temptation. Forbid with savage earnestness the introduction of foul or shameful words into conversation, and resent with contempt and scorn every ambiguous suggestion, every equivocal act.

If you have sinned in thought or in deed in respect of this evil thing, at once seek forgiveness and redemption. This forgiveness will not be withheld by Him who is ready to redeem unto the uttermost, yea, far more ready to redeem than we are to seek redemption. None was ever so tender to the fallen in this respect as the Divine Master Himself. Moreover, it is easier to find deliverance now than later. For, if we persist in evil-doing, a time may come when the power of our will will be broken, and we shall become the easy but self-loathing victims of every such temptation that besets us. Such sins, of course, carry with them their physical penalties, but the spiritual are the worst—a heart steeped in impurity, a befouled imagination, and a soul dishonoured and made a thing debased almost beyond the bounds of recognition or belief.

Deeply conscious of the horrors of these sins which dominated the ancient Greek world, and intensely convinced that Christianity was the only possible and yet at the same time the assured remedy for such evils, St. Paul implored his disciples in Corinth to flee the sins of the flesh.

Protesting against their sensuality, he cries out: " Know ye not that your body is a temple of the Holy Spirit ? (1 Cor. vi. 19) . . . ye are not your own." If it is an impious thing to profane a temple reared to God by human hands, how immeasurably greater is the impiety, the sin, to profane deliberately a habitation of God's Spirit, a temple reared and fashioned not by human hands, but by God Himself.

Let this thought then abide with us continually. However we may have fallen and sinned in the past, let us keep through God's help the temple of our body undefiled in the days to come. Each temptation surmounted and overcome will make the conquest of those that follow easier. Even failure itself will, if our chief desire be purity, make our heart more resolute in the battle before us, and so we shall come more and more to be filled with a passion for purity, and, as the faithful of all times, we shall do our part to bring in the glorious age when impurity will be driven forth from our land, and righteousness and purity and truth and love be established for evermore.

As Christianity won its earlier victories over unnatural vice, gambling, slavery and drunkenness, so assuredly it shall win this victory if we are faithful. Wherefore let us be strong and of a good courage. Christ Himself will be with us in the strife—He who is the Great Comrade, the Great Companion, that never faileth.

EIGHTH COMMANDMENT

"Thou shalt not steal."—Ex. xx. 15.

THE moment we read this Commandment, the question at once arises, What is the property here designed which one is forbidden to steal?

Seeing that various other kinds of property are dealt with in the other Commandments, such as a man's property in his life, in his wife, and in his good name, we may conclude that the property here safeguarded consists of a man's material possessions, though it is allowable in a larger treatment of the subject to make this definition more comprehensive.

Let us consider the question as shortly as we can under three heads: (i) Property considered generally with reference to the community. (ii) With reference to the individual. (iii) The Christian conception of property.

(i) *Property considered generally with regard to the community.* Property may be possessions which we hold through inheritance, or which we acquire through the work of our brains or hands. Since labour of some sort, either of brains or of hands, is the main but not the sole original source of all wealth, so labour should constitute a man's main right to property. Whether a man has wealth to begin with or earns it with the sweat of his brain or hands, in either case he is under the obligation of working, of doing service to the community. The man who has inherited wealth is paid in advance for his services, and should, therefore, under the obligation of *noblesse oblige*, work harder than the wage-earner. The great majority of men belong to the class of wage-earners.

As regards the wage-earners, if every man got exactly what he was justly entitled to, there would be no difficulty as regards the question of property. But seeing that selfishness, organised dishonesty, fraud, theft, covetousness, strife, contention and war are associated in all ages with property, men have from time to time dreamt of abolishing property altogether, in the belief that these evils could be got rid of with the extinction of property. Other evils are the inequalities between the lot of the poor and of the rich : millions are scarcely able to procure the bare necessaries of life, whereas a few thousands live in splendour and luxury. Moreover, much property has been gained by dishonest means ; the rich have exploited the poor, the strong the weak : profiteering has pursued its shameless and inhuman aims, and the cry of the destitute and oppressed has daily risen to Heaven. Such complaints are as old as the world itself, and such wrongs have given birth to the theories of Communism, Socialism, and within the last few years to those of Syndicalism and Guild Socialism. Now in these days no thoughtful man can afford to ignore these theories ; for they are influencing the legislation of every

EIGHTH COMMANDMENT

country and sometimes revolutionising our views on questions of property. Hence I propose to put these theories briefly before you so far as they affect the principle of property, and therefore the Commandment, "Thou shalt not steal."

Some Communists and Socialists have adopted very extreme positions, as, for instance, Proudhon, who maintained that "All property was theft." But the best of these theorists have not adopted this maxim, but have sought in different ways to do justice to the common rights of humanity. These systems, of course, are not of modern birth. Communism was put forward as the ideal form of Commonwealth by Plato, and various forms of Communism or Socialism have been advocated in many countries and nearly in every age by men of the highest character—such as Sir Thomas More, De Foe, Fénelon, Robert Owen—and are to be carefully distinguished from the extremest forms of Communism which are pure anarchism, or individualism run mad. Such baser Communists simply aim at transferring other people's property into their own pockets. We are all familiar with folk of this type, who, having no property of their own to lose, are ever advocating a redistribution of the good things that other people possess. This baser sort of Communism is well defined in the lines:

> "What is a Communist? One that hath yearnings
> For equal division of unequal earnings.
> Idler, or bungler, or both, he is willing
> To fork out his penny and pocket your shilling."

But we are not here concerned with Communists of this crude and base type.

It is only to Communists of a serious character that we can passingly refer, such as, before the Christian era, were the Essenes in Palestine and the Therapeutæ in Egypt. Communism of this type requires that all wealth should be held in common.

From the early chapters of the Acts we learn that the Infant Christian Church in Jerusalem adopted for a short period a voluntary form of Communism. For the past two thousand years attempts have been made to put various communistic schemes into practice in different countries, but sooner or later they have all been wrecked by certain fundamental facts in human nature. To abolish all private property and yet expect all men to work as diligently and conscientiously for the community as they would for themselves, is to require the impossible from human nature in its present ethical condition. Not till men become purely altruistic or angelic in character are such schemes feasible.

But these communistic theories, though they have never shown themselves to be capable of actual realisation, have contributed to the world's progress in the best sense. They have put an ideal before the world. They have influenced economic and social opinion in a right direction, and in several respects have revolutionised legislation : they have given birth to the principle of co-operation, which is now actively at work in England in the form of various co-operative societies. These societies, which seek to economise their outlay by buying in common and to increase their profits by selling in common, adopt as their motto "each for all and all for each," and aim at replacing, so far as possible, individual competition by a voluntary universal league for mutual help.

Though the stricter forms of Communism [1] are incapable of realisation, the same disability does not attach to those of Socialism. Most civilised countries at the present day are adopting Socialist measures in a greater or less degree.[2] Now what is Socialism and wherein is it distinct from Communism? They are often confused in popular thought, though in certain respects they are quite distinct. Socialism [3] may be defined as that theory or policy which seeks through the agency of the State to secure a better distribution of wealth, and also better methods of production than now prevail. Now so far as Socialism would realise these benefits for the community as a whole and not for any portion of it apart from the rest, it has the same end in view as Communism. But whereas the Communist may be an anarchist, the Socialist properly so-called is

[1] Lynden Macassey (*Labour Policy, False and True*, p. 98) states that "there have been at least seventy attempts to carry secular Socialism into effect, of which five only survived their fourth year of life." His short account of the last of these great experiments in Paraguay, where William Lane in 1893 established his "New Australia," should be read. See pp. 98, 99.

[2] On different varieties of Communism, see Lynden Macassey, *op. cit.* p. 74.

[3] Lynden Macassey (*Labour Policy*, p. 40) declares that "Socialism is too amorphous to admit of any workable definition," but that "the one common characteristic (of all Socialistic Creeds) is the abolition of the capitalistic organisation of industry."

not an anarchist; for he is an upholder of the State. And again, whereas the Communists hold all things in common, modern Socialists do not hold all things in common. To a limited extent they recognise private ownership. On the other hand, they demand that property, such as land, raw materials and means of production on a large scale, should be owned by the State, and that the State in taking over such property should give compensation to their owners. Socialists, therefore, as a rule recognise property in some form. This form of Socialism or Collectivism has been advocated by the Fabianists.

And that property in some form is necessary to man in his present stage of development is obvious to every student of history and economics. If it is attended by many evils, the answer is that most of these evils can be restrained or overcome by careful legislation and by the progressive moral growth of the community. On the other hand, private ownership is attended by certain benefits. Thus the stimulus to production, to the exercise of man's physical and intellectual powers, would be destroyed in all save a very small minority of idealists, if the idlers, the inefficients, the good-for-nothings, were as free to use the products of labour as those by whose self-denial and toil they had been produced.[1] But, further, the institution of property

[1] In a note on p. 233, I have referred to the failure of the Socialist colony in Paraguay. The members of this colony decided by vote that the right of private ownership should be restored. A new grant of land was then made by the Government to a large number of the original colonists, who " retrieved their failure and became, under the stimulus of each working for himself, successful farmers."

is a vigorous discipline for good or evil, not only of the physical and intellectual powers of man, but also of his moral powers. A man's loyalty to his conscience cannot be better demonstrated than by the way he gets property and by the way he uses it. You may have been on friendly relations with a man for years, and thought highly of him, and then found that you were obliged to reverse your judgment of him when you were brought into business relations with him. You could not devise a better means of testing a man's integrity than by having business transactions with him. The man that is learning to be faithful in things material is proving himself to be fit to be entrusted with things spiritual. Hence the moral value of private ownership in the development of character.

From this short survey we see that whereas Communism denies the rights of private property, Socialism recognises them within certain defined limits, but expects too much from the State, hoping for its millennium through the nationalisation of the greater part of the property of the nation.

As a reaction against and in opposition to Socialism so conceived, two other theories have recently entered the field, namely Syndicalism and Guild Socialism.[1] As for the first, with which alone we can deal here, Syndicalists are bodies of workmen whose aim is to make themselves masters of the materials and means of production wherewith they work, and of the mines,

[1] On Guild Socialism, see Lynden Macassey, *Labour Policy*, p. 43 sqq.

factories, workshops in which they work, and to transfer the entire profits of such undertakings to their own pockets. But this is not all. The sheer selfishness of this policy is to be initiated by violence, sabotage and dishonesty of every kind. The workmen in each mine, factory or workshop are not only to limit their output, but also to damage the tools and machinery so as to extinguish all profit, and to make the loss incurred in carrying on so great, that the mines and workshops must finally be abandoned by their owners, and, when this end is attained, the Syndicalists propose to secure them for themselves. They further teach that all contracts, however solemnly undertaken, are, when it suits their aims, to be treated as scraps of paper : that the State is to be destroyed, since it maintains the existing order : politics are to be abjured, since they tend to bring the classes together, and a fight to the finish is to be waged against society. Out of the horrors of this war of class with class, and the chaos engendered by interminable strikes, they cherish the delusive hope that a millennium of peace and blessedness will of itself arise—a paradise fit for labour and its leaders. This phase of Socialism originated with the revolutionary phase of Chartism, but owes its extreme developments to Continental Socialists, especially to the Frenchman Sorel. To such a policy none but knaves or fanatics can lend themselves.

Hence, as we have left Communism out of consideration from the fact that it is unpractical, we may leave Syndicalism and Guild Socialism out of consideration on the ground that they are in the main organised roguery.

EIGHTH COMMANDMENT

In the present and in the days to come, therefore, we must reckon with the claims of Socialism; and so far as these claims are just, the State must admit and put them in force. The rights of private property in some form must be maintained—a man's property in his life, in his good name, in his purity and honour, and also in his inherited wealth and earnings so far as these are found to be legitimate. As to inherited wealth, the State has already taxed this severely; but to tax it out of existence, as some propose, would, on the one hand, penalise thrift, self-control and self-denial, and on the other put a premium on improvidence, self-indulgence and every possible form of extravagance, and so destroy the very foundations of national character. What a man's legitimate earnings should be cannot be left wholly to the economic law of supply and demand. The State should sooner or later determine the living wage in every calling when that is found to be possible. What such a wage is can only be ascertained by careful investigation, by wide-reaching experience and equitable judgment on the part of all concerned.

Every man is entitled to so much as corresponds to his contribution to the Community and State and to no more. But it is a very hard problem to define the fair share of each man in the common product when multitudes are engaged in the same enterprise, when some contribute their capital, others their inventive genius, others their organising abilities, others their skill of hand, and others their physical strength. To each worker towards the final product is due just so much as he has contributed towards it and no more. And wherever any artificial combination, whether of employers or of employed, succeeds in getting a larger dividend out of the profits than is their equitable share, they are making a dishonest gain and committing a breach of the Commandment, "Thou shalt not steal."

In fact, so long as employers and employed are out just for what they can get, irrespective of the moral laws involved, they are in principle no better than professional thieves and pickpockets, however specious be the names under which they cloak their filchings from each other or from the common purse.

And this is no less true even when brought about by legislation. If in the teeth of justice and equity any class—whether of employers or employed—succeeds through legislation in wresting from others the benefits which it covets, and which its members have not the capacity to acquire honestly for themselves, they are nothing more than thieves duly authorised and licensed by the State to pursue their immoral practices.

The crimes of employers against labour have been largely and rightly exposed. Many of these have been redressed though much still remains to be done in this field. But, if the employers have been guilty of the spirit of greed and covetousness in the past and are still guilty thereof in many fields of enterprise in the present, the same evil spirit is just as rampant in most, if not in all, the Trade Unions; while in Syndicalism, Guild Socialism and Bolshevism this spirit has taken unto itself seven other spirits worse than itself.

EIGHTH COMMANDMENT 239

Now before I criticise further the Trade Unions, I wish to express my profound admiration for the boundless self-sacrifice these great Corporations have shown in the past in their long struggle for a fairer wage and a fairer share in the products of labour and industry. They have not only taught the nation at large the duty of brotherhood, but they have practised it on a scale without a parallel in the history of Christendom. But, alas! after having achieved these great virtues they are now lending themselves to what cannot be described as other than unquestionable vices. The professed object of the Trade Unions is to get a larger share in the profits of industry. That they should have a larger share than they had in the past no fair-minded man could deny. But has their labour become more efficient in return for the larger wage they have already received? As we are all well aware, with higher wages there has been a distinct limitation of output—a limitation which has been deliberately enforced under mistaken economic views. Herein the influence of the Trade Unions has been detrimental to efficiency. The standard they set up in skill and energy is that of the least capable and the least efficient. A good workman is taught that it is unfair to others to do his best. What would happen if the brain workers, to whom every advance in productive power is due, were to act on the same principle? It is an unpleasant fact that the American miner brings two and a half times as much coal to the surface as the miner in England, and the American bricklayer lays twice or three times as many bricks per day as the English bricklayer. It is true that the American workman is paid higher wages, but this does not affect the question at issue, seeing that the efficiency of the English workman is growing less as his wage grows greater.

Now, however splendid and heroic the history of Trade Unionism has been in the past, such principles and such practices as they are pursuing in the present cannot fail to pervert the moral sense of the workman, to debase his character, and make him forgetful of everything but his own narrow material interest. We have recently witnessed an exhibition of this shameless selfishness on a gigantic scale.

With an astounding meanness and a cynical indifference to everything but their own selfish gains, English miners held this nation to ransom in its hour of supreme danger, when not only its own existence was at stake, but also that of all the best nations of the world. This is a record which cannot easily be forgotten.

While all thoughtful men—manual as well as brain workers—have looked with unmixed sorrow on the adoption of this evil policy by so many Trade Unions, it is with unmixed joy that they have read in a recent number of the *Democrat*—a new Labour journal—a calm criticism and an implicit condemnation of this policy. The writer declares that " it is our duty to increase the national output, and to use our best energies for that purpose. . . . We must work or otherwise watch the nation drift into bankruptcy." These are wise and brave words, and we look forward with no little confidence to the time when the Trade Unions as a whole will act upon them.[1]

Now it is just such facts as these that the average politician and average Trade Union leader will not face, though they are fully aware of them. They will not bring them before the workers, for the workers would resent such unpalatable facts. Truth requires courage, but the Trade Union leaders are so often lacking in courage : hence they shirk this duty and are silent.

The present Government also has been lacking in courage, and in addition to their lack of courage they have exhibited an ignorance of the most elementary laws of economic science by its repeated and uncalled for interventions between the employers and the employed. It can claim, however, the credit of helping the working classes in the period of abnormal employment which set in soon after the close of the War. But these grants have been made on too gigantic a scale and assumed too often the nature of doles. These doles have made it possible, and in some cases profitable, for thousands of people—especially of women—to forego all active work and become idle and injurious pensioners of the State. These grants should have been better secured against abuses, for the abuses have been multitudinous ; a class of subsidised idlers has been created, and the moral tone of large sections of the workers has been distinctly lowered. It is to be hoped, however, that a wise statesmanship will provide against

[1] This lecture was delivered on May 11, 1919.

the continuance and recurrence of this evil, and supersede this uneconomic and demoralising system by a policy that will deal with periods of extraordinary and abnormal employment, such as prevails in the present, and the ordinary and normal periods of unemployment which recur from time to time. The solution of this difficulty will probably be found in some system of insurance, in which each industry will organise its own insurance in co-operation with all other industries under the supervision of and with a liberal subvention from the State.[1]

(ii) I have dealt so far with the duties of bodies of men in relation to the Commandment, " Thou shalt not steal." Let us now treat it more in reference to the individual. What then is theft in reference to the individual ? Theft consists in getting what belongs to others without giving the return they were permitted or led to expect. To give short measure or short weight, to supply an article, whether material or intellectual, of a worse quality than it was understood you would furnish, to use your superior knowledge or skill to pass off on others things they would not give the price you ask but for their trust in your integrity—all these are common cases of theft.

Certain practices condoned by trade are no better than commercial thefts. It is true, unhappily, that, once certain forms of fraud have won the sanction of trade usage, they are regarded as practically irreprehensible, and entail but little disgrace when exposed.

[1] See Lynden Macassey, *op. cit.* p. 258 sqq.

EIGHTH COMMANDMENT

But dishonesty does not become honest because it has hardened into custom, and truth and honour are not things that can be voted into or out of existence by a show of hands. Other forms of theft are adulteration, false labels affixed to goods, and lying advertisements. Sharp practice is essentially of the nature of theft, and the formation of rings, in order to create monopolies and raise prices above their fair and natural level, is a conspiracy to defraud, is theft on a large scale.

Again, the practice of fraud in rendering service for what we have been paid—and ninety-nine out of a hundred of us are in service, serving individual masters or corporations in Church or State—the practice of fraud in rendering such service is just as frequent as in the sale of material or other goods. We are paid for certain duties and the men—whether they are great dignitaries in Church or State, Army or Navy or Finance, leaders in great enterprises or Trade Unions, or simple hewers of wood or drawers of water—all these, so far as they withhold the full measure of service they have covenanted and are paid to give, are just as guilty of theft as the tradesman who gives short measure or the huckster who gives short weight.

Again, to make false returns to the Income-Tax officials is a very common form of fraud, but there is one of a darker hue. This is to live in this country for six months and spend the remaining months of the year in another and so legally escape the payment of Income Tax in both countries. The artful dodgers who can without breach of the law practise this species of theft may think it a clever one, but it is a mean one; for thereby a man takes advantage of all the help his country can give him, and deliberately evades every obligation in return.

(iii) We now come to the third division of our subject —*Christ's conception of property*. Hitherto we have dealt with the obligations of men one to another with regard to property mainly from the standpoint of the Old Testament. We have seen how most classes, if not all, amongst us come short of the standard of honesty therein required.

But there is a higher standard still—that set by our Lord. Christ's teaching runs counter to the glorification of private ownership of things material and the claim to do what one likes with one's own. Whilst others speak with bated breath of the magic of property, our Lord teaches implicitly and explicitly a certain fear of material riches. He instructs His followers not to look with respectful awe on wealth, but rather to regard it as a dangerous possession, and one that may at any moment prove hostile to its possessor. How hardly, He declares, can they who have riches enter into the kingdom of God. He repelled the rich young man because his heart was set on riches. Ye cannot, He declared, serve God and mammon. In the parable of Dives and Lazarus He paints in never-to-be-forgotten words the doom of the well-to-do, whose givings to those who have real claims upon them are, like those of Dives, but the crumbs that fall from the table of their self-indulgence. Christianity deprecates luxury and ostentation—nay more, condemns all lavish expenditure save in so far as it makes men fitter for the work committed to them : it insists on the duty of self-restraint in our expenditure : it forbids waste : it requires work of some kind from all without exception, and insists that the labourer is worthy of his hire and should receive it. If a man work not, neither should he eat, whether he be prince or peasant. It requires from every man according to his ability, hence there can be no limitation of output; and it would award to each according to his real need—hence there should be an equality of opportunity. Those who can work and do not, however exalted or lowly their rank may be, are simply parasites, living on the labour of others, and are therefore no better than pilferers from the common stock. Christianity does not, as we know, abolish private ownership, but it represents all such property as a trust, as a stewardship, and brings home to its owner a sense of definite responsibility for his rightful use of it. You may declare with regard to what you possess : Such and such a thing is mine own. And Christianity will reply : Yes, it is yours, but yours not to do what you like with ; but yours in this sense, that just from you and from none other, God will require an account of its use.

NINTH COMMANDMENT

'Thou shalt not bear false witness against thy neighbour.'—
Ex. xx. 13.

THIS Commandment refers first of all to false testimony given in courts of justice. On this question further directions are given in xxiii. 2, 3, where we read, " Thou shalt not follow a multitude to do evil ; neither shalt thou bear witness by turning aside after a multitude to do evil, neither shalt thou favour a poor man in his cause." If we translate the thought here and not the words, we shall discover that the counsel given is in the highest degree just and equitable. First, we are bidden not to accommodate our conduct to that of the majority when they are in the wrong; secondly, we are not to accommodate our witness to what the majority wrongly desire. In these two cases we are to take the side of right, however many they be that are against us. There is only one course for a just man to adopt, and that is to do the truth and bear witness to the truth, though all others be opposed to him therein. Having so enunciated the duty of the just man when confronting an unscrupulous and powerful majority, the lawgiver next lays down his duty when the interests of the poor man are at stake. " Neither shalt thou favour a poor man in his cause." Here the witness is not to act from any sentimental pity or false sympathy. The testimony given is to be given wholly irrespective of the man's social or financial position. The question of his position or poverty is not to obscure the issue : only the truth and justice of the case are to be considered and witness given accordingly. These were the laws laid down to guide men when giving testimony in Jewish courts some hundreds of years before the Christian era.

But it is not our duty here to dwell on the crime of bearing false witness in courts of justice. We are all aware of the guilt that attaches to the false witness that brings condemnation on the innocent and screens the guilty from the penalties that are their due. Most of us happily have nothing to do with courts of justice, and yet we are not, therefore, exempt from the scope of this Commandment. For this Commandment bears on the whole life of man. It prohibits slander, calumny, defamation, and misrepresentation of every kind. Yet it is not a prohibition of lying generally, but of a specific kind of lying—namely, false witness against our neighbour, not only in courts of justice, but in private life and ordinary social intercourse.

Lying is one of the worst sins of which men can be guilty. Crimes of passion and violence, crimes against the State or against property may be more hurtful in their immediate results to the body politic and so be visited with severer penalties, but such crimes do not necessarily involve half the guilt and moral debasement that attach inevitably to lying. Lying often springs from malice ; it is generally the refuge of the coward, and moral cowardice is worse than other vices, since without moral courage hardly any virtue or Christian grace is possible.

A heroic effort of the will is necessary when we are tempted to falsehood by our vanities, by our fears, by our artificial and often debasing codes of honour, or by the shame we have incurred through our own conscious wrong-doing.

The importance of a nation being true to its covenants in its international relations cannot be exaggerated. It has been well said by an historian of the last century, that " English valour and English intelligence have done less to extend and to preserve our Oriental Empire than English veracity. . . . No oath which superstition can devise, no hostage however precious, inspires a hundredth part of the confidence which is inspired by the " yea, yea " and the " nay, nay " of the British Envoy." [1]

But let us return to the specific form of lying condemned by the Commandment. As we have already observed, this condemnation applies first to false witness given in courts of justice. But there is a more important tribunal than that of our courts of justice to which this Commandment extends, and that is the tribunal of public opinion, a court of which every man is a member whether he will or no, and the character of which, consciously or unconsciously, he is influencing

[1] Macaulay, *Essay on Clive.*

for good or evil. Men are continually pronouncing judgments on each other: and public opinion is the aggregate of such individual judgments. Such judgments create the moral atmosphere in which we live— our moral environment. A sound public opinion is therefore of supreme importance for the moral life of every individual man; for none can escape being influenced by it. Though vague and impalpable, it is beyond all question real.

The value of the court of public opinion depends, therefore, on the individuals which compose it. But the court of public opinion is not a thing one and indivisible. It has many divisions—political, religious, and social, and all these cut athwart each other. And within these divisions there are various subdivisions. Most of us belong to some party or other in State or Church. So far as a party is a confederation of individuals, bound together with the common object of promoting needful reforms in Church or State, party is a good thing. But when the spirit of party degenerates, as it generally does, into partisanship, it becomes a curse; for partisanship sets party before the welfare of the State, or exalts some religious doctrine, some tradition of the elders, or some piece of ritual, above truth itself. The man who surrenders himself to party spirit or party strife cannot fail to break the Commandment alike by what he says and what he leaves unsaid. For this spirit prevents men from seeing what is good in their opponents, while it exaggerates what is evil. It does not set right and truth in the first place, but party interest, and in so doing bears false witness before the tribunal of public opinion. This party spirit finds full expression in the public press. It is the recognised office of not a small section of the religious and political press to vilify and traduce the leaders of the parties opposed to it. They think that they are doing God service in blasting the reputation of their opponents. In fact, the zealots of all parties seem to make a practice of lying for the sake of what they call the truth.

Since then, whether we will or no, we are all raising or debasing the moral tone of public opinion, this consideration brings home to us the importance of this Commandment. This Commandment is in itself a recognition of the immeasurable influence of the moral judgments which men are pronouncing every day upon each other.

Let us now consider some of the various breaches of this Commandment, of which as members of a society we are, alas! so frequently guilty. Many words are required to define these breaches of the ninth Commandment—such as slander, backbiting, calumny, defamation, detraction.

Slander consists in saying maliciously, whether in public or private, things which tend to disparage a man's character or attainments, to lessen his reputation, or to rob him of his good name. When the slander is done in secret it is specifically called *backbiting*. Now in slander and backbiting the things in themselves may be true or false. What constitutes such things—slander

NINTH COMMANDMENT

and backbiting—is not their falsity, but the malicious motive with which they are spoken; and where malice against a neighbour exists, a man can never bear true witness regarding him. He that easily credits a slander shares in some degree in the guilt of its inventor, and he that retails it becomes a partner in guilt. If it is criminal to coin bad money, it is no less criminal to pass it as current coin of the realm.

But if the things we say of our neighbour are false, and we know them to be false, then we are guilty of *calumny*. The calumniator is the forger or propagator of a false report against another, and, like the slanderer, aims at doing him an injury.

Again, if the things we say in public against our neighbour are true, and we know them to be true, they constitute, nevertheless, what is called *defamation*, if they are uttered with a malicious design. The aim of defamation is malicious: its end is not to reform but to destroy. It is wrong to relate to the discredit of others that which is true, if it is not our duty to do so; and if it is our duty, we are sinning against our neighbour if we make the worst of it, or aggravate the mischief its recital may produce.

Another breach of this Commandment comes under the term *detraction*. Detraction is that method of depreciating another in the estimation of individuals or the public, which with seeming honesty accepts the current account of his actions, but interprets them in such a way as to preclude any favourable inferences as to his ability or character. It may even introduce its slanderous depreciation of its victim with some crafty preface of commendation, in order finally with its faint praise to make his damnation surer.

The deepest wounds may be inflicted by this smooth and subtle type of slander. In fact, its most malicious and effective method is to insinuate something and yet to say nothing definitely : to create in unwary folk a belief that the something insinuated is a thing very bad, though in point of fact it may be morally indifferent or even non-existent.

There is perhaps no Commandment in the Decalogue —certainly none in the second table—so frequently broken by us as that with which we are dealing. The Christian conscience is very lax as regards this Commandment. To speak evil of others is one of the commonest sins of society : it forms a large factor of conversation in most companies. In every social centre there are sure to be certain individuals that suffer from moral astigmatism, who can see nothing in the wise man but his follies, nothing in the learned man but his errors, and nothing in the good man but his sins and shortcomings. And yet these folk profess to be conscientious ; but their conscience is so busily engaged in criticising the conduct and character of their neighbours that they have no leisure for taking account of their own.

To keep conversation going, stories are frequently retailed to a neighbour's hurt which are false or exaggerated or susceptible of an innocent explanation. Every centre of gossip is a workshop of scandal, where

NINTH COMMANDMENT

the virulence of the evil varies directly with the character of the company; and the conversation is often accounted dull and flat when it lacks the piquancy of anecdotes bristling with personalities, and that of no kindly sort. And thus, not only through malicious and wilful lying, but through idle and hurtful gossip retailed in sheer wantonness or for the sake of pastime, confidence is destroyed, reputations are ruined, friendships are wrecked, and the peace of homes broken up.

And yet to take away a good name is to take away the most valued possession of the upright man, the last comfort and stay of the unfortunate. The vice of slander is one of the most execrable of all the vices. It is allied to murder and poisoning, save that these affect only the physical life, whereas the effect of slander is to destroy the moral and spiritual life. This evil side of slander has been finely described by Shakespeare in the words:

"Who steals my purse steals trash; 'tis something, nothing;
'T was mine, 'tis his, and has been slave to thousands;
But he that filches from me my good name
Robs me of that which not enriches him,
And makes me poor indeed."

Besides the incurable mischiefs wrought by slander there is another circumstance to which I have just referred that characterises its venomous activities. It is true, indeed, that it is not infrequently begotten of malice and born of envy, and finds its reward in the ruin it has wrought, but it is likewise true that it often acts without provocation, and pursues its deadly work without any thought of reward except the passing gratification of the moment.

The ancient lawgiver in Lev. xix. 16 represents, perhaps with unconscious humour, the slanderer[1] as a pedlar on his rounds amongst the people, whose stock-in-trade consists of the malicious anecdotes which he gathers from one group of customers and retails to another.

In this connection we may note that in the ancient Assyrian language and in at least two forms of the Aramaic—the latter language being that which was spoken by our Lord—the ordinary phrase for the slanderer is "one who eats up another man piecemeal"—that is, eats up his character and destroys it. A similar phrase is found in Arabic.

It is significant also that even the word devil means philologically "the slanderer," being derived from the Greek word διάβολος. The devil is thus the slanderer *par excellence*, and so far as men slander their brethren they betray a nature akin to his.

Slander, then, being so evil a thing and so widespread, it is our duty to be on our guard against it. First, we should be careful to form just judgments on others before we say anything to their discredit. And in framing such judgments we should not strain a man's words to his disadvantage, nor draw conclusions from any unfortunate expression that may have fallen from his lips in some passing heat or some unguarded moment, nor attribute his actions to the worst motive

[1] In Hebrew, רכיל.

they could conceivably bear. In any case we should give him the benefit of the fairest construction that can be put upon his conduct.

Secondly, we should beware of thoughtlessly circulating injurious rumours regarding others, which somebody has related to us. For thoughtlessness is criminal when it gives currency to falsehood.

Again, we should not delight in hearing evil of others. Such a delight is symptomatic of spiritual disease. It behoves us, then, to deal with this evil at its source. The symptom often, though far from always, shows that we are actually hating our neighbour, or on the verge of doing so. Therefore it is a matter of life and death to recover the right attitude towards him. That is, we are to love our neighbour as ourselves : treat him as we would wish ourselves to be treated in similar circumstances : do unto him as we would that he should do unto us. In that case we shall not delight in hearing evil of him, whatever else we may do. Hence we should give no countenance to busybodies, to tattlers and tale-bearers, to those who trade in slander and traffic in calumny and dishonour, to the moral pests of the secular and religious press, of society and the body politic.

But it may seem that, according to the conclusions we have arrived at, we are all but forbidden to express any judgment at all on others. But this is by no means the case. There are times when a man should have the truth told either to him or about him. When the evidence of a man's inefficiency in his particular work is undeniable and we are called to give our judgment thereon, it is our duty to speak out; or again, when a man's wrong-doing is beyond question, and it is necessary to defend those who are likely to be injured by his example, it is nothing less than criminal to be silent. It is our duty to deal out to vice the infamy it deserves, to unmask hypocrisy and to hold up to public execration, oppression and wrong. If such evils were not denounced, vice would march unrebuked and in triumph along all the ways of men, and lying, deceit and profligacy would have nothing to apprehend from the tribunal of public opinion.

But to tell the truth about others is one of the hardest things in the world, and especially when we stand in some personal relation with the man on whom we are proposing to sit in judgment. Now, if we have wronged a man, we are almost certain to do him further wrong if we sit in judgment upon him. An ancient Roman historian has finely observed that it is natural to hate the man we have wronged. And if, in addition to wronging the man we hate him to boot, it is practically impossible for us to speak justly or truly regarding him. Here silence is obligatory till hatred is banished and the wrong repented of. If, instead of having wronged a man, we have been wronged by him, the resentment we feel makes it very difficult to judge his conduct dispassionately and with equity.

In the New Testament the misuse of the tongue is held up to the severest reprobation. St. James writes (iii. 8), "The tongue can no man tame; it is a restless evil: it is full of deadly poison." Notwithstanding, this

NINTH COMMANDMENT

unruly member, he maintains, can and must be subdued (i. 26): "If any man thinketh he is religious while he bridleth not his tongue . . . that man's religion is vain."

St. Paul classes slanderers and revilers with fornicators and murderers (Rom. i. 29, 30), and declares that they shall not inherit the kingdom of God (1 Cor. vi. 10). On the other hand, St. James beatifies the goodness of him who offends not with his tongue : " If any man offend not in word, the same is a perfect man " (Jas. iii. 2).

A permanent significance attaches to the words we utter, because that, as a rule, out of the fulness of the heart the mouth speaketh. Our Lord declares : "For every idle word that men shall speak, they shall give account thereof in the day of judgment" (Matt. xii. 36). Not only, then, for the deeds done in the body, but for the words spoken shall men be brought into judgment. As for words uttered heedlessly in the heat of passion, or spoken deliberately in the spirit of envy, hatred, malice, covetousness or lewdness, we shall learn one day what hopes these words have blasted, what evil passions they have kindled, and to what sin and recklessness and despair they have driven the souls of men.

On the other hand, words can minister to the spiritual well-being of man : they can bring relief to the repentant, strength to the faint-hearted : they can bind up the broken in spirit, and bring home to despairing souls the quickening power of the Spirit. "By thy words," our Lord declares, "thou shalt be justified, and by thy words thou shalt be condemned."

TENTH COMMANDMENT

" Thou shalt not covet [thy neighbour's house, thou shalt not covet thy neighbour's wife, nor his manservant, nor his maidservant, nor his ox, nor his ass, nor anything that is thy neighbour's]."[1]—Ex. xx. 17.

IN dealing with this subject I propose to consider this law under three heads. (i) As directed against covetousness in the individual. (ii) As directed against covetousness in bodies of individuals, such as corporations or trade unions within the State. (iii) As directed against covetousness in the relations of one State to another.

I begin with the individual, seeing that reforms in society and in law within the State as well as reforms in international relations must be preceded by reforms in the individual. Religion must work on the individual and alter the raw material of which society is composed.

(i) *As directed against covetousness in the individual.* First of all, we remark that this Commandment does not refer to any new department of human conduct nor to any new relationship of society beyond those dealt with in the first nine Commandments. The first nine Commandments have dealt with man's duty to God, with the keeping of the Sabbath, with parental authority, and the rights of the individual to his property in his own

[1] See p. xlvii sq. for the original form of this Commandment.

TENTH COMMANDMENT

life, in his wife, in his material possessions and in his good name. To these different provinces of duty the tenth Commandment makes no addition whatever. So far as it specifies one's neighbour's wife, it is a repetition of the seventh; so far as it specifies one's neighbour's house, his menservants and maidservants, it overlaps the eighth; while in its concluding phrase ("nor anything that is his") it is at best only a vague reinforcement of the sixth and ninth, which maintain a man's right to his life and his good name. But these clauses may be safely regarded as a later addition. The original Commandment was no doubt simply: "Thou shalt not covet."[1]

Now to have been a blameless member of the religious commonwealth of Israel would have been no very difficult matter but for this tenth Commandment. Every Israelite who observed the *letter* of the first nine Commandments, being outwardly faithful to the religious, moral and civil obligations therein enforced, could have justly declared: All these have I kept from my youth up, and walked in all the ordinances of the Law blameless. The standard set being a low one—namely, conformity to certain negative outward rules, self-complacency and self-satisfaction would have been inevitable—but for this tenth Commandment. Though, as we have already stated, this Commandment adds no fresh province to the area covered by the preceding Commandments, nevertheless, since it passes from the letter to the spirit, it has in its short compass

[1] See Introduction, pp. xlvii–xlviii.

more than doubled the claims of the entire Decalogue; for it has brought within its purview the inner as well as the outer life, the hidden desire as well as the overt act, every thought and intent of man's heart as well as all his outward conduct. In the preceding Commandments of the second table we are forbidden to get for ourselves by illegitimate means the property of our neighbour, but in this Commandment we are forbidden even to covet or desire it wrongly.

That our Lord reinterpreted the Ten Commandments, we cannot but infer from the Sermon on the Mount. This reinterpretation He made by subjecting the external precept of the law to the principle that all sinful conduct has its root in sinful desire—the very principle that St. Paul finds in the tenth Commandment. Hence sinful desires, even though they may not issue in sinful acts, come in for the same condemnation as the acts themselves. "Ye have heard," our Lord declares, "that it was said ... Thou shalt not commit adultery; but I say unto you that every one which looketh on a woman to lust after her hath committed adultery with her in his heart," and in similar manner He reinterprets the sixth Commandment, "Thou shalt not kill."

Even the first and second Commandments can be reinterpreted from this standpoint. For if covetousness is opposed to our duty to our neighbour, it is still more opposed to our duty to God. This fact was recognised in Judaism before the advent of Christianity. Thus in an ancient Jewish book,[1] written in the second

[1] Test. Judah xviii. 2, xix. 1.

TENTH COMMANDMENT

century B.C., we read, "Beware, therefore, my children, of . . . covetousness [1] . . . coveteousness leadeth to idolatry." But the connection of covetousness and idolatry is still closer; for, according to St. Paul (Col. iii. 5), "covetousness is idolatry." That is, the covetous man sets up another object of worship than God, and thus becomes an idolater. He surrenders his soul to the lust of getting, and to greed. If the covetous man is also religious, then he strives to serve God and mammon—a task which none can achieve.

For such a man there is no freedom, no peace; for there can be no greater plague than to be always baited by the importunities of growing desires and lusts, which are at war with the religious ideals to which the unhappy man would fain hold fast. The universal bearing, therefore, of this Commandment on man's duty both to God and man is thus clear when reinterpreted from the New Testament standpoint. The covetous man is an idolater as regards God, and a transgressor in manifold ways as regards man.

Now it is remarkable what an important part this Commandment played in the spiritual history of St. Paul. As touching the righteousness which is in the law, St. Paul declares himself blameless (Phil. iii. 6); and we may take this statement as literally true in regard to the first nine Commandments. But in his Epistle to the Romans, St. Paul confesses that there was one Commandment which convicted him of sin before God, namely, "Thou shalt not covet": that through this

[1] φιλαργυρία.

Commandment he had first learnt the sinfulness of covetous or wrong desire, and he proceeds to say that the more he struggled against this sinful desire, the more conscious he became of his powerlessness to overcome it, till his troubled soul, torn in its conflict with the evil thoughts it could not expel, and the evil passions it could not dislodge, cried out in the extremity of its despair, "Who shall deliver me from the body of this death?"

Thus, though he was able to prevent his evil desires from realising themselves in outward acts of hatred, or impurity or greed, or slander, he was powerless to check, and still more powerless to destroy, the growing fount of such lawless desire within him or to free himself from inward longings after the sins in which he refused to indulge outwardly. And so for him there was no peace. His personality was rent in twain.

In this way the Law, which made nothing perfect and disclosed to man his inward sinfulness, however righteous he might outwardly appear, served as a schoolmaster to bring him to Christ. In Christ the Apostle found the power of a new and endless life. His nature was regenerated in Christ, being transformed from within; his heart was made the habitation of God's Spirit, and hence arose the new power of loving God and goodness for themselves. From the region of law he had ascended into that of love. And so the Apostle closes this psychological account of his conversion with the words: "I thank God through Jesus Christ our Lord."

In Christian conversion we have the supreme realisation of what psychologists call the expulsive power of a new affection. Love of Christ is the greatest of all the affections, and delivers man from the thraldom of all lesser desires.

The last of the ten Commandments, "Thou shalt not covet," reaches forth when thus interpreted to the characteristic precept of the New Testament, "Thou shalt love thy neighbour as thyself." The command, "Thou shalt not covet," cannot be fulfilled without it. This requires at all events that we should deal as fairly and equitably with our neighbour as we would that he should deal with us. If we fulfil this precept we shall not covet what is our neighbour's. But if we do not love our neighbour, we cannot fulfil the law. By the strongest effort of the will apart from love, we are not capable even of abstaining from doing wrong to our neighbour. Can any man who loves not his neighbour and yet would keep the law, maintain that never by silence, or gesture, or tone, or look, or word had he done anything to injure his neighbour? In fact, in order to fulfil the requirements of the law we must rise into a region above law, namely, into that of love; for love is infinitely more than law: it creates law as one of its minor expressions, and makes its fulfilment possible. Hence St. Paul says: "Love worketh no ill to his neighbour: therefore love is the fulfilling of the law." Seeing, then, that a man is powerless to keep the law without rising into the region of love to his neighbour, it is no less true that he cannot love his neighbour unless he rises higher still. In God alone can we truly meet and appreciate and love our neighbour. Only in God can we come to love our neighbour as ourselves.

But there are some of our neighbours, most people will rejoin, who are not only unlovable but are distinctly objectionable and even detestable. Now it is quite true that no man is unobjectionable in all respects, that all men are unlovable in some respects, and that some men are detestable in most respects. Notwithstanding the Commandment holds good : " Thou shalt love thy neighbour as thyself." Hence the love here enjoined is not based on our neighbour's good qualities ; for to the outward eye he may have none at all. We cannot love many a man for what he appears to be or actually is at present, but we are bound notwithstanding to love him for what he can become and potentially is, as a child of God. The possibilities of indefinite goodness are within the reach of every child of man ; because that he also is a child of God. Hence, however unworthy our neighbour may be, we are to act towards him in such a way as to encourage and strengthen the elements of goodness in him and to discourage and eliminate the elements of evil. Therefore, on the one hand, it may be our duty to give him our entire sympathy and admiration while he marches far ahead of us in the way of righteousness ; or, on the other hand, it may be just as clearly our duty to withstand him to the face and administer in unmistakable terms the rebuke that befits his unchristian conduct. And herein we are to do unto him as we would that he should do unto us. This is the golden rule, and to observe this rule is in a real sense to love our neighbour as ourselves.

Thus the negative and rugged prohibitions of the

TENTH COMMANDMENT

Ten Commandments prepare the way for and find their completion in the gracious and positive legislation of the Sermon on the Mount.

(ii) But the law is directed not only against the covetousness of individuals, but also against the covetousness of any group or combination of individuals within the State.

These combinations may consist of capitalists or workers, of employers or employed. With the former class I am not concerned here further than to remark that the general feeling of society is now directed against all undue exactions, all covetous practices on the part of the employers, and all exploitation of the workers by them. It has taken generations to bring about this revolution in the public mind, but, having come, this revolution has come to stay. Unscrupulous capitalists and unconscionable employers have at last turned public opinion against themselves—at all events in England. In other words, the trend of public opinion in England is making for righteousness and against covetousness so far as these classes are concerned. Let us now turn from the employers to the employed. There are two organisations of workers who have undertaken to solve the labour problem of the present day. These are the Socialists and the Syndicalists. In my lecture on the eighth Commandment I dealt briefly with this question, but it calls for some further consideration. The public generally have not learnt to distinguish the legitimate Socialist from the Syndicalist. The latter has no claim to the designation Socialist in any sense.

I wish you to observe that I here use Socialist in its true and earlier sense, as one who is concerned for the well-being of the nation as a whole and works towards this end by constitutional means.

The Socialists are reformers working on legitimate lines, and as such they send their representatives to Parliament. They are or should be in the main constructive. Their aim is to build up a new nation. They seek by legislation to reform society and to emancipate the State from the control of narrow individual groups.

Hence they seek to bring under the control of the people in its corporate capacity, that is, the State, the natural wealth of the country and the means of production, and to do this, not by confiscating the property of the present owners of such property, but by indemnifying them to the full. In other words, they seek to nationalise this property in the interests of the nation. The true Socialist, therefore, is a constructive reformer, working on constitutional lines, and preoccupied with the interests of the nation as a whole. The main aim he sets before him, therefore, is a political good, that is, a good affecting the whole nation, not merely an economic good affecting only his own class or craft or his own pocket. So far as he is true to this aim and pursues it by equitable means he is not guilty of a breach of the tenth Commandment. But whether the nationalisation of land and the means of production is the best method for attaining the end in view is in the highest degree doubtful—in fact, our recent experience of government control of large industries has forced multitudes, whose sympathies and speculations had led them hitherto in this direction, to abandon such a policy and to regard the nationalisation of industries, not as a remedy, but as a further intensification of our industrial evils. But this practical question does not concern us here, since our subject deals, not with practical politics, but with principles.

So much for the true Socialists. Let us now turn to the Syndicalists and consider in what respects they differ from Socialists properly so called. The Syndicalist movement originated with the more impatient, rapacious and fanatical Socialists, to whom constitutional methods seemed slow and ineffective. Discarding these methods as futile, they have proclaimed the bankruptcy of political Socialism, they have entered the field against the leaders of such legitimate Socialism and trade unionism, and frankly avowed their own methods to be revolutionary. Some revolutionaries have high ideals, leading to the well-being of the nation, but to no such ideal can the Syndicalists lay claim. Their interests are not political but economic. They are working, not for the advantage of the nation, but of certain groups within the nation. In short, they are mainly selfish. Their object is to get into their own hands the entire industries in which they are engaged, and to get them by dishonest means. They expect to achieve this end by limitation of output and constant strikes, and where these fail, by violence and sabotage. Strikes in the hands of the earlier Socialists were undertaken to secure better wages and better conditions of labour and distribution, and when such objects were secured, these Socialists felt themselves morally bound to observe the covenants by which they had secured them. But the Syndicalists acknowledge no moral obligations, they teach that such covenants are not binding, they declare them to be nothing better than scraps of paper. In fact, the General Confederation of Labour in France has deliberately claimed for itself the right of breaking any covenant it makes and of breaking it at any time it may choose. The frequent breaches of contract and the quick succession of wholly unjustifiable strikes in England during the last few years [1] show clearly that the poison of Syndicalism has affected the entire Socialist movement, and indeed most of the Trade Unions in this country. This is a tragic fact, and most of the Labour members have come to recognise the suicidal character of such a policy and are seeking to bring about co-operation between the employers and the employed. But the Syndicalist minorities, disowning every claim of duty and conscience, have shamelessly abandoned themselves to the lust of an unlimited covetousness as the guiding principle of their conduct. Between them and all honest men there is a great gulf fixed. They are ready to go to any length to gratify their greed, and are carrying into effect the words of the labourers in the Parable of the Vineyard : " Here is the heir : come, let us kill him, that the inheritance may be ours." This monstrous and infamous greed has robbed these workmen of all

[1] Preached in June 15, 1919.

true sympathy for their fellow-workmen in other industries.

Hence to promote their own material interests they are ready, as the miners were recently, to cripple every other trade interest in the country to subserve their own interests : and to increase their dishonest gains the most thoroughgoing Syndicalists are prepared to sacrifice their country itself. Syndicalism, therefore, is not merely an offence against religion and morals, it is a criminal movement pure and simple, which draws its inspiration, not from heaven, but from the pit.

There will, therefore, be no industrial peace within the nation till the various industrial organisations come to be guided, not by covetousness, but by a sense of equity and truth and honour ; till they acknowledge that not selfishness but love is lord of all, and, learning that love worketh no ill to its neighbour, discover for themselves that love is the fulfilling of the law and so come to do unto others as they would that they should do unto them. Whilst, therefore, we sympathise heartily with every attempt to improve man's physical surroundings, knowing as we do that physical misery tends to degrade and brutalise, we cannot, notwithstanding, trust to mere legislation or to any purely material improvements for the regeneration of man. For this there is needed a change in man himself, the creation within him of a right spirit, and this new life in Christ is to be had, not at some far distant time or in some other and happier environment, but—here and now by every heart that earnestly seeks to win it. "Seek ye first the kingdom of God and His righteousness, and all things else shall be added unto you."

(iii) Again the Commandment is directed against the spirit of covetousness in the relations of one State to another. Now what is the State as distinct from the Nation? For the State and Nation are, of course, distinct. The State is the corporate expression of the nation's character. It is the body politic, but not a body without a soul. It is not a fortuitous aggregate of individuals and families welded together mainly by material interests and owning no higher affinities. So long as the people exist in this barbarous condition, the State has not as yet won a moral personality, and so cannot be treated as a nation, but must during this period of its nonage be entrusted to some mandatory power till it attains its moral and political majority. It is on this principle that the authority of civilised nations over savage and undeveloped races can be justified. And it is on this principle that every civilised nation has a personality of its own, that no nation can disclaim in the present its responsibility for its own evil deeds in the past, no matter what change of government it may have undergone in the interval. A nation is linked together not by its fears and selfishness, but by its heritage of a common language, by a common ancestry, by common laws and literature, by the pride and glory of its traditions, and by the character it has impressed on the history of its time. Since the State, then, is the corporate expression of a nation's character, its task is to express the common conscience of the

TENTH COMMANDMENT

nation in its laws, and, where needful, to use the strong arm of the nation to enforce them. The more highly developed a nation is, the more fully will its higher aspirations find expression in its laws. The idea that moral convictions and ideals belong only to the individual members of the nation, and that only self-interest should determine the nation's policy, is a wicked doctrine, and can find no justification either in man's nature or in the history of the world. Here, as well as in relation to the individual, the Commandment standeth sure : " Thou shalt not covet." Between State and State as between individual and individual, the right and the true are of eternal obligation. No majority of individuals or of nations has voted these verities into being, and none can vote them out of it. And yet covetousness and not justice and equity has, with some exceptions, been the guiding principle of all governments from time immemorial down to the present day, and this covetousness has hardly ever failed to lead to aggression and crime.

Is it, then, a matter for wonder that in God's world the history of every great empire since the world began has closed in sheer tragedy ? Since history is a record of Divine judgment on the nations, then clear beyond measure is the lesson we are to read from the fall of ancient Nineveh and Babylon, of Tyre and Carthage, of mighty Rome, holding all the kingdoms of the earth in fee, of Spain supreme in the Old World and the New, of imperial France, which all but succeeded in making the nations of the entire earth its thralls, nay more, and from the fall but yesterday of Russia, of Germany and Austria, swollen with the insolence and blindness that centuries of unchastened covetousness and triumphant wrong-doing alone could breed. Surely God's doom on covetous nations is writ so large and clear that even he that runneth may read.

Since, then, each nation is forbidden to covet what belongs to its neighbours, it is clearly the Divine will that all the nations should regard themselves as being families in the great Commonwealth of God, wherein the strong are not to enrich themselves at the expense of the weak, but to protect them from wrong and injustice, wherein the civilised and cultured are not to exploit the less cultured for their own advantage, but to train them to higher forms of intellectual and moral life.

But such noble and lofty ideals can be realised neither by Courts of arbitration nor elaborate treaties even though sealed and ratified by all the great Powers of the world, nor brought about by the obvious advantages of commerce and civilisation, nor even by the dread lessons of the greatest and cruellest of wars in all human experience. This end cannot be achieved till the nations recognise that they are members of a body so organised, physically and spiritually, that, if one member suffers, all the members must suffer with it, and, if one member rejoices, all the members rejoice with it. Hence no nation can really fulfil its true destiny by advancing its wealth or power or culture at its neighbour's expense, but only by doing to its neighbours as it would that they should do unto it.

INDEXES

I.—INDEX OF SUBJECTS

Adonai = " Lord," reverent use of, as synonym for Yahweh, 3.

Adoration, absolute worship, addressed to God, 55 n.

Adultery, 212–228 (see Commandment VII.); extended by our Lord to cover all impurity, and to include thought as well as deed, 215.

Alcohol, abuse of, 191 ; legitimate use of, 191, 192 ; traffic in, 191, 192 ; prohibition not best means of reform of, but State Purchase, limitation of hours, etc., 192.

Anger, in danger of being a breach of Commandment VI., 200–207 ; need of removing personal element in, by prayer and appreciation, 204 ; for fear of it becoming hatred, 204–205 (see Forgiveness); moral value of, 205. See Hatred, Indignation, Wrath.

Aniconic worship. See Commandment II.

Anthropomorphism, crude, of second conception of Sabbath, 115, 116.

Aristeas, Letter of, xvi.

Art, destruction of, by Jewish fanaticism, 29 ; realistic, danger of, in religion, 44–48 ; arouses sensuous and morbid feelings to exclusion of conscience and understanding, 45.

Asherim, 27.

Asylum, right of, 189. See Sanctuary.

Augustine, division of Commandments into groups of three and seven by, 17 n. See Commandments, numbering of.

Authority of parent transcends that of ruler, 176.

Babylonian parallel to Decalogue, xxv, lii ; order of Commandments in, xxv, xxvi, notes.

Backbiting = secret slander, 250. See Slander.

Basil the Great, wrongly appealed to in support of reverence to images, 48 ; Ep. ccclx. of, spurious, 49 ; formula of, as usually cited, taken out of its context, 49, 49 n. See Image Worship.

Bethel, sanctuary at, 22, 23.

Blood, avenging of, a primitive form of justice, mitigated by provision of sanctuaries and cities of refuge, 186–188 ; generally superseded as between individuals, but still prevalent as between nations, 187.

Book of Covenant. See Covenant.

Book of Sports, 150. See Lord's Day.

Brazen Serpent, worship of, 25, 51. See Commandment II.

Bulls, golden, symbolic of Yahweh, 22–24 ; apparently not objected to by Micaiah, Elijah,

INDEXES

Elisha (or Amos ?), 23 n., 24, 24 n.; but denounced by Hosea, 25.

Cæsar, ensigns of, excluded from Jerusalem by Jews, 28.
Calumny, a deliberate false slander, 247, 251. See Slander.
Candour, duty of, 101. See Outspokenness.
Canonical Law, iniquitous immunity of clergy under, 188, 189.
Capital punishment, necessity of, 197.
Capitalism, 265. See Communism, Socialism.
Caroline Books, the, forbid image worship, 61, 62 n.
Catacombs, discovery of, 41 n.; not altogether authentic memorials (as restored by Furius Philocalus) of fourth cent. A.D., 41 n.; no image or crucifix found in, 41, 42; Christ represented in, only as Good Shepherd, or crowned with thorns, 42.
Catechisms, of Luther, Justus Jonas, English Church, 71; of Roman Church, 72-74. See Commandment II.
Chemosh, god of Moab, 3, 4 n., 5, 22.
Christian Church, early, opposition of to idolatry, 36-40 (see Image Worship); worship of, 142-144. See Eucharist.
Christian view of property as stewardship, 245.
Cities of refuge, 187, 188.
Clergy, immunity of. See Canonical Law.
Codes, various, of Decalogue, 1, 2. See Decalogue.
Commandment I., 1-13; consistent with polytheistic belief, but ultimately interpreted only in monotheistic sense, 2-9, 14 (see Monotheism); given a positive content, as duty of loving God, by Deut $6^{4, 5}$, 10.

Commandment II., 14-88; (a) *textual questions concerning*, Ex. and Deut. agree in, ix; ungrammatical Hebrew in, Deuteronomic phrases in, marginal gloss of fifth cent. B.C. incorporated in text of D, and then of Ex. of, ix, xi, xxxv-xxxix; form of, in eighth cent. B.C., xli, xliv.

(b) *teaching of*, forbids worship of God through iconic means, as images; or aniconic means, as unfigured symbols, sacred stones, pillars, trees, 19; not at first considered as forbidding golden bulls, 22-25 (see Bulls); nor brazen serpent, 25, 25 n.; later extended to cover unworthy conceptions of God, 35.

(c) *in Christian Church*, observed by Early Church, 36-40; later explained away by the Eastern and Western Churches, 68-70; omitted by the Western Church, 70, 71; restored by Council of Trent, A.D. 1566, 69, 71; omitted generally by Roman Church since, 72-75; in English Church at first transferred to end of Commandments, later omitted by Peckham, etc., A.D. 1281, as by Luther, 70, 71; restored by English Church in A.D. 1552, 71; Eastern Church limits reference to statues, 56. See Image Worship.

Commandment III., 89-109; addition to, xlv; earlier than 750 B.C., lxii n.; parallel to, in Egyptian Book of Dead, li; connected with Commandments I. and II., 89; forbids false oath, but also implies prohibition of all falsehood, 89-109; meaning of " in vain," 89 n.

Commandment IV., 110-172; two distinct versions of, in Ex 20 and Deut 5, x, xxxix, xl, 110-117; with distinct con-

INDEXES

ceptions of Sabbath, 111 (*see* Sabbath); extrusion of ancient D clause (D 5^{14}), x, xxxix, xl; interpolation of Ex 20^{11}, x, xviii, 113; form of, in eighth cent. B.C., xi, xl; original brief form of, xlv–xlvii. *See* Lord's Day, Sabbath, Sunday.

Commandment V., 173–184; Babylonian parallel to, xxv *n.*; Deuteronomic additions in, xxxv; parallels to, in Book of Covenant, lix; importance of (*see* Family Life, Parents); positive form of, unique in Decalogue, 173, 174.

Commandment VI., 185–211; *ground of*—for State—loss of property in life of citizen, 194, 195; for religion—inherent dignity of man, made in image of God, 195, 196 (*see* Life); *inadequacy of*, as external law only, 199, 200; expanded by Jewish elders to cover cases of murder and contemptuous language, 201, 203; by our Lord to cover spirit and temper from which such actions spring, 203; *order of*, placed after VII. in many authorities, and three times in N.T., 15 (*see* Commandments, order of); *origin of*, primitive (*see* Blood); avenging of, 186; *scope of*, covers cases of criminal neglect leading to loss of life or harmful conditions, *e.g.* vicious bull, dangerous buildings, wrongful liquor traffic, slums, congested populations, excessive hours or hurtful conditions of toil, 190–193. *See* Capital Punishment, Murder.

Commandment VII., 212–228; originally very limited in reference to outward act only and to unfaithfulness in married women only, 212, 213 (*see* Unfaithfulness); and so regarded not so much the sin against purity as that against property, 213; Babylonian and Egyptian parallels to, xxvi, li. *See* Adultery, Fornication, Impurity, Vices; *also* Commandments, Order of.

Commandment VIII., 229–245; Babylonian and Egyptian parallels to, xxvi, lii; concerned with property. *See* Property.

Commandment IX., 246–257; Babylonian and Egyptian parallels to, xxvi, lii; parallel in Book of Covenant, lix; D has primary form 'vain,' Ex. secondary, 'false,' xxxv; forbids lying against neighbour in court, and also in private life and social intercourse, hence prohibits not only false testimony but also calumny, defamation, detraction, and slander, 247; the most frequently broken commandment, 252. *See* Slander.

Commandment X., 258–272; additions to, as early as 900 B.C., lxii *n.*; original form brief, xlvii; text of D secondary in, xxxv; divided into two, 17, 17 *n.*, 18 (*see* Commandments, numbering of); forbids covetousness, and so includes VI.–IX., 259; passes from letter to spirit, and so gives key to our Lord's interpretation of Law, 260; convicted Paul of his inward sinfulness, 261; covetousness regarded as (i) in individual, 258–265; (ii) in bodies and groups, 265–270; (iii) in States, 270–272.

Commandments, *numbering of*, varies, 15; in Judaism, 16; in Roman and Lutheran churches, following Augustine's arbitrary division, 16, 17 *n.*; hence X. divided into two, 17–19, and neighbour's wife precedes neighbour's "house," 19; in other Christian Churches, 18; *order of*, varies, 15; Egyptian origin of inversion of VII. and VI., xxv n., 15, 16; paralleled in Babylonia (?), xxvi n.; widely attested in certain Greek MSS of Ex 20 and Deut 5, also by Luke 18[20], Ro 13[9], Ja 2[11], Philo, Jerome, Augustine; explanation of by Philo, xxv n., by Dr. Peters, xxv n.

Commandments all negative, except one (V.), 173, 174; reinterpreted by our Lord, 200, 203, 215, 260. *See* Reinterpretation. *See* Decalogue, Ten Commandments.

Common worship on Lord's Day, 162-172.

Communism and property, 230-236; theories of, influencing legislation everywhere, 230-233; extreme views of, "all property theft," 231; baser adherents of, 231; serious exponents of—Plato, Essenes, Therapeutæ, early Christians for a time in Jerusalem, 231, 232; sets up an ideal, has developed principle of co-operation, 232, 233.

Communistic experiments, failure of, 233 n.; in Paraguay, 233, 234 n.

Conceptions of God, 32-35.

Concubinage, 213, 214. *See* Polygamy.

Constantine and the paganising of Christianity, 26.

Contempt, a breach of Commandment VI., 200-203, 207; hurtful to others, begets censorious and presumptuous judgments, and so hurtful to self, 210, 211.

Covenant, Book of, presupposes Decalogue of Ex 20, therefore later than it, liv-lix. *See* Decalogue.

Covetousness connected with Idolatry, 260, 261; slavery of, 261. *See* Commandment X.

Cross, an honoured symbol from middle of second cent. A.D., 42; but not prominent in Catacombs, 42.

Crucifix, unknown in worship until sixth cent. A.D., 42; earliest representations of at Gaza, Tours and Narbonne, 43; veiled by order of bishop at Narbonne, 43 n.; first authorised in A.D. 692, 43 n.; worship of, arose in Syria, 43 n.; arguments for, 43; against, 44; ministers to the morbid or sensuous, 45-46 n.; wrongly interprets appeal of Christ, 46, 47; a false symbol, 104, 105. *See* Symbol.

Dan, sanctuary of, 21-23.

Decalogue, *various versions of*, in Ex 20, Deut 5, Ex 34, Book of Covenant, and in Egypt, vii; *Hebrew text of*, as in Egypt 300 B.C. discoverable from LXX text; as in Ex 20, in fifth cent. B.C., and in Deut 5 about 621 B.C., viii, ix; their divergences, ix, x; *Greek text of*, an authority for Hebrew text, viii; corruptions in, viii; *present text of*, in Ex 20 goes back to fifth cent. B.C., in Deut 5 to 621 or earlier (omitting gloss 5[8b-10]), x; Deuteronomic additions in, ix-xi; original shorter form of, xi-xii, older than Book of Covenant, older than Decalogue in Ex 34, xii; so presupposed by E and J, tenth cent. B.C., so attributable only to Moses, xii, 2; *relations of Ex 20 and Deut 5*—agreement in I., III., VI.-VIII., difference in II., IV., V., IX., X.; in V., X. Deut. secondary, in IX. primary, in II. large interpolation in Ex. from Deut., xxxiv-xxxix; in IV. large interpolation in Ex. from P (Gen 2[26], Ex 31[17]), also in Deut. addition from D, and preservation of phrase omitted by Ex., xxxix-xl; *an older form of*, presupposed in Book of Covenant, and a different Decalogue in Ex 34, 1 ; *text of Ex* 20 and *Deut* 5 in eighth and seventh cent. B.C., x, xi, xli–xliv; explanatory clauses in, are accretions, xlv ; originally each Law a few crisp words in tenth cent. or earlier, containing about 159 letters as against the present 620 letters, xlviii, xlviii n. ; *early origin of*, arguments for, *e.g.* parallels in other early religions, xlix–liii ; presupposed by Book of Covenant, liv–lix ; by Ex 34, lix–lxii ; arguments against, *e.g.* non-observance of Commandment II. (but this paralleled in Christian Church), lii, liii ; and silence of eighth cent. B.C. prophets (not conclusive), liii, liv ; *parallels to*, in Egyptian Book of Dead, li, lii ; in a Babylonian document, xxv, xxvi, lii ; *daily recital of*, in Temple, xv ; later abolition of, then attempted restoration of, xv ; alone claimed as divine revelation by Minim, xv.

Decalogue of Ex 34, later than and far removed from that of Ex 20, presupposes settlement of Israel in Canaan as agricultural people, lx, lx n.; reconstruction of, by Wellhausen and Kennett, lix–lx n. ; influence of, on later form of Deut 5 and of Ex 20, and on Book of Covenant, lxiii, lxiv.

Declension from true faith, in Israel, in Christian Church, in Buddhism, 26. *Contrast* Development.

Defamation, a true statement maliciously made, 251.

Deities, [independent, outside Israel, acknowledged in preprophetic times, 3 ; national worship of, 3 ; confined to national territory, 4. *See* Henotheism.

Detraction, unfavourable interpretation of act or character, often a mere insinuation, 251.

Deuteronomic additions, ix–xi, etc. *See* Commandments, Decalogue.

Development and reaction in religion, xlix–li (*see* Declension); in knowledge of God, 1–13 ; in eschatology, 8, 9 ; of worship, by stages, 29–31 ; hence lower forms permissible in earlier times but not tolerable in later, 30 ; of Commandment II. to spiritual worship, 35. *See* Growth, Reinterpretation.

Early Christian worship, 142–144.

Egypt, Hebrew text of Decalogue about 200 B.C. in, (*a*) represented in Nash Papyrus, vii; (*b*) presupposed by LXX of Ex 20 and Deut 5, viii; phrase " out of house of bondage " omitted in Nash Papyrus, xxii n. *See* Decalogue, Nash Papyrus.

Ephod, meaning of, 21 n.

Eschatology of Israel remains heathen to second cent. B.C., in case of Sadducees to A.D. 70, 8.

Eucharist, Pliny's possible reference to, 142 ; Justin's description of, 143, 144 ; held every Lord's Day, 143, 144.

Evidential value of miracles as such *nil*, 108, 109.

Experience, not intellect, the best teacher of religious truth, 8, 9.

Faith, true and lasting, founded on truth alone, 108, 109.

Falsehood, xviii, xxvi, xxxv, 89 n. *See* Commandment III., Lies, Vain.

Family life, importance of, in war against impurity, 225, 226 ; dependence of State and every human association on, 173 ; hence first in duties to neighbour, 173. *See* Parents.

Fetichism, 20.
Fighting on Sabbath Day, 125, 125 n.
Fool, meaning of word, equivalent to Raca, 201, 202.
Forgiveness, not only attainment of forgiving spirit, but winning to repentance and restoration to communion, 205, 206.
Fornication, placed by our Lord on the same level with adultery, 215; though not directly included in Commandment VII., nor so strongly denounced in O.T. as adultery, 213.
Frankfort, Synod of, A.D. 794, forbade image worship, 62, 63.
Future life, knowledge of, gained through religious experience, 9. *See* Eschatology.

Games, Sunday. *See* Recreation.
God, as Father of individual, a Christian revelation, 10, 11; fully mediated only through Son, 11, 12; revealed fully only as Father, Son and Holy Spirit, 11-13. *See* Yahweh.
Good Shepherd, Christ represented as, 42, 42 n.
Growth of Israelite Religion—Israelites at first Semitic heathens, 5; received revelation of henotheism through Moses, 6; but heathen views to eighth cent., of future life persisted to second cent. B.C., 6-9.
Guild Socialism and Syndicalism, 235-238.

Ḥammurabi, Code of, 190, 191 n.
Hatred, a breach of Commandment VI., 200, 204, 205. *See* Anger, Wrath.
Healing on Sabbath forbidden by Rabbis, 129, 133-135.
Heathenism. *See* Constantine, Declension, Image Worship, Prostitution, Solomon.
Henotheism = worship of one god, distinguishable from Monotheism = belief in one god, 2-9; of Moses, xlix.
Holiness not limited to any day, place, food, calling, nation or person, 158, 159.
Honour to parents includes respect, obedience, love, 178; duty not cancelled by parents' shortcomings, 182, 183; duty of giving honour to others and seeing the good in them, 204, 209-211; an incentive to them to improve, 208.
"House," originally included all possessions, xx, xlvii, 19; hence prior to "wife" in Commandment X., 19. Cf. xix.

Icon, after the Iconoclastic controversy, means only picture, 56 n.
Iconic worship. *See* Commandment II.
Iconclastic controversy, 41, 51-56. *See* Image Worship.
Idol, meaning of, extended to include unworthy conception of God, 35.
Idolatry, connected with covetousness, 261; forms of, 31; cf. 55, 57; heathen arguments for, borrowed by Christians, 31, 32, 60, 65; invades Christian Church after "conversion of" Empire, 40.
Image of God, material more harmful than intellectual, because incapable of growth or sublimation, 32; both of these contrasted with mental and formless conceptions, 34, 35.
Image Worship, *in Israel*, Jeroboam not originator of, 22 (*see* Bulls); revolt against, begins under Asa in Judah, 25; develops under prophets, 27; culminates in entire prohibition of all images, pictures and likenesses in second cent. B.C., which though allowed in Solomon's

temple are excluded from Herod's, 27, 28; though still appearing on Jewish tombs in Diaspora, 28; satirised by Philo, 29 n.; *in Christian Church*, denounced by early Christian writers, 37; forbidden by Synod of Elvira, 38; heathen arguments for, 65–67; Christian arguments against, 66, 67; first appears among Gnostics, 37, 59; objected to by Eusebius and Epiphanius of Salamis, and Augustine, 38–40; and all the Christian Fathers for four centuries, 60; began among ignorant classes, leavened gradually the Church, 60, 61; revives practices denounced by Hebrew prophets, 31, 55, 57; explained away as use of symbols, 31, 32; Basil the Great no authority for, 48, 49 n.; formula "honour rendered to image passes to prototype" has no reference to a material image, but essential nature of our Lord, 49 n.; lamented by Augustine, 40, 50; championed by Pope Gregory II., A.D. 729, 51, 52; by John of Damascus, 52–54; opposed by Byzantine Emperors, 51, 54; refusal of, regarded as deadly sin, 53 n., 54; commanded by Second Council of Nicæa, A.D. 787, 55, 61; 200 years later in prevailing in France, Germany and England, 61; condemned by Charlemagne and Alcuin, 62; by Synod of Frankfort, A.D. 794, and Conference at Paris, A.D. 825, 62, 63; in East insisted on by Empress Irene, 56; supported by Theodore of Studium, A.D. 823, 58; controversy settled by Synod of Constantinople, A.D. 842, worship confined to paintings by Second Council of Nicæa, as by Greek Church since, but extended later to statues by Roman Church, 56, 56 n.; modern instances of, in recent eruption of Etna, 58 n.; modern arguments for, 72 n., 73 n.

Images, religious, approved of by Leontius, bishop in Cyprus (*floruit*, A.D. 582–602), 50; defended by Pope Gregory I. as books of the unlearned, 50; championed by Pope Gregory II., 51, 52; actual use of, as godfathers, 58.

Immaculate conception, denied by Augustine, first taught by Franciscans, 83. *See* Mary.

Impurity, most ignored of sins, 215; most persistent of temptations, 215, 216; struggle against, sets in before maturity, 216; insidious appeal of, to imagination, 217; intimate connection of, with higher powers of man, 218; stimulated by excitement of war or even religious revivals, 219, 220; rife in periods of greatest artistic or intellectual activity, 219; destructive of empires, 220; connection of, with housing question, 222, 223; war against, not hopeless, 222; to be waged by nation legislatively, 222–225; by family by parental care, 225, 226; by individual by life and influence, 226; protection against, not sufficiently afforded by dread of consequences, by frank teaching, by artistic or intellectual education, 217–219; but materially given by patriotic and self-denying preoccupations, 220; and effectually provided by Christ and Holy Spirit, 226–228. *See* Adultery, Fornication, Vices.

Incarnation, adduced as justifying suppression of Commandment II, 63 n.

Incense, use of, in image worship, 31, 55–57.

Indignation, righteous, need of, 198, 205–207.
Individual, importance of, in war against impurity, by private example and public witness, 226.
Infallible authority, belief in, fatal to truth of thought, 102–107. *See* Ultramontanism; unquestioning submission to, biases or atrophies judicial faculty, and leads to superstition and ignorance, 104–106.
International relationships, truth in, 248; God's laws apply to, 270–272.
Invocation of saints, 75; of the Blessed Virgin Mary, 75–88.
Irene, Empress, evil character of, 56, 57, 61; supporter of image worship, 55, 56, 61.

Jehovah, an artificial spelling of the divine name Yahweh, written with the vowels of Adonai, 3. *See* Yahweh.
Jeroboam, revolt of, against foreign cults of Solomon or Rehoboam, 22. *See* Image Worship.
Judgment, private, duty of, 107; limitations of—vast field of truth, impossibility of absolute impartiality or absolutely open mind, 107, 108; yet indispensable on things within our ken, 107.

Lamb, figure of, replaced by Crucifix, 43 *n.*
Law, Jewish, alone to be read on Sabbath, 129, 130.
Legislation, inability of, to regenerate man, 269; following on advance in public opinion a corrective of intemperance, 191, 192, 223; of impurity, 222–225; of gambling, 223.
Lies, prevalent in primitive and barbarous times, 94; of courtesy, as "not at home," 94–97; of covetousness, malice and hatred, 98; of flattery and harmful exaggeration, 97; of weakness and fear, inevitable evils results of, 98.
Life, not an absolute but relative and potential good, 196, 197; sacredness of, an unsatisfactory principle, 195; inferior to sacredness of honour and truth, 196; saving of, supersedes Sabbath restrictions, 130, 131, 135. *But see* Healing.
Likeness, a Deuteronomic phrase, xxxviii.
Lord's Day, distinctive Christian weekly festival, 139; *title*, origin of, 139, 140; parallels to in Egypt and Asia Minor, 139, 140 *n.*; *observance of*, instituted by Early Church because Christ manifested Himself to the Apostles on first day of week, 160, 161; therefore Sunday is a weekly commemoration of Resurrection, 161, 162; and a fresh creation of Christianity, not a substitute for the Sabbath, 164; observance of, not commanded in N.T., 140, 141; but kept by Paul, 140; observance of, necessarily limited to early and late hours of day for bulk of early Christians, as slaves and subordinates, 141, 142; evidence of Pliny's letter to Trajan, 142; observed with celebration of Eucharist, after lessons, sermon and prayers, according to Justin Martyr, 143, 144; evidence of Tertullian, 144; religious observance made compulsory at Council of Illiberis, A.D. 305, 145; civil observance by Constantine's decree, A.D. 321, 145; games and litigation on, prohibited by Theodosius, A.D. 386, 146; growing severity of rules for, 146; thus at first a day of worship, after 300 years a day also of rest, 165; *identified*

during two periods with Jewish Sabbath; (*a*) seventh cent. A.D. to Reformation, *e.g.* in West by Alcuin and Charlemagne, in East later (A.D. 900) by Emperor Leo, 146 *n.*; Reformers, *e.g.* Luther and Calvin, refused to equate with Sabbath, and regarded it as institution of Church, 148, 149; (*b*) from sixteenth cent. in England, Holland and America by Puritans, 165; lax observance of on Continent due to equation of all holy days with Sabbath, *e.g.* by Bernard of Clairvaux and Thomas Aquinas, 147; hence eclipse of Sunday by holy days, and amusements more and more freely indulged in, 147, 148; licence encouraged by Book of Sports of James I. and Charles I. led to Puritan reaction, 150, 151; *modern questions concerning*—physical need of rest on, 165, 166; claims of others to rest on, 167; mental needs, 168–170; recreations on, to whom essential, 168; spiritual needs, 168, 170–172; danger of commercialisation, 169; need of special days and common worship, 170, 171; problem of those who refuse to observe any fixed festivals, 171. *See* Puritans, Sabbath.

Love of God, 10. *See* Commandment I.

Love, the supreme principle of conduct and reform, 269, 270; fulfilment of law, 263; difficult in regard to unlovable persons, but a duty still, 264.

Lying, deep guilt and baseness of, often due to cowardice, 248.

Maccabean leaders and Sabbath fighting, 125.

Mariolatry, 75–88. *See* Mary.

Mary, the Blessed Virgin, worship of, *evidence of monuments*—no trace of, in Catacombs, 76; nor in mosaics at Rome of A.D. 435 and 441, nor at Ravenna of A.D. 451 and 462, 76, 77; nor elsewhere till sixth cent. A.D., 77, 78; first appears in Syria, 78; far advanced by ninth cent. in Rome, 78; fully developed in twelfth cent. in mosaics of St. Nicholas in Urbe, 78, 79; *evidence of Fathers*—no trace of, in New Testament, where very subordinate position assigned her, 80, 81; nor in Basil, Chrysostom, Cyril of Alexandria or Augustine, 82, 83; prepared for by Apocryphal works condemned by Pope Gelasius (A.D. 492–496), 82; cult first appears in Thrace, Syria and Arabia, condemned in fourth cent. A.D. by Epiphanius, 82; later appears at Ephesus and Constantinople, about A.D. 450, 82; developed by, *e.g.*, Peter Damian, the Franciscans, Bonaventura, Bernardinus de Bustis, and especially Liguori, 83–88; decreed by Council of Trent, exceeding worship of saints, but differing from worship of God, 84; extravagances of Liguori, 86–88. *See* Immaculate Conception.

Massoretic text of Decalogue, viii, xvii–xxxii, xxxvi, xl, xli, xliii, xlvi *notes*.

Mendacity, and infallible authority, 102–104.

Mesha, king of Moab, inscription of, 5.

Milcom, god of Ammon, 3.

Miracles no proof of truth, 108, 109.

Mishnah, rules in, regarding Sabbath observance, 127.

Molech, worship of, 22.

Monotheism, not formally asserted in Commandment I., but a result of it, xlix, 6, 14; first taught explicitly by 8th cent. B.C.

prophets, 9; dispels superstition, sorcery, opportunism, 9, 10. See Henotheism.
Moral sense, liable to perversion, 198.
Moses, founder of pre-prophetic ethical Yahwism of Israel, xlviii; author of Decalogue in original form, xlviii, 2; henotheism of, xlix; acquainted no doubt with Egyptian ethical teaching, l, li.
Murder = killing from personal feeling, intentionally, 186; distinguished from manslaughter = killing by accident or in self-defence, 186. See Blood, Commandment VI.

Nash Papyrus, written towards close of first cent. A.D., used probably as Service Book or Catechism, vii, xiii, xv; discovery of, in 1902, xiii; much older than any Hebrew MS, xiii; works on, xiii; Egyptian character of, vii, xxvii–xxix; found in Cairo, agrees with LXX frequently against Massoretic, has Egyptian order of Commandments, omits " out of house of bondage," xxvii–xxix; as a rule agrees with Deut. against Ex., vii, xxix–xxx, xxxiii; occasionally with Ex. against Deut., xxx, xxxi, xxxiv; twice right against Ex. and Deut., xxxi; has readings and forms of its own not affecting the sense, xxxi; agrees with LXX more than with any other authority, viii, xxxii, xxxiii, xxxiv; represents a form of Hebrew text in Egypt 200 B.C., xv, xxxii, xxxiii; Hebrew text of, restored, xvi, xvii; critical notes on, xvii–xxii; translation of, xxii–xxvii.
Nation, character of, expressed in State, 271; if barbarous, still without moral responsibility,

270; if civilised, has moral convictions, ideals and duties, 270; linked together by language, ancestry, laws, literature, traditions and character, 270.
Nations, duty of, to one another, 270–272; selfishness of, 271; tragic history of, 271, 272; justice between, not ensured by courts of arbitration, treaties, commerce, civilisation or fear of war, 272; under Divine law, 271, 272; families in commonwealth of God, 272.

Oath, definition of, by Philo, " an invocation of God," 89; false, sin of, 89–92, penalty of, 90, 91; taking of, forbidden by our Lord, but not absolutely, 92, 93; by Philo, Essenes, 92, 93; necessary in courts of law, 90–94.
Obedience to parents, 173–176, 178–184; of child, unquestioning, 178; of youth, discriminating, 179.
Obscurantism, 101–109.
Observances, religious, not an end in themselves, 137, 138.
Opinion, public, an ever open court, 248, 249; has many divisions, 249; is aggregate of individual judgments, 249; tone of, being ever raised or lowered by us all, 250.
Order of Commandments. See Commandments.
Oriental cults, prepare way for Christianity, 40 n.
Output, increase of, 240; limitation of, 239. See Trade Unions.
Outspokenness, duty of, 255, 256; but inadvisable when hatred is present, 256. See Candour, Truth.

Paintings, religious, approved of by Gregory of Nyssa and Paulinus of Nola, 49, 50. See Pictures.

INDEXES

Parents, obedience to, 173-184; continuity of society bound up with, 174; based on factors of heredity and environment, 175, 176; authority of, 176, 177; honour due to, 178; children's debts to, 179, 180; duty of, to children, 180; need of careful training by, to overcome impurity, 225, 226; example of, 178; love of, a type of God's love, 184; God's earliest medium of revelation,178. *See* Authority, Obedience.

Partizanship, prejudices and blindness of, 249, 250; prominent in religious and political press, 250.

Paul, moral struggle of, 261, 262; conviction of, by Commandment X., led to his conversion, 262.

Perjury, 91, 92. *See* Oath.

Physical pain and agony, a favourite subject for representation in Eastern religions, 45, 46.

Pictures of Christ and saints forbidden by Eusebius and Epiphanius, 38, 39; allowed by Eastern Church. *See* Icon, Image Worship.

Pliny, letter of, to Trajan, 142, 143, 163. *See* Lord's Day.

Polygamy, common in O.T., 213, 214; tends to low moral code for men, 212.

Polytheism. *See* Deities, Henotheism, Monotheism.

Priests' Code, date of, 114 *n.*; based on pre-exilic usage, 114 *n.*

Private judgment. *See* Judgment.

Profanity, due to want of self-control, a limited vocabulary, or a lack of education, 92.

Prohibition, undesirability of, 192. *See* Alcohol.

Property, *considered with regard to community*, entails responsibility for service for community, 229, 230; banned by Communists, 231-234; recognised in some form or degree by Socialists, 234; attended by certain evils, *e.g.* selfishness, dishonesty, fraud, theft, covetousness, contention, war, inequality of lot, exploitation and profiteering, all of which amenable to legislation and moral advance, 230, 234; attended also by certain benefits, *e.g.* stimulus to production, discipline of physical mental and moral powers, 234, 235; *with regard to individual*, duty of giving full measure and supplying full quality, rendering full service, submitting to full taxation, 242-244; *Christ's conception of*—dangers and responsibilities of wealth, 244; wrongfulness of luxury, ostentation and waste, 245; requires from all according to ability and awards to all according to need, 245. *See* Stewardship.

Prophets, Hebrew, two schools of in Northern Kingdom, 23 *n.*; monotheism of, 9; earlier prophets, *e.g.* Elijah, do not denounce images, 23; later do, 25-28.

Prostitution, religious, sanctioned by Rehoboam, 22, 23; banished by Asa, Jehoshaphat and Josiah, 23 *n.*

Prototype and image, 49 *n.*, 55 *n. See* Image Worship.

Puritan view of Lord's Day, value of, 150, 151, 156; not prevalent on Continent, 149; rejected by English Church, which, however, holds to principle of sanctification of one day in seven, 153; this not ultimately provable, 156; contrary to Paul's teaching, 157; and our Lord's, 157, 158. *See* Holiness, Lord's Day.

Raca, meaning of word, 200-203.

Recreation, Sunday, problem

of, 168–170; State control of, 167.
Reformed Churches and Sunday, 148, 149.
Reinterpretation of Commandments by our Lord, 260; of VI., 200–203; of VII., 215.
Rest, day of, weekly, essential to physical health, 165, 166. *See* Lord's Day, Sabbath.
Rites of idolatrous worship, 31, 55, 61, 62, 65, 68.
Roman Church, sanctioned image worship earlier than France, Germany or England, 61; permits statues as well as pictures, 56, 65 (*see* Image Worship); Mariolatry in, *see* Mary; equates holy days with Sundays, 147. *See* Lord's Day.

Sabbath and Lord's Day, differences between—Sabbath commanded, Sunday not; Sabbath seventh day, Sunday first; Sabbath lasts from sunset to sunset, Sunday from midnight to midnight; Sabbath commemorates God's rest, Sunday Christ's resurrection; Sabbath observed by cessation of work on penalty of death, Sunday by worship (not rest, at first), without penalty, 153, 154.
Sabbath, name of, connotes rest and cessation from toil, 117; no doubt also implied sacred rites, and therefore rest with a view to worship, 117, 118; connected with weekly division of time, 118 (*see* Weeks); observance of, two different reasons given for (*a*) older, humanitarian, for man, in Deut 5 (and Ex 23¹²); (*b*) later (about 500 B.C.), theological, for God, in Ex 20, 110–114; crude anthropomorphism of, 115, 116; after Exile more important than New Moon, 119; ultimately the distinctive Jewish festival, 119,
120; strict rules regarding, became intolerable burden, 124; actual danger to life overrode rules, 130; but this principle limited both for men and animals, 130, 130 *n*., 135 *n*.; in N.T., corrected by our Lord on principle "Sabbath made for man," 133; Jewish parallel to this saying, 133 *n*.; Jewish delight in, 131 *n*.; classical authors' slighting references to, 131 *n*., 138 *n*.; Gentile Christians rejected, as part of law, *e.g.*, Ignatius, Justin, Athanasius, 139, 139 *n*.; though recognised in *Apostolic Constitutions* and by Council of Laodicea, A.D. 363, 139 *n*. *See* Healing, Lord's Day, Puritan.
Saints, days of, equated with Sunday, 147 *n*.; worship of, 41, 75. *See* Worship.
Samaritan Pentateuch, presumably escaped later corruptions of Jewish text, xxviii *n*.
Samaritan text of Decalogue, viii, xvii–xxxii, xliii *n*.
Sanctuary, right of, for homicide, 187; under Hebrew law, not available for murderer, 188; under mediæval canon law, offered to murderers and all criminals, with deplorable results, 188, 189.
Scorn. *See* Contempt, Honour.
Sensuous, the, in religion, 45. *See* Art, Crucifix, Physical Pain, Symbols.
Septuagint, viii, xvii–xxxiv, xxxvi, xxxvii, xxxix, xli, xlvi, lv. *See* Nash Papyrus.
Sermon, danger of sensuous appeals in, 47, 48; contrast reserve of Gospels, 48; on Mount. *See* Mount.
Sex, appetites of, 218.
Sexes, equality of, in Christian view, 224.
Sexual development precedes maturity, 216. *See* Impurity.

Shema', xv; form of, xx, xxi; ascribed to sons of Jacob, xxi. *See* Temple Service.

Slander, 247; disparaging statement, true or false, with malicious motive, 250, 251; how differing from backbiting, calumny, defamation and detraction, 251; an execrable vice, condemned by Paul and James, 256, 257; description of, in Shakespeare, 253; in Leviticus, 254; striking idiomatic expression for, in Semitic languages, 254; frequently irresponsible, 252-255; methods of guarding against—judging others fairly, avoiding hearing or repeating evil of others, 255. *See* Backbiting, etc.

Socialism, distinct from Communism, 233, 265-267; seeks through State agency better distribution of wealth and services, and better means of production, 233; aims at abolishing capitalistic organisation of industry, 233 *n.*; recognises to some extent private ownership, 234; works on legitimate lines, constructive and equitable, 266; aims at nationalisation of land and means of production, 266, 267. *See* Communism, Property, Syndicalism.

Solomon, introduction of foreign cults by, 22. *See* Jeroboam; their persistence to reign of Asa, 23.

State, duty of, in regard to Sunday observance, 167-169. *See* Legislation.

Statue of Peter, described as " a god upon earth," 52.

Stewardship, Christian view of property as, 245.

Sunday games. *See* Lord's Day, Recreation, Sabbath.

Sunday Observance Act, A.D. 1625, 149 *n.*

Symbols, stir and quicken thought, 44; but owing to associations of reverence may tend to idolatry, 44; and prototypes, 49, 55, 57; mediæval, mistake of reviving to-day, 105. *See* Cross, Crucifix, Good Shepherd, Images.

Syndicalism, originated with Sorel, 236; aims of, 235, 236; methods of violence and sabotage, 236; constant strikes and limitation of output, 267; opposition of, to State, 236; constitutional methods discarded by, 267; disregard of agreements by, 267, 268; invasion of Trade Unions by, 268; selfishness the bane of, 267-269. *See* Communism, Socialism.

Talmud, rules regarding Sabbath observance in, 127, 128; absurdity of certain rules in, 129; Babylonian, xxi.

Targum, Samaritan, xvii-xxi, xxiii-xxxii, xxxvi, xxxvii, xliii; Jerusalem, xxi, etc.

Targums, Babylonian, xxi, etc.; Palestinian, xxi, etc.

Temple, of Solomon contained representations of natural objects, 28; of Herod contained none, 28; prostitutes in, 23 *n.* (*see* Prostitution); daily recital of Decalogue and Shema' in, xv. *See* Decalogue.

Ten Commandments, cf. tenfold laws of Manu, ten conditions of heart of Buddhism, ten admonitions of Zoroastrianism, l, li.

Teraphim, image in human form, 21, 22.

Trade Unions, long struggle of, for fair wage, 239; self-sacrifice of, 239; brotherhood of, 239; limitation of output by, 239; selfishness of, 239; and Sunday labour, 166.

Trent, Council of, 64, 65, 68, 84. *See* Image Worship, Mary.
Truth, duty of, for truth's sake, 94; of word, 94–99; need of courage and unselfishness for, 98, 99; of life—expressing convictions, being ourselves, fulfilling our trust, avoiding finesse and chicaneries, 99–101; of thought, rarest and hardest to attain, 101; incompatible with ignorance, conceit, expediency, 102; or submission to an infallible authority, 102, 103; the only lasting foundation of faith, 108, 109.

Ultramontanism, promotion and inculcation of mendacity by, 102, 103; testimony of Lord Acton concerning, 103. *See* Infallible Authority.
Unemployment, relief of, dangers of, 241; insurance against, by industries, 242.
Unfaithfulness of man to wife, no Hebrew or Greek term for, 212; owing to polygamy and conception of wife as property, 212. *See* Adultery.

Vain, 89 *n*. *See* Falsehood.
Veneration=relative worship, addressed to images, 55 *n*.
Vices, unnatural, regarded as inevitable and incurable by Plato, 221 *n*.; by Greece and Rome generally, 221, 222; but eradicated by Christianity within three centuries, 222.

Wages, the problem of, 237; not to be wholly determined by supply and demand, 237. *See* Employers.
War, necessity of, 197, 198; excitement of, leads to impurity, 219, 220.
Wealth, difficulties and dangers of, 244.
Weeks, Hebrew origin of, 119; connection of, with Babylonian holy days of rest possible, 118, 119; but Babylonian seventh day an "evil day," while Babylonian Sabattum=fifteenth day, *i.e.* "resting" of moon, 118, 119.
Westminster, right of sanctuary at, till James I.'s reign, 189.
Wife, originally regarded as a piece of property, 212; and subsumed at first under "house" in Commandment X., xix, 19. *See* Woman.
Woman, oriental view of, a low one, 213; still prevails among Jews, 214, 215.
Worship of gods, confined to territory, 4, 5; to tribe or nation, 2, 3; of saints, led to image worship, 41, 75; spiritual, 35; outward, forms of, 31, 35 (*see* Adoration, Idols, Rites, Veneration); of early Christians, 142–144. *See* Eucharist.
Wrath, distorts judgment, disorganises body and nerves, 205.

Yahweh, God of Israel, 3; name of, not pronounced except as Adonai or Elohim, nor written with own proper vowels, 3. *See* Jehovah; originally an Amorite deity, but name found in Babylonia under first dynasty, xlviii *n*.

INDEXES

II.—PASSAGES QUOTED

(a) From the Old Testament

Gen 1–2³	.	113, 114, 121, 122 n., 133
2²,³	. . . . .	113 n.
2³	. . .	xxiv n., xlii n.
2²⁶	. . . . .	xxxix
9⁶	. . . . .	195
Ex 1¹⁻⁵	. . . .	114 n.
1¹³⁻¹⁴	. . . .	114 n.
2²³ᵇ⁻²⁵	. . . .	114 n.
6²⁻7¹³	. . . .	114 n.
7¹⁹⁻²⁰ᵃ	. . . .	114 n.
7²¹ᵇ⁻²²	. . . .	114 n.
8⁵⁻⁷	. . . .	114 n.
8¹⁵ᵇ⁻¹⁹	. . . .	114 n.
9⁸⁻¹²	. . . .	114 n.
11⁹⁻¹⁰	. . . .	114 n.
12¹⁻²⁰	. . . .	114 n.
12²⁸	. . . .	114 n.
12³⁷ᵃ	. . . .	114 n.
12⁴⁰⁻⁴¹	. . . .	114 n.
12⁴³⁻⁵¹	. . . .	114 n.
13¹⁻²	. . . .	114 n.
13²⁰	. . . .	114 n.
14¹⁻⁴	. . . .	114 n.
14⁸⁻⁹	. . . .	114 n.
14¹⁵⁻¹⁸	. . . .	114 n.
14²¹ᵃ	. . . .	114 n.
14²¹ᶜ⁻²³	. . . .	114 n.
14²⁶⁻²⁷ᵃ	. . . .	114 n.
14²⁸ᵃ	. . . .	114 n.
14²⁹	. . . .	114 n.
16¹⁻³	. . . .	114 n.
16⁶⁻²⁴	. . . .	114 n.
16²³	. . . .	124
16²⁹	. . . .	123 n.
16³¹⁻³⁶	. . . .	114 n.
17¹ᵃ	. . . .	114 n.
19¹⁻²ᵃ	. . . .	114 n.
20	.	vii, viii, ix, x, xxxiii, xxxiv, xxxv, xli, xlv, lx, lx n., lxi, lxiii, lxiv, 1, 8, 111
20²		xvi, xvii, xxii, 16
20³	.	xvi, xxii, lxi, 1, 1–11
Ex 20⁴	.	xvi, xvii, xxii, xxxvi, xxxvii, xxxviii, lxi, lxii
20⁴,⁵	. . .	36, 59
20⁴⁻⁶	. . .	14
20⁴⁻¹², ¹⁷	. . .	xli
20⁴ᵇ⁻⁶	. ix, xxxix, xli, lv, lxiii
20⁵	.	xvi, xxii, xxiii, xxxi
20⁶	. . .	xvi, xxiii
20⁷	.	xvi, xxiii, lv, lxii n., 89
20⁷ᵇ	. . . .	lv
20⁸	.	xvi, xvii, xxiii, xxx
20⁸⁻¹⁰	.	xxxix, xl, xli–xlii
20⁸⁻¹¹	. .	x, xxxix, 110
20⁸⁻¹²	. . .	xxxix
20⁹	. .	xvi, xxiii, 17 n.
20⁹,¹⁰	. . .	lv
20¹⁰	. xvi, xvii, xviii, xxiii, xxiv, xxviii, xxix, xxxi, xl, xli n., xlii n., xlvi, xlvii
20¹¹	. viii, x, xvi, xviii, xxiv, xxviii, xxx, xxxii, xxxix, xlii n., lv, lxiii, 113, 113 n.
20¹²	. viii, xvii, xviii, xxiv, xliii, xliii n., 17 n., 173, 174
20¹²ᵇᶜ	. . . .	lv
20¹³	. xvii, xviii, xxv, xxv n., 185, 200, 260
20¹³⁻¹⁴	. .	xxv n., xxviii
20¹³⁻¹⁵	. .	viii, xviii, xxxii
20¹⁴	. xvii, xviii, xxv, xxv n., 212
20¹⁴⁻¹⁷	. . . .	xviii
20¹⁵	. xvii, xxiv, xxv n., 17 n., 229
20¹⁶	. xvii, xviii, xxvi, xxix, xliii, 246
20¹⁷	. viii, xvii, xix, xx, xxvi, xxvi n., xxix, xxx, xxxi, xliii, xlviii, 17 n., 19, 258
20²²⁻²³	. . . .	lvi n.
20²²⁻²⁶	. . . .	lvi

INDEXES

Ex 20^{22}–23^{33}	liv, lvii, lxiii, lxiv, 1, 112	
20^{23}	lvii, lviii	
21^2–22^{17}	lvi	
21^6	lviii	
21^{12-14}	lix	
21^{14}	188	
21^{15}	lix	
21^{16}	lvi n.	
21^{17}	lvi n., lix	
21^{18-25}	lvi n.	
i.e. Ex. $21^{18-19.\ 23-25.\ 22.\ 20-21}$		
21^{20}	lix	
$21^{23.\ 24}$	lix	
21^{29}	lix	
21^{29-31}	190	
22^{1-4}	lvi n.	
22^{1-5}	lix	
22^{7-8}	lix	
22^8	lviii	
22^{12}	lix	
22^{16}	lix	
22^{17}–23^{19}	lvi	
22^{21}	xlii n., lvi n.	
$22^{23.\ 21b.\ 24}$	lvi n.	
22^{27}	lvi n.	
22^{28}	lviii	
23^1	xix	
23^{1-2}	lix	
23^{4-5}	lvi n.	
23^9	xlii n., lvi n.	
$23^{10.\ 11.\ 13b}$	lvi n.	
23^{12}	xxiii, xxxix, xl, xli n., xlii n., xlvi, xlvii, lviii, 112, 113, 115, 115 n., 120 n., 133 n.	
23^{13}	lvii	
23^{14-19}	lvi n.	
23^{24}	lvii	
23^{32}	lvii	
23^{33}	lvii	
24^7	liv	
24^{15-18a}	114 n.	
25^1–31^{18a}	114 n.	
31^{13}	122 n., 133 n.	
31^{14}	133 n.	
31^{14b}	123 n.	
31^{15}	123 n.	
$31^{16.\ 17}$	115	
31^{17}	xviii, xxxix, 113 n., 115 n., 121, 122 n., 133 n.	
Ex 34	xii, xlvi, xlvii, l, liv, lvi, lix n., lx, lxi, lxii, lxiii, lxiv, 1	
34^{1-28}	lxii	
34^6	34	
34^7	xxviii, xlv, lxiii	
34^{11-26}	lx	
34^{14}	lix n., lxi, lxii	
$34^{14.\ 7}$	lxiii	
34^{14b}	xxxviii	
34^{17}	lix n., lxi, 25	
34^{18}	lvi n., lix n.	
34^{19}	lix n.	
34^{21}	xxiii, xli n., xlvi, lx n., lxii, 120 n., 123 n.	
34^{21ab}	xlvi, xlvii	
34^{22}	lx n.	
$34^{22.\ 23}$	lvi n.	
34^{22a}	lix n.	
34^{22c}	lix n.	
$34^{25.\ 26}$	lvi n.	
34^{25a}	lix n.	
34^{25b}	lx n.	
34^{26a}	lx n.	
34^{26b}	lx n.	
34^{29-35}	114 n.	
35–40	114 n.	
35^2	123 n.	
35^3	124	
Lev 18^5	130	
19^{12}	92	
19^{16}	254	
Num 12^8	xxxviii n.	
14^{18}	34	
15^{32}	124	
15^{32-36}	123 n.	
Deut 1^{19}	xl	
1^{41}	xl	
4^5	xl	
4^{12}	27	
4^{16}	xvii, xxxvii	
4^{18b}	xxxviii	
4^{21}	xliii n.	
4^{23}	xvii, xxxvii	
4^{25}	xvii, xxxvii	
4^{34}	xxxix	
4^{39c}	xxxviii	
4^{40}	xxv n., xxxv, xliii n.	
4^{44}	xxi	
4^{45}	xvii, xx, xxvii, xxvii n.	

INDEXES

Deut 5	vii, viii, ix, x, xxxiii, xxxiv, xxxv, xli, xlv, lxi, lxiii, 1, 111, 112	
5^8	. xvii, xxxvi, xxxvi n., xxxvii, xxxviii, lv	
$5^{8-16, 21}$	 xli	
5^{8b}	 xxxviii	
5^{8b-10}	. ix, x, xxxviii, xxxix, xli n., lv, lxiii	
5^9	. xxiii, xxxi, xxxii, xxxviii	
5^{9-10}	 lxiii	
5^{10}	 xxxviii	
5^{11}	. . . . . lxii n.	
5^{12}	. . . . . xxx, xl	
5^{12-14}	. xxxix, xl, xli–xlii, 110, 132	
5^{12-16}	. . . . x, xxxix	
5^{14}	. viii, x, xvii, xxiii, xxiv, xxix, xxxi, xxxii, xxxix, xl, xlii n., lv, 111, 121	
5^{14c}	. . . xxxix, xlii n., lv	
5^{15}	. xviii, xxxix, lv, lxiii	
5^{15bce}	 lxiii	
5^{16}	. viii, xxiv, xxv n., xxix, xxxii, xxxii n., xxxv, xxxvii, xl, xliii, xliii n.	
5^{16b}	 lv	
5^{16bce}	 lv	
5^{16ce}	 lv	
5^{16d}	. . . . lv, lxiii	
5^{17}	. . . . xxv n., xxix	
5^{17-19}	. . . . viii, xxxii	
5^{18-21}	 xviii	
5^{19}	 xix	
5^{20}	. xviii, xxvi n., xxix, xliii	
5^{21}	. viii, xix, xx, xxvi n., xxix, xxx, xxxi, xliii, 19	
5^{29}	. . . xxv n., xxxv	
5^{32}	 xl	
5^{33}	. xxv n., xxxv, xl, xliii n.	
6^1	 xxi	
6^2	. xvii, xx, xxv n., xxvii, xxvii n., xliii n.	
6^3	. . . . xxv n., xxxv	
6^4	. xv, xvii, xx, xxi, xxii, xxvii, xxviii, xxxiii, xxxiv	
$6^{4, 5}$	 10	
6^5	. . . xvii, xxvii	
6^{17}	 xl	
Deut 6^{18}	. . xxv n., xxxv
6^{21}	 xxxix
6^{25}	 xl
7^8	 xxxix
7^9	 xxxviii
11^9	. . . . xliii n.
12^{12}	. . . . 112 n.
12^{18}	. . . . 112 n.
12^{25}	. . xxv n., xxxv
12^{28}	. . xxv n., xxxv
13^{6-9}	 27
14^{26b}	. . . . 112 n.
15^{15}	 xxxix
16^{11}	. . . . 112 n.
16^{12}	 xxxix
17^{2sqq}	 27
17^{20}	. . . . xliii n.
19^{13}	. . xxv n., xxxv
19^{15-21}	 90
19^{19}	 90
20^{17}	 xl
21^{10sqq}	 xix
22^7	. xxv n., xxxv, xliii n.
22^{13sqq}	 xix
23^{17}	. . . . 23 n.
24^{1sqq}	 xix
24^8	 xl
24^{18}	 xxxix
24^{22}	 xxxix
25^{15}	. . . . xliii n.
27^{16}	 180
30^{18}	. . . . xliii n.
31^{12}	. . . . xlii n.
32^{47}	. . . . xliii n.
Jos $2^{12, 14}$	. . . xxxviii n.
Judg 11^{24}	 4
17–18	 21
18^{30}	 21
1 Sam 19^{13-16}	. . . 21
26^{19}	 4
2 Sam 16^{14}	115, 115 n., 133 n.
1 Kings 11^{1-8}	. . . 22
$14^{23, 24}$	 23
15^{12}	. . . . 23 n.
15^{12-13}	. . . 23, 25
18^4	. . . . 23 n.
19^{10-14}	. . . . 23 n.
19^{18}	. . . 23 n., 31
22	. . . . 23 n.
22^6	. . . . 23 n.
22^{12}	. . . . 23 n.

INDEXES

1 Kings 22⁴⁶		23 n.
2 Kings 4²³	118 n., 119 n.,	120 n., 123 n.
5¹⁷		5
9⁷		23 n.
13⁶		27
18⁴		25 n., 51 n.
23⁶		27
23⁷		23 n.
23¹⁵		27
1 Chron 23³¹		119 n., 120 n.
2 Chron 2⁴		119 n., 120 n.
26¹⁶		51 n.
31³		119 n.
Neh 10³¹		123 n.
13¹⁵		124 n.
13¹⁶, ¹⁷		123 n.
13¹⁹		124 n.
13²³⁻³¹		xxviii n.
Job 31¹		213
Ps 10³		203 n.
31¹		83, 84
50²¹		34
150⁶		84
Prov 7²⁷		213
30¹⁷		180
Isa 1¹³	112, 118 n.,	119, 120 n.
2⁸		25
2²⁰		25
14		7
19¹⁹		25 n.
40¹⁸⁻²⁰		27
40²⁸		116
41⁶ˢᑫᑫ·		27
44⁹⁻²⁰		27
44¹⁵		31
46¹		31
46⁶ˢᑫᑫ·		27
46⁷		31
57¹⁵		35
58¹³		126 n.
Jer 10²⁻⁵		27
10⁵		31
10⁹		27, 31
10¹⁴ˢᑫᑫ·		27
17¹⁹⁻²⁷		120, 124 n.
17²⁴		xxiii
17²⁵		124 n.
Ezek 8¹¹		31
14³		34
16¹⁸		31
Ezek 20¹²		122 n.
20²⁰		122 n.
45¹⁷		119 n.
46³		119 n.
Hos. 2¹¹	112, 118 n.,	119 n., 120 n.
8⁴⁻⁶		25
10⁵		25
13¹⁻³		25
13²		31
Amos 8⁵	118 n., 119,	120 n., 123 n.
8¹⁴		24

THE TEN COMMANDMENTS

(*Supplementary to* (a))

Introductory formula as I. Commandment, 16, 18.

I. ix, xxxiv, xliv, xlvi, lvii–lviii, lxi, lxii, 1–13, 16, 17, 18, 24, 89. See Ex 20³.

II. ix, x, xi, xxxiv, xxxv–xxxix, xli, xliv, xlvii, lv, lviii, lxi, lxii, lxiii, 14–88, 16, 17, 18, 21, 24, 68–75, 89. See Ex 20⁴⁻⁶.

III. ix, xi, xii, xxxiv, xliv, xlv, xlvii, li, lv, lviii, lxi, lxii, lxii n., lxiii, 89–109. See Ex 20⁷.

IV. viii, ix, x, xi, xii, xxviii, xxxii, xxxiii, xxxiv, xxxv, xxxix–xliii, xliv, xlv, xlvi, xlviii, lv, lviii, lxi, lxii, lxiii, 8, 110–172. See Ex 20⁸⁻¹¹.

V. viii, ix, x, xi, xxvi n., xxxii, xxxiii, xxxiv, xxxv, xliii, xliv, xlvii, lii, lv, lix, lxiii, 173–184. See Ex 20¹².

VI. viii, ix, xxvi n., xxviii, xxix, xxxiv, xliv, xlvii, li, lii, lix, 185–211. See Ex 20¹³.

VII. viii, ix, xxvi n., xxviii, xxix, xxxiv, xliv, xlvii, li, lii, lix, 212–228. See Ex 20¹⁴.

INDEXES

VIII. viii, ix, xxvi n., xxviii, xxix, xxxiv, xliv, xlvii, li, lii, lix, 229–245. See Ex 20^{15}.

IX. ix, xxxiii, xxxiv, xxxv, xliii, xliv, xlvii, li, lix, 246–257. See Ex 20^{16}.

X. viii, ix, xi, xii, xxxiii, xxxiv, xxxv, xliii, xliv, xlvii, xlviii, lv, lvi, lvi n., lxi, lxii, lxii n., lxiii, 17, 18, 19, 70, etc., 258–272. See Ex 20^{17}.

VII.-VI.-VIII., viii, xxviii, xxix, xxxii, xxxiv, 15, 16,

VII.-VIII.-VI., xxv, xxxii, 15.

(b) *From the New Testament*

Matt 5^{21}	16
$5^{21,\,22}$	199, 200–203
5^{22}	207
5^{27}	16, 260
5^{28}	212, 215
5^{34}	92
5^{39}	92
6^{24}	244
6^{33}	269, 270
7^{12}	272
$12^{4,\,5}$	134
$12^{11,\,12}$	130 n., 135
$12^{36,\,37}$	257
12^{46-50}	80
19^{18}	xxv n., 16
21^{38}	268
26^{63}	93
27^{62}	126 n.
Mark $1^{21,\,23}$	126 n.
$2^{23\text{sqq}}$	134
2^{27}	116, 132, 133, 135, 152, 157
3^2	135
$3^{4,\,6}$	135
3^{31-35}	80
7^{14-21}	159
$7^{21,\,22}$	215
10^{19}	xxv n.
10^{23}	244
12^{31}	263, 264
15^{42}	126 n.
Luke $4^{31,\,33}$	126 n.
6^4	136
Luke 6^6	126 n.
$11^{27,\,28}$	80
13^{10}	126 n.
18^{20}	xxv n., 15
23^{28}	47
23^{54}	126 n.
John $2^{4,\,5}$	79
4^{21}	159
4^{23-24}	35
4^{24}	36
5^{10}	128
5^{37}	35
8^{32}	106, 107
$9^{6\text{sqq}}$	128
Acts 1^{14}	80
10^{10-13}	159
$13^{14\text{sq}}$	126 n.
13^{43}	126 n.
15^{10}	124
20^7	140
Rom $1^{29,\,30}$	257
$2^{1,\,3}$	136 n.
$2^{25,\,27}$	136 n.
7^7	261
$7^{24,\,25}$	262
13^9	xxv n., 15
13^{10}	263
14^5	132, 136, 152, 157
$14^{5,\,6}$	137
1 Cor 6^{10}	257
6^{19}	227
12^{26}	272
16^2	140
2 Cor 1^{23}	93
13^{14}	1
Gal 1^{20}	93
3^{28}	158
4^4	80
$4^{10,\,11}$	137, 157
Eph 3^{15}	178
4^{26}	205
6^2	175
Phil 1^8	93
3^6	261
Col 2^{16}	157
$2^{16,\,17}$	132, 137
3^5	261
3^{11}	158
Jas 1^{26}	257
2^{11}	xxv n., 15, 136 n.
3^2	257

Jas 3^8	. . . .	256
5^{12}	. . . .	92
1 John 1^5	. . . .	35
3^{15}	. . . .	204
4^8	. . . .	35
5^{21}	. . . .	35
Rev 1^{10}	. . .	140, 141
19^{10}	. . . .	81
22^9	. . . .	81

(c) *From the Apocrypha and Pseudepigrapha*

Wisd 2^{16}	. . . .	10 *n.*
14^{12-21}	. . . .	27–28
Sir 17^{17}	. . . .	10 *n.*
23^1 51^{10}	. . . .	10 *n.*
Ep. Jer. 4, 6, 19, 26	. .	31
1 Macc 2^{34-38}	. . .	125 *n.*
9^{34-43}	. . .	125 *n.*
2 Macc $5^{24\mathrm{sqq.}}$	. .	125 *n.*
8^{25-28}	. .	125 *n.*
$15^{1\mathrm{sqq.}}$	. . .	125 *n.*
Jub 1^{6-13}	. . .	125 *n.*
2^{17-32}	. . .	125 *n.*
2^{18}	. . .	123 *n.*
2^{19-21}	. . .	123 *n.*
2^{31}	. . .	123 *n.*
50^7	. . .	xviii
Test. Levi 4^2	. . .	10 *n.*
Test. Judah 18^2	. .	260
19^1	. . .	260
2 Enoch 49^{1-2}	. .	92

(d) *From Talmud, etc.*

Aboda Zara, 27*b*	. .	130 *n.*
Berachoth, 3*c*, 11*a*	. .	xv
12*a*	. . . .	xv
Beza, 2*b*	. . . .	129
Gittin, ix. 10	. . .	214
Mekilta on Ex 31^{13}	.	133 *n.*
104*a, b*	. . .	123 *n.*
Peah, viii. 7	. . .	126 *n.*
Pesach, 56*a*	. . .	xxi
Sanh. vii. 6	. . .	31
Shabb. i. 2	. . .	129
vii. 2	. .	127, 127 *n.*
x. 6	. . . .	129
xvi. 2	. . .	126 *n.*
xxii. 5	. . .	129
Shabb. xxiv. 3	. .	127, 128
19*a*	. . . .	125 *n.*
74*a*	. . . .	134 *n.*
107*b*	. . . .	129
108*b*	. . . .	128
117*b*	. . . .	135 *n.*
119*b*	. . . .	122 *n.*
128*b*	. .	130 *n.*, 135 *n.*
Sot. (Jer. T.) i. 16*b*	. .	214
Tamid, iv. *ad fin.* v. 1	.	xv
Yad. ii. 23–25	. .	125 *n.*
Yoma, viii. 6	. . .	130
85*a*	. . . .	133 *n.*

(e) *From Patristic Writers and Philo and Josephus*

Apostolic Constitutions, vii. 23. 36	. .	139 *n.*
Arnobius, *adv. Nationes*, vi. 8, 9	. .	66
Athanasius, *de Sabb. et circum.* 4	. . .	139 *n.*
Athenagoras, *Legatio pro Christo*, xv–xvii		37
Augustine, x. 1133 A, 2101 C	. .	83
de Civ. Dei, iv. 31. 2	.	39
vi. 10. 1	. . .	39
Epistolæ, ii. 55. 20	.	17 *n.*
de Mor. Eccl. Cath. i. 75	40, 50
in Psalmum, xcvi. 7	.	67
Quæstiones in Exod. 71	.	17 *n.*
de Sancta Virginitate, 3	83 *n.*
Sermo ix. 7	. .	17 *n.*, 15
Sermo cxcviii.	. .	39 *n.*
Sermo ccl. 3	. .	17 *notes*
c. Faustum, xv. 4	. .	15
Barnabas, Ep. of, xv. 8, 9	140
Basil the Great, *de Spiritu Sancto*, ix.	. .	49 *n.*
de Spiritu Sancto, xviii. 49, 49 *n.*
Comm. in Esaiam, cap. xiii. 267	. .	49 *n.*
Ep. ccclx. (spurious)	.	48, 49
Bede, *H.E.* iv. 376	. .	43 *n.*
Chrysostom, Migne, *P.G.* viii. 141	. .	80 *n.*
Hom. ix. in Acta Apost.	93 *n.*
Clem. Alex. *Strom.* iii. 15. 99	. . .	139 *n.*

Clem. Alex. *Strom.* iv. 3. 8   139 *n.*
Strom. vi. . . .   15
Cyprian, *de Idolorum vani-*
tate, vii. . . .   38
Testimonia, 51 . .   38
Cyril of Alexandria, Migne,
P.G. iv. 1064, 1065 .   80 *n.*
Didache, ii. 2 . . xxv *n.,* 16
   iii. 2 sq. . . . xxv *n.,* 16
   xiv. 1   144
Diognetum, Ep. ad, ii. .   37
Elvira, Canon xxxvi. of .   38
Epiphanius, *Ep. ad Joann.*
Hieros. . . .   39
Hær. lxxix. 7 . . .   82 *n.*
Eusebius, *H.E.* iii. 27 .   138 *n.*
   H.E. iv. 26 . . .   144 *n.*
   H.E. vii. 18 . . 39, 39 *n.*
   Præp. Evang. iii. 7 .   65
   Præp. Evang. viii. 7 .   126 *n.*
Evangelium de Nativitate
Mariæ . .   82 *n.*
Gregory I., *Ep. ad Se-*
verum   50
Gregory II., *ad Leonem*
Imp. i. ii. . . . 51, 52
Gregory of Tours, *de gloria*
martyrum, i. 23 . .   43
Ignatius, *ad Magn.* 9 . 139 *n.*
Irenæus, *Hær.* i. 25. 6 .   37
Jerome, Migne, *P.L.* xxv.
   Jerome v. 437, 438 .   60 *n.*
John of Damascus, *de Im-*
aginibus oratio, i. 328   53 *n.*
   de Fide orthodoxa, iv. 16   49 *n.*
John Moschus, *Pratum*
Spirituale . . .   53 *n.*
Justin Martyr, *Apol.* i. 9 .   37
   Apol. i. 65 . . .   143
   Apol. i. 67 . . 142 *n.,* 143
   Apol. xvi. . . .   93
   Cohort. ad Gentiles .   37
   Dial. c. Tryph. xii.. . 139 *n.*
   Dial. c. Tryph. xci. .   42
Lactantius, *Institut.* ii. 2 .   38
   Institut. vi. 2 . . .   31
Leontius, Bp. of Neapolis
   in Cyprus . . 50, 50 *n.*
Liber de Infantia Mariæ et
Christi Salvatoris .   82 *n.*
Melito of Sardis, *Chroni-*
con Paschale, p. 483
   (ed. Dindorf) . .   37
Minucius Felix, *Octavius,*
   10   38
   Octavius, 23 . . .   38
Origen, *c. Celsum,* vii. 62,
   64, 65   38
   c. Celsum, vii. 66 . .   66
Paulinus of Nola, *Carmen*
   ix. and x. de S. Felicis
   Natali   50
Peter Damian, *Sermo de*
Nativ. Mar. (*P.L.*
   cxliv. 740) . . .   83
Proclus, *Laudatio Deiparæ*
Virginis, iv. p. 343 .   82
Protevangelium Jacobi .   82
Tatian, *ad Græcos,* iv. .   37
Tertullian, *adv. Judæos,* iv. 139 *n.*
   adv. Nationes, i. 12 .   42
   de Fuga in Persecutione,
   11, 14 . . 142 *n.,* 144 *n.*
   de Idol. i. 3. 4 . . 37 *n.*
   de Idol. 14 . . . 145 *n.*
   de orat. 23 . . 144, 145
Theodore of Studium,
   Migne, *P.G.* xcix. 962–
   963   58
Theophilus of Antioch, *ad*
Autolycum, ii. 2 . .   37
Philo, *de decem Orac.* xiv.   29 *n.*
   de decem Orac. xv. . .   29 *n.*
   de decem Orac. xvi. .   29 *n.*
   de decem Orac. xvii. 89, 90, 93
   de decem Orac. xviii. .   91 *n.*
   de decem Orac. xxiv., xxv. 15
   de decem Orac. xxix. . xxv *n.,*
     29 *n.*
   de Vita Contemplativa,
   i.–ii. . . . .   29 *n.*
Josephus, *Ant.* iii. 5. 5   xxv *n.,* 16,
     28 *n.,* 89 *n.*
   Ant. viii. 7. 5 . .   28 *n.*
   Ant. xi. 7. 8
   Ant. xii. 1 . . . 125 *n.*
   Ant. xii. 6. 2 . . . 125 *n.*
   Ant. xiv. 4. 2 . . . 125 *n.*
   Ant. xiv. 10. 11–19 . 125 *n.*
   Ant. xvi. 2. 4 . . . 126 *n.*
   Ant. xvi. 6. 2 . . . 126 *n.*
   Ant. xvii. 6. 2–4 . . 28, 28*n.*

Josephus, *Ant.* xviii. 3]	28, 28 *n.*
c. *Apion.* ii. 40	138 *n.*
B.J. i. 33. 2–4	28, 28 *n.*
B.J. ii. 8. 5	93 *n.*
B.J. ii. 9. 2	28, 28 *n*
B.J. ii. 10. 4	28 *n.*
B.J. ii. 17. 10	125 *n.*
B.J. ii. 19. 2	125 *n.*
Vita, 12	28

(f) *From Classical Writers*

Cicero, *de off.* iii. 29–30	91
de Orat. ii. 68	95, 96
Dio Chrysostom, *Orat.* xii. 407	65, 66
Juvenal, xiv. 96, 105 sqq.	131 *n.*
Martial, iv. 4. 7	131 *n.*, 138 *n.*
Maximus of Tyre, *Dissertatio*, viii. 2	65
Ovid, *Ars Amatoria*, i. 415	138 *n.*
Persius, v. 179–184	131 *n.*
Plato, *Laws*, viii. 841	221
de Republica fragment, iv. 5. 10 (ed. Noble), p. 1196	221 *n.*
Pliny, *Ep. ad Trajan*, 96	142, 163, 164
Plotinus, *Ennead.* iv. 3. 11.	66
Plutarch, *de Superstit.* 8	131 *n.*
Seneca, *Epist.* ix. 47	131 *n.*
Strabo, *Hist.* x. 3. 9	117
Suet. *Aug.* 76	131 *n.*
Tacitus, *Hist.* v. 4	131 *n.*
Hist. v. 5	28
Tibullus, i. 3. 18	138 *n.*